COPYRIGHT FUTURE COPYRIGHT FREEDOM

Marking the 40th Anniversary of the Commencement of Australia's *Copyright Act 1968*

Edited by Brian Fitzgerald and Benedict Atkinson

Queensland University of Technology

SYDNEY UNIVERSITY PRESS

Published 2011 by SYDNEY UNIVERSITY PRESS
University of Sydney
NSW 2006 Australia
sydney.edu.au/sup

Publication date: March 2011
© Individual authors 2011
© Sydney University Press 2011

ISBN 978-1-920899-71-4

National Library of Australia Cataloguing-in-Publication entry
Title: Copyright future copyright freedom : marking the 40th
              anniversary of the commencement of Australia's Copyright
              Act 1968 / edited by Brian Fitzgerald and Benedict
              Atkinson.
ISBN: 9781920899714 (pbk.)
Notes: Includes bibliographical references and index.
Subjects: Australia. Copyright Act 1968.
              Copyright--Australia.
              Intellectual property--Australia.
Other Authors/Contributors:
              Fitzgerald, Brian F.
              Atkinson, Benedict.
Dewey Number: 346.940482

The digital version of this book is also available electronically through the Sydney
eScholarship Repository at: ses.library.usyd.edu.au and The Queensland University of
Technology ePrints Repository at: eprints.qut.edu.au.

ACKNOWLEDGEMENTS

Cover image and design by Elliott Bledsoe.

Cover Image credits: 'USB Flash Drive' by Ambuj Saxena, flic.kr/ambuj/345356294; 'cassette para post' by gabriel "gab" pinto, flic.kr/gabreal/2522599543; untitled by 'Playingwithbrushes', flic.krcom/playingwithpsp/3025911763; 'iPod's' by Yeray Hernández, flic.kr/yerahg/498315719; 'Presentation: Free Content for a Free Societey! 11/12' by Matthias Mehldau, flic.kr/wetterfrosch/130493803; 'BCN Street Art 30' by SlapBcn, flickr.com/slapbcn/2172264138; 'My digital camera Sony DSC-V3' by Shashwat_Nagpal, flic.kr/shashwat/183232807; 'Clip Art' by eliazar, flic.kr/eliazar/43127676; 'Wikipedia – Art Historian', 'Wikipedia -Musician' and 'Wikipedia-Gamer' by quartermane, flic.kr/mikeeperez/2453225976, flic.kr/mikeeperez/2453225040 and flic.kr/mikeeperez/2452395177; '132/365' by riot jane, flic.kr/riotjane/2331106291; 'StudioSix Brushes' by geishaboy500, flic.kr/geishaboy500/408711459; 'Swoon Drown (59)' and 'Swoon Drown (32)' by Lord Jim, flic.kr/lord-jim/2390489851 and flic.kr/lord-jim/2391324534; 'Film Strip' by Hamed Saber, flic.kr/hamed/407909486; 'Kindle 2' by Joe Shlabotnik, flic.kr/joeshlabotnik/3309641856; 'photo.jpg' by TJ Ryan, flic.kr/48994449@N00/3487765466; 'Lawrence Lessig Remix Party' by José Carlos Cortizo Pérez, flic.kr/josek/2985192607; 'Free Desktop Background – 1600-1050 Wide' by pookado, flic.kr/pookado/2957955605; 'Free Texture, by Paul Phung, flic.kr/rephotography/2666338958; 'Coelacanth (evolutionary undead / ghost fish)' by craneboy, http://flic.kr/justinbaldwin/1393868618; 'Pirates & the Kraken' by roctopus, flic.kr/hownowbrowncow/2889267815; "Stop Sign" by thecrazyfilmgirl, flic.kr/thecrazyfilmgirl/3248283617; '* Garbage *' and '* Star Grunge Texture *' by pareeerica, flic.kr/8078381@N03/2878994524 and flic.kr/8078381@N03/3034189660; 'Floral Pattern 2' by Sarai!WoaH Photography!, flic.kr/wingsofahero/3327601814. All images are licensed under a Creative Commons Attribution 2.0 Generic licence. Full terms at, creativecommons.org/licenses/by/2.0.

'fusion' by TFDC, tfdc.deviantart.com/art/fusion-90172576. Licensed under a Creative Commons Attribution-Noncommercial 3.0 Unported licence. Full terms at creativecommons.org/licenses/by-nc/3.0.

'icons from Silk Icons' by FamFamFam, www.famfamfam.com/lab/icons/silk; and 'Big Buck Bunny' poster by Blender Foundation, http://www.bigbuckbunny.org. Licensed under a Creative Commons Attribution 3.0 Unported licence, creativecommons.org/licenses/by/3.0.

CONTENTS

PREFACE

Professor Brian Fitzgerald

This book arises from a conference that I convened along with Benedict Atkinson at Old Parliament House in Canberra.

The conference was held near to the day of the 40th anniversary of the commencement of the Australian Copyright Act of 1968.[1]

Ben Atkinson's work – The True History of Copyright – had encouraged me to assemble key figures in Australian copyright history at Old Parliament House to discuss the past, present and future of copyright law.

I am thankful to the presenters for their generosity and insights and to the enthusiastic participants for making the conference a lively forum of discussion.

I am also thankful to the Australian Research Council (ARC) Centre of Excellence for Creative Industries and Innovation (CCi) and QUT (my home institutions) for supporting the conference and the many people who helped make the conference a success including Ben Atkinson, Tanya Butkovsky, Anne Fitzgerald, Steven Gething, Rami Olwan, Elliott Bledsoe, Kylie Pappalardo, Xiao-Xiang Shi and Nic Suzor.

A special thank you to Ruth Bell of the Ngunnawal people for her Welcome to Country.

While I had high hopes that this would be an interesting event I had not anticipated the excitement that the conference would generate.

The essays we have collected in this volume are only a selection of what was on offer.

We trust that you will enjoy them.

Professor Brian Fitzgerald

Brisbane

October 2010

---

[1] The Act commenced on 1 May 1969.

FOREWORD

The Hon Michael Kirby AC CMG[1]

COPYRIGHT WILL CONTINUE

Towards the end of this book, in his second contribution on national, regional and international perspectives of copyright, Professor Adrian Sterling shares with the reader an anecdote from his long career in the world of copyright law.[2]

He describes the conclusion of the conference of the World Intellectual Property Organisation (WIPO) in 1996, at which the WIPO treaties on copyright and related rights were approved. According to his recollection, the Director of WIPO at the time, Dr Arpad Bogsch, greeted him in what was to be their last meeting. Dr Bogsch declared: "Sterling, these treaties are only a step in the history of copyright. You and I will disappear, but copyright will continue". Affirming that "Dr Bogsch was always right", Adrian Sterling draws comfort and encouragement from this prediction.

Partly in consequence of the exponential growth of technology in recent years (and especially the development of the internet), the challenges to copyright law, as it has evolved, are daunting. Traditionalists, even of the most devoted kind, must sometimes wonder how the fabric that they have built, and loved, can remain intact under the multiple assaults launched against it. Criticisms have been conceived in ideology, nurtured in politics and self-interest and delivered by a never-ending stream of technological changes. So it has been in the past thirty years. So it will probably be in the decades ahead.

Just to show that miracles can still happen to retired judges, when I departed Barwick's High Court building, I had no computer on my desk. Not far from the building could be seen the art deco elegance of Old Parliament House, Canberra. That was where the conference was held whose papers are collected in this book. Not long before I attended the conference, I could not open a computer, still less send an email or conduct a Google search. Well, necessity is not only the essential ingredient for an

---

[1] Justice of the High Court of Australia (1996–2009). One time chairman of the Australian Law Reform Commission (1975–84); Judge of the Federal Court of Australia (1983–4); Laureate of the UNESCO Prize for Human Rights Education (1998).

[2] A. Sterling, "Current Issues: National, Regional and International Perspectives", this volume, p200.

implication that a statutory licence will be implied as a matter of law under the *Copyright Act* 1968 (Cth) s183 into a contract between a creator and its clients in favour of a State[3], it is also the mother of a retiree's inventiveness. So now, like more than a billion others of my species, I lock my mind every day into the internet. It trawls and searches through cyberspace, opening up original works of countless others, available for the most part free online.

THE DYNAMIC OF TECHNOLOGICAL CHANGE

My newfound capacity with the internet has brought me into acquaintance with all the fashionable outlets, even YouTube. A video doing the rounds on this network reveals, amongst other things[4]:

> If you were one in a million in China, there would be 1300 people just like you.

> China will soon be the number one English-speaking nation on earth.

> The top ten in-demand jobs in 2010 did not even exist in 2004.

> One in eight couples in the United States who married in 2010 met on line.

> Every month in 2010, 31 billion searches were conducted using Google. In 2006, the figure was 2.7 billion.

> The number of years that it took to reach a market of 50 million was: in the case of radio, 38 years; of television, 13 years; of the internet, 4 years; the iPod, 3 years; Facebook, 2 years.

> 200 million users of Myspace, if they were a nation, would be fifth largest in the world, ranked between Indonesia and Brazil.

> The number of internet devices in 1984 was 1000. In 1992, a million. In 2008, 1000 million.

> The amount of new technological information is doubling every two years. For students taking a four year technical degree, this means that half of what they have learned in their first year of study will be outdated by their third year of study.

> By 2013, a super computer will be built that exceeds the computational capacities of the human brain. Predictions are that by 2049, a $1,000

---

[3] *Copyright Agency Limited v State of New South Wales* [2008] HCA 35; (2008) 233 CLR 279 at 305–6 [92]-[93], citing *Concrete Pty Ltd v Parramatta Design & Developments Pty Ltd* [2006] HCA 55; (2006) 229 CLR 577 at 584 [13]-[14] per Gummow ACJ; and at 606 [96], per Kirby and Crennan JJ.

[4] www.youtube.com/watch?v=cL9Wu2kWwSY.

computer will exceed the computational capacity of the entire human species.

During the course of this presentation, 67 babies were born in the US; 274 in China; 395 in India and 694,000 songs were downloaded illegally.

From the point of view of experts in the law of copyright, the sting in the tail of this YouTube presentation (which lasted all of four minutes) was to be found in the concluding statistic. All of those worthy individuals and citizens, many of them children (some maybe even judges), are knowingly, ignorantly or indifferently finding themselves in breach of international and national copyright law. And they intend to keep on doing exactly as before.

THE LEGAL AND THE ILLEGAL

The fact that this is so and is of such little concern to so many, profoundly interests Professor Laurence Lessig, whose keynote address is featured in this book.[5] Young people, especially, view remixes, for example, as a type of conversation. Just as in earlier days, young people sang the songs of the day, or old songs together. As Professor Lessig describes it:

> Instead of gathering in the corner, or on the back lawn, people from around the world are using this digital platform to engage in a form of read-write technology.

Some activities of the new generations are unregulated by law. But some are definitely contrary to law. Just as in earlier generations, buying tea at Boston Harbour, upon which royal tax had not been paid, was contrary to law. Or just as adult private homosexual activity was (as it still is in many places) contrary to law. Or providing sterile injecting equipment to minimise the spread of HIV/AIDS was (and often still is) contrary to law. Law is not everything. But lawyers tend to consider that it is rather important that it should be obeyed and respected. Otherwise, if it is ignored or defied, that fact might bring down the whole edifice of the rule of law.

In the same chapter, Adrian Sterling quotes the recent report *Digital Britain* as making this point:[6]

> In the new digital world, the ability to share content legally becomes ever more important and necessary ... There is a clear and unambiguous distinction between the legal and illegal sharing of content which we must

---

[5] L. Lessig, "Culture Wars: Getting to Peace, this volume, p116.

[6] Sterling, n2 above at p221 citing BERR, Interim Report, *Digital Britain*, (January 2009, The Stationery Office), par.[3.2].

urgently address. But we need to do so in a way that recognises that, when there is very widespread behaviour and social acceptability of such behaviour that is at odds with the rules, then the rules, the business models that the rules have underpinned and the behaviour itself, may all need to change … Our aim, in the rapidly changing digital world is a framework that is effective and enforceable, both nationally and across borders. But it must be one which also allows for innovation in platforms, devices and applications …

How can international and national copyright law be changed to conform not just with the technology that is with us now, but with the amazing pace of technological expansion that is happening so fast that we cannot even imagine where we will be in a couple of decades? The slow-moving pace of legislative change, bureaucratic decisions and judicial opinion-writing makes it difficult, if not impossible, to cope with the current pace of technological innovation in informatics. And if this is true of municipal law, how much more true in the case of international law, where the economic, social, cultural and other diversities are such that consensus (with all its subtle nuances) can only be achieved through intensely time-consuming negotiations, trade-offs against competing interests and overcoming hurdles presented by countless obstacles?

THE WARM EMBRACE OF SOFT LAW

In my early days as chairman of the Australian Law Reform Commission, I was introduced to the challenges of the impact of technology on the law in several of the projects of the Commission. They included the reports on human tissue transplantation[7] and privacy.[8] Thus, scientific developments suddenly helped to overcome the previous human immune rejection of transplants. And just as the Commission was about to deliver its report on transplantation law, a baby, Louise Brown, was born as a result of *in vitro* fertilisation. The use of foetal tissue already then loomed as a new challenge for gaining a local consensus over the shape that Australian law should take. Prudently, perhaps, the Commission elected to leave these issues aside, for separate attention. Safer by far to limit our recommendations to the transplantation of corneas and kidneys. A foetus seemed to raise different and more controversial questions.

---

[7] Australian Law Reform Commission, *Human Tissue Transplants*, (ALRC 7, 1977).

[8] Australian Law Reform Commission, *Privacy* (ALRC 22, 1983), 206.

In the privacy report, the Commission recommended (and the Australian Parliament accepted[9]) certain 'information privacy principles' to guide decisions on the protection of privacy in the then new world of computer processing. These principles were, in turn, derived from a report of the Expert Group on Privacy of the Organisation for Economic Co-Operation and Development (OECD) which I had chaired in Paris 1978–80.[10]

There was wisdom at that time in proceeding along the path earlier charted by "soft law", in the form of the OECD Guidelines. This is a point that has been made in the context of copyright law by Professors Bernt Hugenholtz and Ruth Okediji, when conceiving a future international instrument on limitations and exceptions to copyright.[11] Still, the dangers of soft law, when translated into the hard law of national statutory texts, was quickly demonstrated to the Australian Law Reform Commission by supervening advances in information technology. Suitable to the technology as it stood when the OECD report was completed (and endorsed by the Council of that organisation in 1980) was the 'use limitation principle'. For protection of individual privacy, this principle limited the later use of [private] personal information to a use for which the information had earlier been [lawfully] collected or any other use to which the data subject had given consent or specific approval was granted by law. But with the advent of search engines, such as Google, that principle, at least in the terms originally expressed, became unsuitable, if not unworkable and probably unthinkable. So enormous were the utilities of the search engines that no-one could hope to turn back the clock.

Although this meant the active use of information with personal identifiers for purposes other than those first given (necessarily some of it out-of-date and gathered for quite different and even alien purposes) the marginal utility of the facility of the search engine was far greater than the marginal cost in the loss of privacy or in any (futile) attempt to restore the old legal regime so as to apply to the new informatics.

In this sense, therefore, the problem now faced by intellectual property lawyers in general (and copyright lawyers in particular), because of the advance of technology and the huge public engagement with it, is nothing new. What is new, as the report *Digital Britain* explains, is the "very widespread behaviour and social acceptability"

---

[9] Organisation for Economic Co-operation and Development *Guidelines on the Protection of Privacy and Transborder Flows of Personal Data*, OECD, Paris, 1981.

[10] See M.D. Kirby, "The History, Achievement and Future of the 1980 OECD Guidelines on Privacy" (2010) 20 *Journal of Law, Information and Science* 1.

[11] P.B. Hugenholtz and R.L. Okediji, *Conceiving an International Instrument on Limitations and Exceptions to Copyright* (Final Report), March 06, 2008, Uni of Amsterdam and Uni of Minnesota, 5.

that comes in the train of the new technology and effectively demands the acceptance of a new legal paradigm.

COPYRIGHT AND THE PUBLIC INTEREST

What should that paradigm be? This is a question that recurs throughout the contributions collected in this book. Professors Hugenholtz and Okediji have pointed out that, certainly in our legal tradition of the common law"[12]

> It is a well-established principle of copyright doctrine that the qualified grant of proprietary rights over the fruits of creative enterprise is directed first and foremost at the promotion of the public interest. Most countries around the world explicitly recognise this vital goal as a foundational element of their copyright systems.[13] Indeed, from the very first formal copyright law, the British *Statute of Anne* (1710), the encouragement of learning and dissemination and knowledge as a means to enhance the general welfare has been the chief objective behind the grant of exclusive rights to authors[14]. For over 100 years, this public-centred rationale of copyright protection has been recognised and clearly articulated in all major instruments for the global regulation of copyright[15]. The currently pre-eminent Global Intellectual Property (IP) Treaty, the Agreement on Trade-Related Intellectual Property Rights[16] (TRIPS) Agreement, concluded under the auspices of the World Trade Organisation (WTO) in 1994, recently reflected and re-affirmed this basic precept by describing the overarching objective of intellectual property protection under the Agreement as "the mutual advantage of producers and users of technological knowledge … conducive to social and economic welfare"[17]

Yet, it is one thing to express, in general language, a commitment to "public interest", "learning and dissemination of knowledge" and "mutual advantage". It is often quite

---

[12] Ibid, 6.

[13] See e.g. US *Constitution*, Art.1, sec8, cl8. Directive 2001/29/EC of the European Parliament and of the Council of 22 May 2001 on the *Harmonisation Of Certain Aspects Of Copyright And Related Rights In The Information Society*, OJ No.L167 at 10 (2001), pmbl 3.

[14] See *Statute of Anne*, 8Anne c19 (1710), pmbl and art.[2] 1.

[15] See *Berne Convention on the Protection of Literary and Artistic Works*, September 9, 1886 as last revised, July 24, 1976; 828 UNTS 221; *Universal Copyright Convention (WIPO) Copyright Treaty*, December 20, 1996.

[16] TRIPS Agreement, April 15, 1994, Marrakesh Agreement establishing the World Trade Organisation, Annex.1C; 33 ILM 81 (1994).

[17] TRIPS Agreement, n15, art.7. See also id. Art 8.1.

another to translate these aspirational phrases into activities that are accepted by the several competing interests that are at stake. The competition of interests will include such practical concerns as respective economic advantages. They will offer perceptions of what is right, derived from legal history and doctrine that can differ quite markedly between nations. They will sometimes include a particular element offered by competing assertions of the requirements of international human rights law. Because this is an area of law with which I have had some involvement over three decades, I must refer to it in this context.

THE NEW PARADIGM OF HUMAN RIGHTS

The language of international human rights is not antagonistic to intellectual property protection. Providing legal protections for intellectual property (including patents of invention, trademarks and copyright) is by no means alien to the objectives of universal human rights. To the contrary, from the very start of the attempts in the post-Second World War era, to express and uphold universal human rights, a place has always existed for the defence of those interests that are conventionally safe-guarded by intellectual property law.

Thus, in the *Universal Declaration of Human Rights*[18] (UDHR), prepared in 1947–8 by a committee chaired by Eleanor Roosevelt of the United States of America (and brought into operation in the General Assembly of the United Nations by a vote over which an Australian, Dr. H.V. Evatt, presided), the following article was included:

Article 27

1. Everyone has the right freely to participate in the cultural life of the community, to enjoy the arts and to share in scientific advancement and its benefits.

2. Everyone has the right to the protection of the moral and material interests resulting from any scientific, literary or artistic production of which he is the author.

The potential juxtaposition of, and tension between, the foregoing paragraphs was immediately noted. When the UDHR was transformed into a treaty, relevantly the *International Covenant on Economic, Social and Cultural Rights* (ICESCR)[19], the states parties to the treaty committed themselves to "achieving progressively the full

---

[18] *Universal Declaration of Human Rights*, United Nations, GA Resolution 217A(iii), 1948.
[19] 993 UNTS 1453 (1976).

realisation of the rights recognised in the present Covenant by all appropriate means, including particularly the adoption of legislative measures".[20]

Amongst the rights recorded in the ICESCR were:

Article 15

1. The States Parties to the present covenant recognise the right of everyone:

(a) To take part in cultural life;

(b) To enjoy the benefits of scientific progress and its applications;

(c) To benefit from the protection of the moral and material interests resulting from any scientific, literary or artistic production of which he is the author.

2. The steps to be taken by the States Parties to the present covenant to achieve the full realisation of this right shall include those necessary for the conservation, the development and the diffusion of science and culture.

3. The States Parties to the present covenant undertake to respect the freedom indispensible for scientific research and creative activity.

4. The States Parties to the present covenant recognise the benefits to be derived from the encouragement and development of international contacts and co-operation in the scientific and cultural fields.

Again, within the very same article, principles are stated that appear to pull in differing, and even opposite, directions, so far as the award of exclusive rights to creative authors is concerned. However, it is not always appreciated that international human rights law includes provisions expressly recognising and accepting the fundamental, universal and morally justifiable character of the nominated intellectual property rights.

Of course, in the attainment of those rights, it is necessary to secure a reconciliation of each such right with the other rights provided elsewhere by international human rights law, according to their terms. Thus, the rights of some persons must be reconciled with those of others. The rights afforded by some articles of the human rights treaties must be reconciled with the rights of others under other treaties. Notably, in apparent competition with a provision such as that in Article 15 of the ICESCR are the following rights contained in the *International Covenant on Civil and Political Rights* (ICCPR)[21]:

Article 19

---

[20] ICESCR, Art2.1

[21] 999 UNTS 171 (1976), 16 December 1966 (emphasis added).

1. Everyone shall have the right to hold opinions without interference.

2. Everyone shall have the right to freedom of expression; this right shall include freedom to seek, *receive* and impart information and ideas of all kinds, regardless of frontiers, either orally, in writing or in print, in the form of art, or through *any other media of his choice.*

3. The exercise of the rights provided for in paragraph 2 of this article carries with it special duties and responsibilities. It may therefore be subject to certain restrictions, but these shall only be such as are provided by law and are necessary:

(a) for respect of the rights or reputations of others;

(b) For the protection of national security or of public order (*ordre public*), or of public health or morals."

Many of the contemporary debates about the shape and direction of international and national copyright law involve an endeavour to reconcile the foregoing rights. I am sure that some intellectual property lawyers, particularly those of a parochial kind who have never ventured outside their intellectual specialty, will have little sympathy for my mention of this backdrop of international human rights law. However, it is reassuring to see the attention given to the subject in this book by, amongst others, Adrian Sterling.[22] Correctly, he invokes international human rights law to rebuff the more extreme assertions of IP-phobic commentators, calling for the abolition of IP protection altogether, or, at least, modification in relation to material freely available on the internet.[23]

Just as reminders of the aspirational core value of "public interest" in copyright law can sometimes give little practical guidance to municipal lawyers or lawmakers, so appeals to the broad language of the UDHR or the ICESCR may sometimes send different signals to different minds, according to their susceptibility, backgrounds and interests.

An important point has been made in this connection by Professors Graeme Austin and Amy Zavidow[24] in an article on "Copyright Law Reform Through a Human Rights Lens".[25] Whilst accepting that international human rights law will not necessarily resolve the tensions between proponents and critics of copyright law, the authors suggest, for the purpose of reform (in my view correctly), that international law

---

[22] Cf. Sterling, n2 above p200.

[23] Ibid, p227.

[24] Both of the University of Arizona, James E. Rogers College of Law.

[25] "Intellectual Property and Human Rights", 2008, *Arizona Legal Studies*, Discussion Paper No.0734.

affords unexplored territory, potentially useful for defenders of global copyright regimes. Moreover, Austin and Zavidow assert that:

> Debates about the domestic law reform agenda in the copyright field could be richer and more salient if they were accompanied by deeper engagement with public international law – both the public international law of intellectual property and international human rights law.

This is an appeal that I would endorse. Unfortunately, it sometimes needs endorsement in countries, such as Australia and the United States, which tend to be rather parochial and even a tad self-satisfied about their law in general, and their intellectual property law in particular.

DESTABILISING PREVIOUS BALANCES

A special difficulty that is peculiar to the need, which international human rights law recognises, to reconcile competing human rights norms, is the fact that, in many countries, particularly in the developing world, there are inadequate provisions either in constitutional law or the domestic legal tradition and practice, to speak up for the right of access to information when it comes into conflict with intellectual property rights asserted by powerful commercial interests. This is a point which has been made by Professor Michael Birnhack in his article "Global Copyright, Local Speech"[26]. Birnhack argues that, whatever its original history, copyright law today is less a means of promoting progress in science (as the words of the United States Constitution proclaim) so much as protecting established national interests in the matter of trade. The TRIPS Agreement of the WTO has effectively produced a global copyright regime which, Birnhack concludes, has "de-stabilised previous balances". He argues that the shift to a global trade environment requires an urgent re-evaluation of the previous balances, particularly because, in the face of expanding trade-related copyright, the competing norms of international human rights law (access to information, research and free speech) tend to be "left unattended".

Professor Birnhack argues that this result is especially true in developing countries, mostly with neither express nor effective constitutional provisions to uphold free speech and usually with inadequate political will to do so. In short, Birnhack's special concern is about the effective imposition of copyright obligations, through TRIPS and bilateral free trade agreements, whereby, as he puts it, as "the trade benefits to The North have a cost in limiting access to information, use thereof and formation of new speech, or more generally, it has a cost in freedom, in The South".

---

[26] 24 *Cardozo Arts and Entertainment Law Journal* 491 (2006).

Not all writers in this field are as pessimistic as Professor Birnhack. Professors L.R. Helfer and G.W. Austin, in an excellent review: "Human Rights and Intellectual Property: Mapping the Global Interface",[27] conclude that the intersection of human rights and intellectual property law is now "unavoidable".[28] They classify the responses of lawyers in the field into four groups:

- The first are those human rights lawyers who declare that, basically, IP law does not fit into the new world of human rights. By reference to the history and the texts of the UDHR and ICESCR, it is suggested that such opponents "understand the discourse of one complex legal and political system but not the other".[29]

- Secondly, they identify the IP protagonists who are deeply fearful of, and therefore hostile towards, international human rights law; proclaiming that it will "promote government intervention in private innovation markets and ... radically scale back or even abolish IP protection".[30] They point out that this is simply not likely to happen in the real world.

- The third category includes those lawyers from both camps who worry that the international legal system is being overly fragmented, so that it is difficult to acknowledge the competing values of human rights and IP. The authors accept that there is a specific problem of whether the current decision-makers within WTO, for example, "are adequately equipped" to mediate the conflicting values of international IP treaties and of human rights law[31].

- Finally, they themselves suggest a fourth approach, which they urge should be "empirically grounded".[32] That is, it should recognise that both human rights and IP legal regimes are continually evolving in response to changing conceptions of fundamental legal entitlements and technological progress. They point out that no empirical approach to that reconciliation of international law which will best protect the legitimate interests of all players will occur, without improvement in the process, transparency and predictability of the current techniques.[33]

---

[27] *Arizona Legal Studies*, DP No.10–18 (University of Arizona, May 2010).

[28] Ibid, 10.

[29] Ibid, 11.

[30] Ibid, 11.

[31] Ibid, 12.

[32] Ibid, 16.

[33] For an example of a practical way in which the broad principles of fundamental rights may be used in choosing the preferable construction of municipal copyright legislation and thus securing a reconciliation see e.g. *Metro Goldwyn-Mayer Studios Inc v Grokster Ltd* 75 545 US 913 (2005) per

TOWARDS A NEW RECONCILIATION

In this connection, Professors Helfer and Austin make what seems to me to be a powerful point:

> A salient recent example is the Anti-Counterfeiting Trade Agreement (ACTA), a proposed multi-lateral treaty that would establish new and more robust obligations for states to suppress unauthorised uses of intellectual property. For two years, ACTA negotiations occurred in secret and governments refused to disclose an official draft text of the treaty. Only after a French civil rights NGO leaked the document revealing "contradictions between the text and public comments by [government] negotiators" did governments release an official text. This lack of transparency involving potentially far-reaching changes to domestic and international intellectual property laws and enforcement mechanisms is disturbing, as is the inability of interested constituencies to, in the words of the Committee on Economic Social and Cultural Rights, "take part in ... any significant decision-making processes that have an impact on their rights and legitimate interests.[34]

Whilst secrecy on the part of powerful national interests (doubtless egged on by the sometimes even more powerful interests of transnational corporations) may be understandable, it is intolerable as a matter of global policy and principle. It may itself be a breach of international human rights norms. Little wonder that many observers of international copyright law, and of its current directions and indecisions, are suspicious and antagonistic. Nevertheless, Professors Helfer and Austin, make very useful suggestions. It is essential to know exactly how in practice the current international regimes operate. There is no doubt that intellectual property protections are still useful and justifiable in principle. Moreover, in the international context, they have the support of express provisions in international human rights law itself.

At the end of their analysis, Professors Helfer and Austin conclude in words that I would endorse:[35]

> [T]here may be no incompatibility if individuals retain the right to be acknowledged as creators and to receive remuneration for at least some

---

Breyer J (with whom Stevens and O'Connor JJ joined) and *Stevens v Kabushiki Kaisha Sony Corp* [2005] HCA 58; (2005) 224 CLR 193 at 255–258 [213]-[221] per Kirby J.

[34] United Nations, Committee on Economic, Social and Cultural Rights, General Comment No.17, *The Right of Everyone to Benefit from the Moral and Material Interests Resulting from any Scientific, Literary or Artistic Product of which he is the Author*, Art.15(1)(c). UN Doc.E/C/12/2005, par.[34] (November 21, 2005).

[35] Helfer, Laurence, and Austin, Graeme, *Human Rights and Intellectual Property: Mapping the Global Interface*. New York: Cambridge University Press, 2011, p 522.

uses. The more fundamental point, however, is that although creators and innovators do indeed possess a narrow class of inalienable economic and personality rights, they can choose how best to exercise those rights so as to construct a zone of personal autonomy that is both self-empowering and conducive to the broader public values that the human rights framework for IP seeks to achieve.

Those broader frameworks will include creative commons, incentives designed to reduce poverty, disease, misgovernment and other afflictions as well as limitations and exceptions to copyright protection, yet to be worked out.

The working out is, of course, a major enterprise. It will not happen overnight. Indeed, it will not happen any time soon. But a step in the right direction is to collect the informed experts. To encourage amongst them a constructive clash of opinions. To lift the thinking of all so as to take them outside their comfort zones, shaped by current international and municipal law and perceptions of past practice and present national interests. And to stimulate bold and inventive thinking.

THE URGENCY OF LAW REFORM

This was the objective of the conference convened at Old Parliament House, Canberra on the 40th anniversary of Australia's *Copyright Act* of 1968. It is what makes this book, collecting those proceedings, so interesting, topical and valuable. It is all here. Anecdotes. Analysis. History. Optimism. Pessimism. Ways forward. Scepticism. Hostility. Infatuation. Fierce reformism. And passionate defence of the status quo. The editors and organisers deserve praise. But, the greatest reward for the contributors will be if this book helps to stimulate consideration of law reform, both at an international and national level.

Michael Kirby

February 2011

CONFERENCE OPENING SPEECH

The Attorney General of the Commonwealth of Australia,

The Hon Robert McClelland, MP

First, may I acknowledge the traditional owners of the land we meet on – and pay my respects to their elders, both past and present.

> Professor Brian Fitzgerald, Queensland University of Technology
>
> The Honourable Michael Kirby AC CMG
>
> The Honourable Greg James QC
>
> Professors Lessig, Cohen and Sterling
>
> Distinguished guests
>
> Ladies and gentlemen

Good morning and thank you for your welcome to this important conference.

It is now 40 years since the commencement of the 1968 Copyright Act.

When former Attorney-General, Nigel Bowen, introduced the Bill into Parliament in 1967, which completely revised Australia's copyright law, he acknowledged that:

> the law of copyright is assuming a greater practical and economic importance both within Australia and internationally.

His statement is just as relevant today.

Studies prove that point, including recent research by Price Waterhouse. Their 2008 report[1] found that Australia's copyright industries have grown considerably over the past twelve years.

It may not be widely known that in 2006–07 alone, Australian copyright industries employed more than 830,000 people – 8 per cent of the Australian workforce.

They generated $ 97.7 billion – 10.3 per cent of our Gross Domestic Product. And earned more than $6.8 billion in exports – that is, 4.1 per cent of the Australian total.

---

[1] Price Waterhouse Coopers, *Making the Intangible Tangible: the Economic Contribution of Australia's Copyright Industries*, November 2008.

I know that successive Attorneys-General have worked to develop reforms to copyright law in response to the impacts of new technologies or changing circumstances in society.

That need for copyright reform continues – particularly in response to the development of new technologies now largely driven by the internet and digital devices.

We have international obligations to meet, incentives to establish for creators, and consideration of the broader public interest of access to copyright materials.

These factors create a challenging mix as we work to find a "balanced" copyright regime.

Overall, I think Australia is acknowledged internationally as having a strong, comprehensive and balanced copyright law.

Despite this, we must also be open to the need to re-examine the present balance as circumstances change.

ACHIEVING BALANCE

One of my challenging tasks as Attorney-General lies in creating a fair and workable copyright system that ensures the right balance between the often conflicting interests of copyright owners and the needs of copyright users.

Traditionally, copyright owners have tended to argue that the law should protect their copyright, in response to innovations that facilitate greater copying or sharing of copyright material.

On the other hand, copyright users generally oppose any tightening or increased control of access to copyright protected materials.

Some have argued that copyright not only comprises the copyright owner's private property rights, but also certain "public rights".

This is not a novel debate.

Just as Nigel Bowen's comments about the importance of copyright are relevant today, so too is the observation of Victor Hugo in the 1870s:

> Before the publication, the author has an undeniable and unlimited right ...
> but as soon as the work is published, the author is not any more the master.
> It is then that other persons seize it ...[2]

As Minister responsible for copyright almost 150 years later, I do not profess to have the ultimate resolution to this issue.

---

[2] Victor Hugo, when chair of l'Association Littéraire Internationale.

But it is my view the balance is best achieved by adopting a principled approach to policy development.

In effect, this means not being captive to one interest group or point of view.

The Government needs to reach a reasonable middle ground when interests have worked together to find a solution but genuinely cannot agree, and when the public interest is at risk.

The key here is about working genuinely to come to agreement.

Copyright interests are often diametrically opposed. But that is no excuse for not seeking compromise and fair outcomes.

In this respect, I see copyright as essentially about players acting in good faith.

This is not to say that Government does not have a role in guiding policy and finding legislative solutions. But Governments can never purely be arbiters between two competing interests; there are broader considerations to take into account.

Governments also have an obligation to consider individual rights as well as the social benefits and implications of copyright when developing policy.

Government must also act according to international obligations arising from multilateral and bilateral copyright agreements.

The guiding statement for today's conference mentions that:

> Copyright should underpin freedom by promoting the optimal flow and dissemination of knowledge.

I will be interested to learn more from your discussions about how copyright can be "free", yet part of a balanced system that recognises owners' rights and Australia's international obligations.

ENGAGEMENT WITH STAKEHOLDERS

The task of assessing what aspects of copyright law should be examined is a difficult one.

There is clearly a wide range of stakeholders.

Only last week I held a roundtable forum with about 30 of the key representative groups to hear their perspective on copyright reform and what their key issues were.

Their views are important and I found it a very efficient way to gauge stakeholder views. I was also struck by the broad range of issues aired.

There was some commonality of issues.

This will lead me to think further about key themes.

For example:

- whether the Government would benefit from an independent source of advice in addition to my Department, especially for technology and competition issues
- access to justice considerations for individual creators and also the effectiveness of the Copyright Tribunal
- addressing piracy in the online environment
- the roles and responsibilities of declared collecting societies
- whether there should be new rights for visual artists, indigenous creators and audio-visual performers
- the relationship between copyright and contract law, and
- whether there should be new exceptions to allow greater access to copyright materials.

These are some of the themes that came through at the meeting and many will be further considered by the Government.

COPYRIGHT AGENDA

In addition to these ideas there are a range of copyright issues facing Government.

These include the issues of resale royalty legislation for visual artists and the review of restrictions on the parallel importation of books.

I am also evaluating proposals on the use of internet material by educational institutions, the role of Internet Service Providers in relation to online infringements, and appropriate enforcement of intellectual property crimes.

There is also the push for Governments to consider how to enhance access to and re-use Government information.

These are just a few of the important copyright issues to address – and in doing so, being mindful that copyright policies influence our wider agenda for innovation, education, the arts, trade and the digital economy.

CONCLUSION

These are interesting times for copyright policy.

We face challenges as new platforms of communication, presentation and distribution sprout almost overnight.

The context for all we do is subject to constant change. The agenda for this conference demonstrates that point.

I commend Professor Brian Fitzgerald for bringing you together and welcome your perspectives on copyright policy to help us achieve an effective and fair balance.

I wish you success in your deliberations.

It is my great pleasure to declare the Conference officially open.

Thank you.

INTRODUCTORY REMARKS

Professor Brian Fitzgerald [1]

Thank you Attorney General McClelland for opening this conference. Your remarks provide a good starting point for us as we move on over the next day and a half to consider the past, present and future of copyright law and policy.

At the outset let me say a few words about why this Conference, why now and why here?

The conference would not have happened if it was not for the excellent work that Benedict Atkinson produced as part of his LLM thesis at Sydney University and which he subsequently published as a book – *The true history of copyright 1905–2005: the Australian experience* (Sydney University Press). The book in my mind is one of the most important contributions to Australian copyright scholarship. It opened our eyes to the nuances of copyright in this country and did so in a concise and learned way with an interesting narrative.

Ben's hours of researching uncovered some interesting facts and threw light on the roles of a good number of people. When I read Ben's work I saw the name Leslie Zines.

---

[1] Professor Brian Fitzgerald BA (Griff) LLB (Hons) (QUT) BCL (Oxon.) LLM (Harv.) PhD (Griff) Honorary Professor – City University of London, Professor – Law Faculty, QUT Brisbane Australia, Barrister of the High Court of Australia, bf.fitzgerald@qut.edu.au Website at: www.law.qut.edu.au/staff/lsstaff/fitzgerald.jsp. Brian Fitzgerald studied law at the Queensland University of Technology graduating as University Medallist in Law and holds postgraduate degrees in law from Oxford University and Harvard University. He is well known in the areas of Intellectual Property and Internet Law and has worked closely with Australian governments on facilitating access to public sector information. Brian is also a project lead of Creative Commons Australia, and Peer to Patent Australia www.peertopatent.org.au From 1998–2002 he was Head of the School of Law and Justice at Southern Cross University in New South Wales, Australia and from January 2002 – January 2007 was appointed as Head of the School of Law at QUT in Brisbane, Australia. Brian is currently a specialist Research Professor in Intellectual Property and Innovation at QUT, Honorary Professor at City University of London and Chief Investigator in the ARC Centre of Excellence for Creative Industries and Innovation. In 2009 Brian was appointed to the Australia Government's "Government 2.0 Taskforce" by Ministers Tanner and Ludwig and to the Advisory Council on Intellectual Property (ACIP) by Minister Carr. Brian's most recent publication is B Fitzgerald (editor and contributor) *Access to Public Sector Information: Law Technology and Policy* (2010) Sydney University Press.

I also saw the name Adrian Sterling and the name John Gilchrist, and said to myself, "I know those people; I didn't realise that they had such an intimate connection with Australian Copyright Law".

I knew John Gilchrist as an academic at the University of Canberra who had come to do a PhD with me at QUT and Adrian Sterling I had met at the Fordham conference in New York over the years and knew of his connection with Australia. And Leslie Zines I knew as our esteemed professor of constitutional law at the Australian National University. But I did not realise that these people had had such interesting roles to play in Australian copyright history. I said to Ben, "I would like to be able to take your work, and those figures, those personalities, and put them together right back where a lot of this happened, in Canberra, and particularly at Old Parliament House (OPH)."

Ben was just as enthusiastic and with his help we have managed to organise this conference.

We did miss a couple of milestones along the way. We had hoped to run the conference in 2005 on the 100the anniversary of the Copyright Act 1905 (our first federal copyright Act) and having failed to get organised by that date we set our sights on the 40th anniversary of the enactment of the Copyright Act 1968. Again, we did not get it organised in time. We then set our sights on running this event as we are now doing on the 40th anniversary of the commencement of the 1968 Act, which was May 1969. We got there in the end.

The research that Ben undertook, and the venue here at OPH, bring us together in unique circumstances and give us an exciting platform upon which to consider copyright law and policy.

COPYRIGHT FREEDOM

What about the title of the conference – *Copyright Future: Copyright Freedom* – what does it mean? On seeing the flyer for the conference some people said to me, "copyright freedom, that is a little provocative". There is no doubt that copyright and freedom have been viewed as enemies in recent history, and I am not convinced that is the way it should be. I am not convinced that is what copyright law demands. To my mind, copyright ought to be about liberating us from ignorance, enriching our culture and therefore the idea of copyright and freedom existing side by side as partners is a natural fit not an aberration. The debates we have had over the last 10 years have certainly pitched copyright and freedom as the opposing ends of a fiercely contested spectrum. The time is right – right now – to put these two words together, copyright and freedom, and see how we can move forward.

As a focal point for our discussion I suggest we might consider the following as a fundamental principle or underlying purpose of copyright law: "Copyright should underpin freedom by promoting the optimal flow and dissemination of knowledge." And then ask how copyright law might facilitate this goal in the future? This is without doubt a significant challenge. In recent times we have seen some interesting developments which I would like to highlight. They show how people and institutions are giving definition to the notion of "copyright freedom" in the digital era.

IceTV

Let me start with the High Court of Australia and the recent case of *IceTV*[2] in which the High Court held that it was not an infringement for *IceTV* to copy the time and title aspects of a television program produced by Channel 9 and to use that in their electronic program guide (EPG). As lawyers will say it is a complex case and there are complex facts in issue but amidst the many judgements and arguments made in the case we get the message. The High Court says, in effect, that where there is a "merger", a term of art used in US copyright law, of content and expression, so that you can really only express something – such as the time and title of the television program – in one way, it's very difficult to say to someone downstream, "you should not be able to re-use the information." And that meets with common sense. Think of people in everyday life creating their own guides – whether it is in a retirement village or a mining canteen or wherever – for their community from an assortment of TV programs; creating their own programs and then being told, "Oh well, look sorry, that's an infringement".

Now, people would say to me "that's technically an infringement but it is tolerated use" and the whole concept of tolerated use is an interesting one. Some American academics, particularly Professor Tim Wu, say there is a lot of copying that goes on out there that owners are not worried about, or they tolerate because it is in their best interests.[3] There is no indication in *IceTV* that the High Court was saying that copying time and title information was tolerated use. To the contrary the Court is saying that this is unremunerated use, a use that you are able to freely make of this particular information. While the High Court has not expressly endorsed the merger doctrine recognised in the United States it goes very close when one considers the essence of what the High Court is saying in the two judgments in the *IceTV* case: "if you can only say something in one way, there is a real question about infringement and proving infringement".

---

[2] *IceTV Pty Limited v Nine Network Australia Pty Ltd* [2009] HCA 14.

[3] Tim Wu, "Tolerated Use" (2008) *Columbia Law and Economics Working Paper No 333*
papers.ssrn.com/sol3/papers.cfm?abstract_id=1132247

IceTV is an articulation of what I might call copyright freedom. At the level of doctrine the High Court is providing the contours of an Australian version of the "merger doctrine". The idea that certain parts of "intellectual infrastructure"[4] must be able to be reused without fear of infringing otherwise the dissemination (and innovation) rationale of copyright is stifled. At a deeper level the High Court hints at but does not expound on its theory of copyright. Ben Atkinson has reminded me of the seminal work of Lyman Ray Patterson in this area[5] and Sam Ricketson has written on this topic many years ago[6] – the idea that copyright is designed to protect against unfair competition (which I would extrapolate to mean) not remuneration for every conceivable use. The scope of remunerable use is a key consideration in evaluating the level of copyright freedom.

GOOGLE BOOK SETTLEMENT

The other development that I find fascinating is the Google Book Settlement.[7] Love it or hate it this event is revolutionising copyright law as we know it and will give us insights as to how things might work in the future. My colleague Larry Lessig has already expressed his concerns with the operation of the proposed Google Books Settlement (GBS). I agree that the GBS needs more work but let us not overlook some of the key aspects of it.

Lessig has been famous for the mantra that copyright is a permission based concept, that is, you cannot do anything without the copyright owner's permission. Google, a very big, powerful company that has entered the copyright politics arena in the last few years, is, starting to change the way we think about copyright and that idea of a permissions culture. In undertaking the Google Library Project[8], the company took

---

[4] Brett M Frischmann, *An Economic Theory of Economic and Commons Management* 89 Minn LR 917 (2005); Peter Lee, 'The Evolution of Intellectual Infrastructure', *Washington Law Review*, Vol 83, 2008.

[5] L Ray Patterson, "Free Speech, Copyright, and Fair Use", *Vanderbilt Law Review*, Jan 1987, Vol 40 No 1

[6] S Ricketson, "Reaping without Sowing: Unfair Competition and Intellectual Property Rights in Anglo-Australian Law" [1984] UNSW Law Journal 1

[7] In 2005, the Authors' Guild and American Association of Publishers launched an action against Google for breach of copyright. The action followed commencement of Google's Library Project to scan books in the collections of five of the world's great libraries. In 2008, the parties agreed a preliminary settlement creating a compensation fund of $125million for authors and publishers and creating a books rights registry. However, the settlement fairness hearing has involved a large number of interested parties speaking for and against the settlement, and the dispute continues.

[8] The project began in 2004. Initially, Google agreed with the libraries of Oxford, Harvard, Michigan and Stanford universities, and the New York Public Library, to digitise the books in

that approach that "we do not need to seek permission; we see something that's innovative, we see something that we can make money out of, we see a new opportunity, we're going to go and do it". Then the copyright owners say, "No, we are going to sue you, you do not have our permission". Google all along has maintained that it is engaging in "fair use" and does not need permission to undertake this activity. Litigation ensues and we now have a proposed settlement.

If we stand back and look at this case study we start to see that we have gone beyond a permission based notion of copyright to a benefit-share model of copyright where Google have said, "we are going to do this, we started out to do this, and we will still continue to do this, but what we are happy to enter a commercial deal with you to share the benefits". People can debate how good or bad that commercial deal is, but it seems to me that the Google Book Settlement represents a fundamental shift in the way we are going to start thinking about copyright in the future. More and more, as I would advocate, and people will no doubt disagree with me, we will move towards an access-based model, rather than a control-based model.

To make the point more succinctly let me say this. Google as a key player in copyright politics has moved the goal posts somewhat. This is where the notion of copyright freedom finds further articulation. Google in this case are in a battle and leading the charge on who controls the redistribution of copyright material. Tradition tells us control is held by the copyright owner – the control model. The digital networks of the 21st century suggest access is the key to dissemination, innovation and wealth in the 21st century. As business evolves to meet this new dynamic one anticipates the need for copyright to be able to accommodate widespread dissemination practices. This is another aspect of copyright freedom.

THE RIGHT TO NETWORK *VS* THE RIGHT TO PRIVATE PROPERTY

The last thing that I would like to mention in terms of this idea of copyright freedom is the idea of the network and innovation in the network. The network, as we call it in the broad sense of the word, is crucial, and if we are not careful in the way we strategise about litigation, and the way we position our business models, if the network is made slower and less effective, we are going to harm the potential for innovation, and the potential for creativity. There is a real question mark over the impact we are going to have on networks and innovation.

---

their collections, in order to facilitate public electronic access to the five collections. Fifteen other university, or university-affiliated, libraries have joined the project.

Many people have made this argument over the last ten years; that when we think about copyright, and when we think about regulation in general around the network, we have to appreciate that there is a fundamental interest not only in private property, but also in the right to network, if you like, the right to be able to use the one of the most incredible networks that we have ever possessed, to be able to innovate, to be able to create, and to be able to do new things.

It is very difficult to work out how we put copyright together with instantaneous worldwide communication and viral distribution and all of the affordances of Web 2.0, but that is one of the great challenges that lie ahead. One of the exciting things about bringing copyright and freedom together (again) is to show us, and focus our attention on what might be able to be done.

THE CULTURE OF THE LAWYERS

Copyright freedom has a broader dimension and an interesting dynamic to navigate.

In my mind copyright and freedom are metaphors for the established and the new wave of copyright lawyers (respectively) and we could go even further and say for business or more broadly social interaction.

Let me stick to the lawyers to make my point.

We have a proud tradition worldwide but especially in Australia of scholars and industry leaders who have spent over 40 years building a tremendous edifice that we know today as copyright. These people spent years and years building a legal framework that can support creative people and creative industries, and they are very proud of it.

I have seen this most recently as part of a copyright reform group – Copyright Principles Project – that has been convened by Professor Pam Samuelson of the University of California, Berkeley. Over a three year period twenty people have come together from "all sides of the fence" to make proposals about the future of copyright law. Lawyers from software companies, practice, film studios, and libraries joined with academics from the leading law schools.. When we meet I see an interesting dynamic. We have the people who built the structure, the people who really see this as their craft, and are very proud of it, and to some extent, they represent a copyright tradition. But on the other hand, we have a brash new generation of people who come forward and say, "you built a great structure, but guess what it's wrong, it's got these problems with it", and the other side bristles, but acknowledges, "you know, I think we can do it better". If metaphors help one side represents "copyright" as we it know it today and the other side represents the call for "freedom" in the network era. Now how can we – like Pam has done – get those two groups together more often and more productively because that is the future of the copyright. I hope we have done that with this conference to some extent.

Take time to listen to and appreciate what is being said over the next two days. We have an interesting line up of speakers and a tremendous group of participants. The venue is remarkable.

Thank you to all who have made this event possible.

PART ONE

THE COMMONWEALTH OF COPYRIGHT: AUSTRALIA, NEW ZEALAND, CANADA

CREATING AND SHAPING THE AUSTRALIAN COPYRIGHT ACT
1968

1

AUSTRALIA'S COPYRIGHT HISTORY

Benedict Atkinson [1]

PSYCHOLOGY AND NATIONS

Psychology, understood as speculation, not science, helps the historian to make sense of what sometimes seems mysterious in national politics. Within limits of reason and commonsense, we may be justified in considering how the behaviour of nations invites analogy with that of individuals, and extrapolate from human psychology principles to explain political conduct. In the case of Australian legislative history, one psychological theory, in particular, commends itself as a partial explanation for the sometimes sabotaging conduct of Australian politicians. This is the concept of the "locus of control", proposed in the 1950s by the psychologist Julian Rotter.[2]

It helps to explain plausibly the elements of passivity and subservience in Australian lawmaking whenever it has involved the interests of two powers, Great Britain and the United States. Those elements are so perceptible in the pattern of Australian copyright legislation that Rotter's theory seems directly to explain why politicians passed copyright laws more accommodating to foreign interests than Australian.

LOCUS OF CONTROL

Although an academic, Rotter observed patients in therapy and noticed that their psychological health to some extent correlated to their perception of control. He

---

[1] Benedict Atkinson is a Fellow of the CCI ARC Centre for Excellence for Creative Industries and Innovation and author of *The True History of Copyright 1905–2005: The Australian Experience*, Sydney University Press, 2007.

[2] Born United States 1916. Spent the majority of his career at the University of Connecticut. In the 1950s helped to develop social learning theory (positive or negative expectations derived from experience influence behavioural choices in ways that may not be rational) – see *Social Learning and Clinical Psychology* 1954.

coined the term "locus of control" to explain why an individual's sense of autonomy is stronger or weaker.

People who observe that certain behaviour is rewarded, and are permitted to engage in that behaviour, come to believe that their behaviour controls reward. If they experience sufficient positive reinforcement, they may believe that reward is the invariable consequence of action. Their locus of control is internalised: they, so they believe, control their environment.

Those who perceive that action does not result in reward, or that if reward occurs, it does so irrespective of individual initiative, tend to become apathetic or avoidant. They are certain that their actions do not, in any way, determine the outcome of events. They externalise the locus of control. External forces, they believe, shape what happens to them.[3]

The idea of a locus of control is helpful in explaining why nations, like humans, may act boldly or timidly, rashly or with foresight, and pursue strategies that may result in prosperity and stability, or poverty and anomie.[4] In Australia's case, the body politic, in the widest sense, has tended to externalise the locus of control. Externalising is not invariable. Australia wears the mask of Janus, at once backward-gazing and self-doubting and forward-looking and optimistic.[5]

AUSTRALIA'S LOCUS

Why externalise? One emotion, scattering or binding the particles of resolution, seems especially to have shaped the European response to the antipodes, and whites, feeling its omnipresence, avoided mention of its name: fear. First settlement in 1788, the primordial act in Australia's political history, seems to have transmitted to politics

---

[3] The locus of control is fixed in childhood, though adults may learn ways to a stronger sense of autonomy. The child who is brought up in a secure predictable way will generally develop a strong sense of autonomy. Its locus of control becomes internal. But a child who experiences fear or rejection, who is treated capriciously or cruelly, may react differently. It may learn to see the external environment as frightening and punitive, inflicting hurt unpredictably. Such a child is likely to externalise the locus of control.

[4] Rotter's schema is conceptually sweeping and critics have noted that a person's perception of control may vary according to environment. For example, some people may believe that external events govern their professional wellbeing, yet confidently expect to control the outcome of events occurring in their private lives.

[5] The theme of Australian identity, explored in national literature over more than 150 years, needs little elaboration. Contrasting themes of optimism and tragedy, youth and decay, extroversion and repression, honesty and concealment, heroism and cowardice, progress and ignorance, acceptance and denial, failure and rebirth, run through the continuing discourse on Australian character and nationhood.

something of the emotions of the convicts, and their overseers and masters, who confronted the mysterious hinterland, human threat, and the everyday possibility of violence, failure and starvation.

Colonial policy in the later part of the 19th century absorbed the traces of their reaction and anticipated, in new hinterlands, and the horizon of the ocean, threat and danger. The imperial power remained far away and not very helpful. But the support of that power was indispensable. Australians, who lived "in the brave sunshine" and for whom life seemed "[r]ich, rude, strong-giving",[6] could not escape their hidden anxiety about a world that could deliver ruin with little warning.

At the end of the 19th century, filled with recorded deeds and unrecorded terrors, colonial politicians faced the necessity for political unity. Though *The Bulletin* and the bush poets sounded the call for the republic, the colonies chose federation and imperial co-option. But long before the creation of the federal commonwealth, politicians responded to their fear of external forces by dependency – a dependency as much psychological as material.[7] Thus, over two centuries, Australia adopted as its protectors Great Britain (19th century until World War II) and the United States (from World War II).[8] In matters of defence, foreign policy and economics, the prescriptions of these two powers powerfully influenced Australian policy.

The requisites of dependency applied with particular force to copyright policy formation.

---

[6] Victor J Daley (1858–1905), *In a Wine Cellar.*

[7] The tension caused by the sense of external threat expressed itself most strongly in reactions to the surrounding environment, powerfully expressed by some of the bush poets in the later part of the 19th century. Authority is dangerous, the moneyed class exploits ruthlessly, life is fragile, nature is overwhelming:

> *Strangled by thirst and fierce privation-*
> *That's how the dead men die!*
> *Out on Moneygrub's farthest station –*
> *That's how the dead men die!*
> Barcroft Boake (1866–1892), *Where the Dead Men Lie.*

[8] When in 1942 General Douglas Macarthur established the Allied Forces' South West Pacific Area headquarters first in Melbourne then in Brisbane, Australia's dependency on the military protection of the United States, protection that the United Kingdom could not offer, became obvious. However, though the control locus passed to the US, and US policy began increasingly to influence Australian, Australia, culturally, and to a significant degree, economically, remained tethered to Britain.

INTERNALISING THE LOCUS OF CONTROL

Australia, in the field of copyright, has been a follower, though twice a leader. On the occasions of autonomous policymaking, Australia internalised the locus of control, once in 1905, when the new federal parliament passed the first federal copyright legislation, and a second time in 1928, when Australia and New Zealand leadership encouraged the Berne Union to permit members to legislate limitations on the author's broadcasting right.

Why, on these two occasions, were policymakers able to internalise the locus of control? Probably because, for distinct reasons, they felt free from the undertow of fear that creates dependency and mental enclosure. A certain poetry, or perhaps romantic self-confidence, can be discerned in the actions of legislators in 1905. In 1928, policy is shaped by national necessity and the federal government determines that on the question of broadcasting, Australia will, if necessary, stand its ground against the world.

FEDERATION

Federation in 1901 created the independent Commonwealth of Australia. The radicals of the 1890s, the great decade of political gestation, who anticipated in Australia a sweeping away of the traces of the old order, heard no birdsong in the new creation. The constitutional device, they said, merely consolidated the self-serving stranglehold exerted over the life of Australia by its seedy politicians, moneygrubs, imperial lickspittles and complacent middle class.

Yet federation produced something remarkable and unimagined: a strain of poetic licence in the behaviour of legislators charged with giving life to the commonwealth. Parliamentarians expressed, in a flood of legislation, the poetry of new nationhood. Death attended new life –the nation continued, until 1902, to grieve at the deaths of Australian soldiers in the Boer War[9] – but joy outweighed sorrow. After federation, the blood, travail and striving of colonial Australia could be forgotten, and for a golden moment in its history, one measured in a handful of years, Australia, the nation, enjoyed gilded youth.

In this moment, politicians grew unafraid. They located control within themselves, and chose boldly to step out of the 19th century's shade, and the penumbra of imperial restriction, to express a nation's freedom to be its own arbiter. The poetry of these post-federation years lies in expression of political emancipation. Political chaos supplied one of the clearest signs of psychic emancipation. Many federal politicians

---

[9] About 1,000 Australian volunteers died in the conflict between the British colonies in South Africa and the adjoining Dutch republics, the Anglo-Boer war of 1899–1902.

refused to be corralled by party discipline, and they forced frequent government dissolutions.[10]

Then, inevitably, accommodations, failures, and tragedies, small and large, swept in like the tide, and youth vanished. Before the vanishing, in the golden moment, a time when everything seemed possible, federal parliament passed the 1905 Copyright Act. It expressed, in full measure, the spirit of the times. Short, coherent, cogent, wasting no words, and written in style attractive to modern readers – and admirably distant in style from obfuscating19th century statutes – it is, so far as any law can be, a poetic achievement.

THE INTERNALISED LOCUS OF CONTROL 1 – THE 1905 COPYRIGHT ACT

In 1905, Australia did not need copyright legislation.[11] Parliamentarians could have waited for the imperial parliament to pass legislation that could be imitated or adopted, and in the meantime left the States to carry on administering copyrights according to their own laws. This was the path of least resistance, or least difficulty. The men of 1905 eschewed this path. The achievements of Australian authors,[12] and the penury of some,[13] urged them to action – a number of senators dilated on the publishers' abuse of monopoly, and their exploitation of writers – though they knew that publishers, predominantly British, would not welcome their initiative.[14]

---

[10] Between 1901 and the outbreak of the Great War in 1914, five different federal parties formed eight governments (a ninth taking office a month after the outbreak of war). Five governments (including three in 1904–1905) lasted for less than a year.

[11] The Australian colonies had enacted copyright laws, principally concerned with registration of local publications, in the later part of the 19th century. The British imperial Copyright Act of 1842, and a miscellany of related imperial statutes, governed the subsistence of British copyright material and its distribution throughout the empire, and also regulated, in lieu of conforming local statutes, copyright in books etc in British possessions.

[12] Beginning with the anonymous folk songs and ballads that record life in early Sydney, and continuing with colonial poetry and the bush ballads, publication of Marcus Clarke's great realist novel, *For The Term of His Natural Life,* and the effusion of diverse, distinctively Australian poetry and prose from 1890 onwards, the literature of nineteenth century Australia is remarkable for its originality and deep poetic feeling.

[13] Christopher Brennan, probably the finest Australian poet of the 1890s, and Henry Lawson, were two great figures of Australian literature whose lives were by 1905 disintegrating in alcoholism and poverty.

[14] The British publishers' grip on the Australian market did not constrain the supply of Australian literature, although publishers, controlling supply of British books to the Australian market, practised ruthless price discrimination. Contrary to contemporary assertions by

The Act said NO to the claims of external powers. It said no to provision for import controls, which, for the avoidance of doubt, British publishers would have wanted carried over from the imperial Copyright Act of 1842. It said no to provision for the new categories of copyright works, and the 50 year posthumous term, advocated by the Berne Convention. And it said no to a conception of copyright as more than the 19th century idea of literary property, thus turning away from expanding the scope of copyright to permit copyright holders to control the production of records.

Viewed in this light, the 1905 enactment can be depicted as an expression of recalcitrance. The unwillingness to adopt the all-encompassing categories of "works" promulgated in the Berne Convention, the insistence on retaining as the principal category of protected subject matter, "books", and the shunning of the idea that copyright extended to so-called "mechanical" reproduction, condemned the legislation to swift obsolescence.

A more accurate way to characterise the legislation is as an act of defiance. The generation of 1905 rejoiced in its volition. The Hansard record shows that in the few years that elapsed between the passing of the 1905 Act and its successor in 1912, party discipline and the interdictions of imperial policy sapped politicians of vitality, independence and forthrightness. Politicians remaining from 1905 were mostly cyphers in the debates of 1912. Senator John Keating, probably the most learned student of copyright law in Australian political history, the sponsor, and possibly author, of the 1905 bill, made a noble and patriotic speech against adoption of import controls. The Government ignored him. The other great figure of 1905, Senator Sir Josiah Symon, kept his silence.

In 1905, however, the Senate engaged in a searching examination of copyright policy that far exceeded in its penetration, and diversity of opinion, any debate, in either chamber, of any Australian parliament, since. Feeling unconstrained by external considerations, politicians concentrated on a principal object: to vest in Australian authors proprietary rights that would, they hoped, allow authors to bargain more effectively with publishers.

They could be called artless for scorning much consideration of the Berne Convention, or the controversy caused by unauthorised recording of musical performances by pianolas or phonographs. On the other hand, their debates showed a sincere concern with ascertaining the rationale of copyright and ensuring that the law created for authors the means to secure economic justice. Subsequent parliamentary debates on these and

---

Australian publishers, British control did not preclude Australian publishing (Angus and Robertson, est 1886, and publisher of Henry Lawson, is an example of a highly successful early Australian publisher). Import controls, however, enabled British publishers to regulate the supply of foreign books – to public detriment.

other subjects of the law were usually characterised by shallow reasoning and glib certitude.

The 1905 Copyright Act lasted on the statute books for a mere seven years. It deserves to be remembered as the outcome of the one great act of legislative independence in Australian copyright history.

THE INTERNALISED LOCUS OF CONTROL 2 – THE 1928 ROME REVISION CONFERENCE

By 1928, the poetry of the immediate post-federation years had long vanished. In 1912, Australia reverted to the policy of imperial dependence, adopting in the Australian Copyright Act of that year the British Copyright Act of 1911. In so doing, it accepted the provisos of the Berne Convention ignored by the legislators of 1905, including the 50 year posthumous term. After 1912, Australia deviated only once, in 1928, from its policy of following the normative examples of the United Kingdom, the Berne Convention (which Britain studiously implemented) and the United States.

The Australian federal parliament of 1928 differed in spirit from its counterpart of 1905. Now the grim factionalism of two party politics (Nationalist and Labor) made impossible the creative anarchy of post-federation, when Protectionist, Labour,[15] Free Trade, and, later, Commonwealth Liberal parties vied for office. Australia's role as a dominion cooperating in the machinery of the British Empire, and its tenderness to the welfare and concerns of the United Kingdom, betrayed the attitude of the obedient child to its distant mother. The locus of control, internalised for a few short years, reposed once again in the bosom of that mother.

For a fleeting period in 1928, Australia snatched back power to make copyright policy for its own sake. This brief reprisal of the 1905 spirit proved too much for the Government, and the control locus soon returned to the imperial power. In the meantime, Australian diplomacy achieved a great deal. The reason for the departure from policy conformism is that the Berne Union's broadcasting policy threatened to wreck the Australian Government's strategy for ensuring the spread of radio broadcasting across the nation. The Government considered the danger to Australia's national interest to be grave and definite. So Australia shrugged off docility. Like the child suddenly aware that self-extinction is the price of automatic obedience, it acted, with decision and acumen, to secure its own interest.

The Berne Union's 1928 Rome revision conference considered, among other things, amending the Convention to vest in authors control over the broadcasting of original works. This proposed extension of authors' rights threatened the policy of countries

---

[15] The Australian Labor Party changed the spelling of its name from 'Labour' to 'Labor' in 1912.

like Australia, which regarded the spread of radio dissemination as a critical element in unifying disparate, often isolated, populations, stretched around and across a vast continent.

If the authors' proposed broadcasting right were adopted in the Convention text without limitation, authors could, thought some, hold broadcasters to ransom. Australian radio stations, embroiled in argument with the Australasian Performing Right Association over fees for playing music, lobbied furiously. If no means existed for restraining APRA, they said, they could be held to ransom, and go to the wall. If APRA, on behalf of copyright owners, demanded inordinate fees for the broadcasting of music, the development in Australia of radio broadcasting could be severely retarded.

The federal Attorney General, John Latham, entertained no doubt, and he instructed the Australian delegate to the Rome conference, Sir Harrison Moore, to resist the conference resolution to adopt an unfettered broadcasting right. Great Britain, while not unsympathetic to the Australian position, offered no particular assistance, and might have voted for the proposition supported by civil law countries. Moore, and his New Zealand colleague, Samuel Raymond (as they pointed out proudly in their conference reports) refused to accept the consensus in favour of an unrestricted broadcasting right.

Eventually, the Union, which depended on unanimity for the passage of resolutions, relented. Article 11 *bis* (2) of the Convention permitted Union members to "determine the conditions under which the … [broadcasting right] may be exercised …" The Australian legislature could thus enact copyright laws imposing certain limitations on the way APRA exercised the performing right. Ultimately, this concession resulted in the provisions of the 1968 Copyright Act establishing the Copyright Tribunal.

As Moore stated in his report, "the interests of the public – that great body of purchasers of copyright wares – were vigorously voiced by the Dominions for the first time in the history of the International Copyright Conferences."

THE EXTERNALISED LOCUS OF CONTROL

After parliament passed the 1905 Act, Australian governments continued, until 1910, to determine copyright policy from the sole perspective of the Australian interest. Then Westminster turned the screws. In 1909, the British Board of Trade appointed a copyright review committee to consider whether to accept in British law the Berne Convention, amended in Berlin in 1908. The Gorell Committee replied in the affirmative,[16] and the Board of Trade oversaw drafting of a copyright bill implementing the Berne provisos. Committed to legislating, the British government turned its attention to securing uniform legislation throughout the empire. Government policymakers had no wish for dominions like Australia and Canada to pursue independent policy. A patchwork of copyright regulations, they reasoned, could only prove inimical to the policy of imperial cooperation, and the preferential trade system on which it was based.

In 1910, at the imperial copyright conference in London, Sydney Buxton, the President of the Board of Trade, made Britain's wishes plain to the assembled dominions. For reasons of "efficiency" and "the imperial connection", the imperial government considered it "highly important to attain as great a degree of uniformity as is reasonably practicable among the principal nations of the world with regard to international copyright." The coda of Buxton's words was clear: commit to legislating in conformity with the imperial copyright bill circulated to conference delegates.

Even so, Australia at first showed no inclination to accept a central precept of the Berne consensus, the 50 year posthumous term, which British publishers embraced enthusiastically. The federal Attorney General, Billy Hughes, instructed Australia's representative at the imperial conference to resist pressure to accept the 50 year term, adding that a long posthumous term benefitted British publishers but conferred "nil" benefit on Australia.

The Prime Minister, Alfred Deakin, also cabled instructions to reject the 50 year posthumous term. Deakin promptly lost office (a month before the conference took place) and his replacement, Andrew Fisher, cabled that his government must examine the British copyright bill before any commitments could be made. Remarkably, Australia's representative at the conference, Lord Tennyson,[17] an Englishman, and a seeming partisan for the British interest, disregarded government communications.

A former governor-general of Australia, he treated federal government communications with condescension and pursued the policy he declared best suited to Australia's interest: that of accepting the resolutions of the conference, including British ratification of the Convention, and the preparation of imperial legislation that could be adopted by all British possessions. The insistence of Australia's first law officer, and its prime minister, that Australia retain the limited copyright term set out in the 1905 Act came to nought, and no Australian politician criticised Tennyson for his wilfulness.

---

[16] Although it rejected enactment of a compulsory licence, a measure countenanced by the revised Convention.

[17] Hallam Tennyson, son of the great Victorian poet Alfred, Lord Tennyson. Governor of South Australia 1899–1902, Governor-General Australia 1903–1904.

The outcome of the imperial copyright conference, which substantially committed Australia to legislate in conformity with new imperial legislation, indicated psychological shift in Australian policy. The unwillingness to discipline Tennyson, indeed the peculiar choice of Tennyson as Australia's representative,[18] the ready acquiescence to copyright policy that, in the words of Billy Hughes, "is of greater relative importance in Great Britain than it is in Australia",[19] betokened return to the tractability that subsumed national interest in that of the perceived external protector.

The change is not surprising. In Australian copyright history, the internalised control locus is anomalous. Externalisation is normal. Once federation's golden moment vanished, and the machinery of politics began to grind predictably, as politicians defined national development and imperial cooperation as inseparable objects, reversion to psychic traits of the 19th century occurred.

The excitement and creative possibility of federation's early years absorbed politicians in nation-building, and they forgot old fears. Australia's dark ontology could be forgotten, but only for a while. Politicians discovered that, in some ways, they forged independence contingently. Seemingly every aspect of Australian life, from railways to sheep stations, relied, in some portion, on British investment. Prosperity depended, to a large extent, on imperial markets, chiefly those of the mother country, and safe passage of cargo guaranteed by the arms and diplomacy of Great Britain.

The recurrence of fear need not have prevented politicians from recognising that while Australian policy must take account of external factors – and external powers – national interest could yet be separated from, and preferred to, foreign. Acceptance of Westminster's primacy in imperial governance need not have entirely stymied the rush of free-wheeling enthusiasm launched by federation. Politicians, presented with the fait accompli of imperial copyright conference resolutions, could yet have fought for, and won, important legislative concessions that benefitted the Australian public. But after 1910, they retreated.

The old fear of annihilation, by nature or humankind, sublimated yet fixed, steered politicians away from the awe-inspiring prospect of genuine self-determination. A person may outwardly display the signs of vitality and resolution and still exist as the mental bondservant of another, crippled by belief that survival without the other is impossible. So it was with Australia, young and free, in the words of the national

---

[18] The former prime minister George Reid became high commissioner in London in 1910. He took some part in debate over the 1905 copyright bill in the House of Representatives and would probably have suited the role of representative better than Tennyson. Keating or Symon could perhaps have attended the conference as Australia's representative. They were still sitting members of parliament but neither was a member of the governing party.

[19] Hughes spoke of the 50 year posthumous term.

anthem written in 1878, yet stepping off the path of adventure and choosing instead to follow that of conformity, certitude, safety – and enclosure.

THE 1912 COPYRIGHT ACT

Great Britain enacted new copyright legislation at the close of 1911 and issued a polite warning to Australia. Any Australian legislation, said a British cable on 1 December, must adopt the provisions of the imperial act (which implemented the amended Berne Convention) or otherwise Australian copyright would no longer be recognised in Britain or the empire. A flickering manifestation of independent spirit prompted the British statement. The Labour Government, perhaps smarting from Tennyson's disobedience in the previous year, drafted a copyright bill in 1911 to give effect to the imperial conference resolutions, but its haste probably indicated a desire for expedition rather than mischief making. At any rate, in 1912, the Government issued a new copyright bill adopting the imperial act of 1911. The bill attracted little critical comment from either house. Legislators concerned themselves mostly with matters of machinery and passed over the substantive portions of the legislation.

The Australian Copyright Act of 1912 adopted the whole of the British Copyright Act of 1911, the latter placed in a schedule to the Australian legislation, offending a number of politicians who expressed dislike of inferior British parliamentary drafting. John Keating called the British legislation "unintelligible to the ordinary person." Together, the statutes swept away the brief legacy of 1905. Keating objected to one part only of the disavowal of legislation with which his name is associated.

He understood, and supported, he said, the passing of new legislation that brought Australia into the community of Berne nations, and brought to authors the benefit of international uniformity in copyright rules. However, he disagreed vehemently with the provision creating import controls, a proviso absent from the 1905 Act.

Import control allowed the copyright holder to control the distribution of copyright material in Australia. Their provenance lay in the 18th century battle against French and Irish book pirates, and principally they benefitted British book and music publishers. They relied on copyright legislation to prevent Australian retailers (or wholesalers) from buying overseas remaindered legitimate copies of British books (or sheet music), and importing them into Australia for sale at prices that undercut the publishers.

The British Copyright Act permitted dominions like Australia to adopt the legislation subject to modifications relating to "procedures and remedies" or "necessary to adapt this Act to the circumstances of the dominion."[20] The notoriously poor drafting of the

---

[20] *Copyright Act 1911*, section 25(1).

1911 Act here created doubt about exactly in what circumstances Australia could modify the terms of the imperial legislation, and the Australian parliament allayed uncertainty by accepting the legislation unchanged.

Keating, though, could not be mollified. Joined by Senator Joseph Vardon, he insisted, that import controls must be resisted, as they had been ignored in 1905. In words that resound in the present day, he demanded that the public interest be satisfied. "We have to realise that copyright legislation affects not merely publishers, printers, and authors, but readers ... the whole community." Keating called section 10 of the 1911 Act, which established controls, "a big blackmailing clause", and he added that, "in adopting this legislation, we are adopting British legislation, and ... Great Britain is a totally different country from Australia."[21]

Keating returned to the theme of blackmail, anticipating modern arguments against parallel importation restrictions. Controls, he reiterated, "open the door to blackmail." They "give a monopoly to a man who chooses to buy the copyright of a song, as far as Australia is concerned."

In the lower house, William Archibald, a Labor MP, and the man responsible for the creation of free libraries in towns, said that section 10 would do "an injustice ... to people in Australia." David Gordon, a member of the ruling Commonwealth Liberal party, submitted that, "we should legislate according to Australian requirements". Section 10, he said, "is all very well from the British aspect, but from the Australian standpoint, it seems to me that we ought to consider the position in this part of the world, and modify the law to suit our own purposes, rather than to suit those of persons who are copyrighting in Great Britain."[22]

These voices of dissent, arguing for the Australian interest, were ignored. A new Australian Copyright Act, superseding the legislation of 1905, and accepting in Australian law, the British Copyright Act of 1911, passed in 1912. The new Act introduced a 50 year posthumous term, the class of "works" recognised in the Berne Convention, the compulsory licence for recording music, and classes of fair dealing. Copyright applied to the production or reproduction of works in any material form, including recording or cinematograph film. Import controls placed in the hands of copyright holders control over the supply of all legitimate product.

---

[21] He continued that, "we are adopting a provision made in the United Kingdom to meet conditions with respect to importation of pirated copies, which are totally dissimilar from those that apply in Australia."

[22] Archibald added that legislators, "should not make away with our rights for the sake of securing uniformity."

THE INTERWAR YEARS

Allowing for the unusual circumstance that Britain ratified the Berne Convention on Australia's behalf,[23] and thus technically only imperial legislation formally implemented the convention, Australia's adoption of the 1911 Act emphasised the nation's rediscovered psychological subsidiarity. That for 56 years, a self-directed British legal instrument constituted the substance of Australian copyright legislation, reflects the external locus of control.

The British Copyright Act of 1911 made Australia safe for British business in three ways:

- import controls enabled British publishers and record companies to control the supply of all licit copyright material to the Australian market
- control, by the Australasian Performing Right Association, of the public performance right, resulted in repatriation to Britain of the bulk of music performance fees collected by APRA
- copyright in records enabled British gramophone companies, which by the early 1930s monopolised Australian record manufacture, to regulate production and supply.

Except in the case of import controls, designed to facilitate the practice of ruthless price discrimination by British publishers, British commercial control in Australia did not result from legislative plotting to subordinate Australian markets to British copyright interests. In 1911, no-one foresaw the rise of radio broadcasting and its extraordinary effect on the increase in the commercial value of the public performance right. However, imperial copyright legislation vested in the publishing and recording industries, by species of copyright control, great economic power. These industries were made up of British companies, and as soon as peace descended on Europe, they exerted control over Australian markets for copyright material.

The history of Australian copyright politicking in the interwar period is complex, and it is sufficient, for present purposes, to record that by accepting imperial legislation, and the obligation to honour the unfolding program of authors' rights in the Berne Convention (and the evolving system of neighbouring rights), Australia's copyright perspective, already governed by the imperial perspective, became fixed.

Considerations of international law and imperial comity now made impossible significant retreat from the legal position determined, at root, by psychic dependency. Even though Australia the nation, seen independently from external considerations, benefitted little from the lengthy copyright term, or a number of other stipulations of

---

[23] Australia became an independent member of the Berne Union in 1928. Until then British accessions or ratifications were done in its own right and on behalf of its imperial possessions.

copyright law, and not at all from import controls, politicians could not contemplate the frightful possibility of separation. The desire for attachment perhaps explains the otherwise mysterious absence of critical thought in Australian policymaking from this time forward.

Though policymakers had plenty to object to, from now on, by and large, they confined themselves to discussing the mechanics of international law and its reception into Australian. They were not disturbed that the structure of the law primarily benefitted a foreign economic interest. They reacted to copyright disputes that broke out frequently between 1920 and 1940, as if the underlying law, which buttressed the arguments of British copyright owners against obstacles to revenue-making, reflected deeper natural necessity.

Between the wars, two copyright-related phenomena disturbed the economic peace. The first, starting in the mid-1920s involved APRA's collection of fees for the public performance of music. Radio broadcasters, instruments of unprecedented mass communication, beneficiaries of advertising revenues and government subsidy, quickly became APRA's favourite collecting source. The second concerned the bitter dispute between commercial radio broadcasters,[24] orchestrated from EMI headquarters in London, which, in the early 1930s, resulted in Australian record companies banning radio stations from playing their records.

Government reacted by conciliation. The Royal Commission on Performing Rights, which reported in 1933, examined the first dispute, and became embroiled in the second. The Royal Commissioner, Sir William Owen, recommended compulsory arbitration as the suitable procedure for resolving performing right disputes,[25] and equivocated on the record companies' claim for a record performing right (on which basis they asserted the right to ban the playing of their records). Owen saw that such a right, if accepted, would lead to necessity to pay two public performance fees but he said the legislature must determine the question.

Reform, however, proved too much. Government ignored the royal commission report and life went on as before. APRA, described as a "dragon devastating the

---

[24] Australia, unusually, established in the early 1920s a broadcasting system split between public broadcasters supported by licence fees, and private broadcasters supported by advertising revenue. By the mid 1930s public broadcasters were consolidated under the control of the Australian Broadcasting Corporation. Public and private broadcasters devoted a large proportion of airtime to the playing of music.

[25] He also recommended, among other things, that APRA publicly disclose non-collection income, public performance fees, distributions, its music repertoire. Government allowed the report to lapse. Over 30 years later, the Coalition Government adopted the first recommendation, for the establishment of an arbitration tribunal, establishing in the *Copyright Act 1968* the Copyright Tribunal.

countryside"[26] continued to court unpopularity by demanding progressively larger public performance fees from the ABC and commercial radio stations. Legally, the broadcasters could do nothing to stop the devastation. The record companies, whose counsel at the royal commission called commercial radio, "a noisome weed", continued – with diminishing interest – their war against radio.

The "gramophone lion", so-called by an interested member of the federal attorney-general's department, blamed the precipitate fall in record sales during the great depression on radio broadcasting of music. In the United States and United Kingdom, the recording industry reacted by instituting bans on the playing of their records. In the UK, EMI asserted that the 1911 Copyright Act conferred on record producers the right to control the public performance of their records, and to general amazement, the English High Court upheld this argument in 1933.[27]

In Australia, Gramophone Company, Parlophone Company, and Columbia Gramophone Company, sustained heavy losses from record sales from the mid 1920s. After their UK parent companies merged in 1931, they constituted the monopoly supplier of records in Australia. Their ban on broadcasting of records thus posed a grave threat to radio stations but over time the record industry saw, in its activities and those of broadcasters, confluence of interest. As EMI eventually realised, broadcasting stimulated, rather than undermined, sales.

By 1940, government, because of difficulty, distraction, and simple ineptitude, had failed in its task of conciliation. Copyright factions were antagonistic but they lived with their differences. The Australian interest in the wide dissemination, via radio and other means, of copyright material could not be said to be a foremost consideration of government policy. Reform would have to wait.

THE EXTERNAL LOCUS STRENGTHENED AND BROADENED

Reform came, slowly, and once again, Australia followed the British lead. Spurred by continued commercial dispute over performing rights, and importuning for recognition of a sports performing right,[28] the British Government commissioned a committee to review the copyright law. The Gregory committee reported in 1952,

---

[26] By Purcell, barrister for the Cinematograph Exhibitors' Association at the royal commission.

[27] *Gramophone Company Ltd v Stephen Cawardine & Co* [1934] 1 Ch 450.

[28] The Association for the Protection of Copyright in Sports (renamed the Sports Promoters' Association) lobbied government hard in the late 1940s and early 1950s, for recognition of copyright in sporting spectacles. Though the sports promoters often did not precisely articulate the species of right sought, they wanted the legal right to control the broadcasting of sporting fixtures. In 1952 they organised a ban on television broadcasting of major events. In the same year, the Gregory Committee rejected the proposal for a sporting performing right.

recommending implementation of the latest amendment to the Berne convention,[29] and reordering of the copyright legislation to recognise analogous copyrights of the recording and radio and television broadcasting industries.

Australia followed by assembling the Spicer committee in 1958 to review the findings of the Gregory committee and the implementing legislation.[30] The committee largely adopted the conclusions of its British counterpart, and recommended new legislation, which, when it finally came in 1968, adopted the structure, categories and terminology of the British legislation.

The Australian Copyright Act of 1968 thus began its life as an analogue of the British Act of 1956. In its present incarnation, multiplied in length about sevenfold, it sets out complex procedures for collecting fees for use of copyright material, as well as expressing imperatives of international law and a bilateral trade agreement with the United States.

Most informed Australians would regard the 1968 Copyright Act as an instrument nicely calculated to enable Australia to benefit from the principle of international mutuality, while supposedly "balancing"[31] the interest of copyright owners in profit, and the public in dissemination. The Act is thus viewed as a beneficial compact, the product of something more than mortal wisdom, uncovered by the exegesis of enlightened foreign lawmakers, and so obviously giving effect to the universal moral law, that reception in Australian law must occur automatically.

Another view, drawn from consideration of Australian copyright history, suggests itself. If the locus of control is hard to shift, if embedded psychologies live in nations through centuries, we have no reason to expect, in the future, more freedom of information than that allowed us, in the century past, by the proprietary interest collectives of larger powers. Two young Canadian scholars, Sara Bannerman (sarabannerman.blogspot.com) and Blayne Haggart (blaynehaggart.blogspot.com), neither lawyers, are drawing attention to a way in which Australia, among other nations, might free itself from psychological subsidiarity, and emancipate its policy for practical benefit. They suggest that even within the constraints of international law and free trade agreements, so-called "middle powers" like Australia and Canada, and less developed countries, can create something like copyright freedom, or more freedom than before, by identifying common interests and interpreting rules to encourage, rather than restrict, information freedom. Theirs is a pragmatic conception of freedom, but it offers more encouragement than the principle of "balance of

---

[29] At a conference in Brussels.

[30] The British *Copyright Act 1956*.

[31] The first reference to a "balance of interests" – now repeated ad nauseum to be the function of copyright law – that I noticed in official literature is in the 1959 report of the Spicer Committee.

interests", which, if the last century is a guide, may encourage more obedience to external restrictions that inhibit rather than emancipate the supply of information.

2

THE SPICER COMMITTEE (1958)

Professor Leslie Zines [1]

INTRODUCTION BY PROFESSOR BRIAN FITZGERALD

Most people here know Professor Leslie Zines as probably Australia's most famous constitutional law professor, having been at ANU for over 30 years. A real genius in the constitutional law area. Many people don't know that he also played an interesting role as a new recruit to the Attorney General's Department in the mid 50s with the Spicer Committee. What we asked him to do, although he was a little apprehensive about this, was to come to the conference and talk a little bit about that time and about his reflections about copyright. So over to you.

PROFESSOR ZINES

As was just said, when I was first asked to attend the conference, I refused on the ground that although I had been heavily involved in the reform of copyright law 50 years ago, I have had nothing to do with it for several decades. As a result of a change in my career, my work and my interests led me into other fields.

I explained that when it came to issues at the cutting edge of copyright, such as the internet and information technology and digital copyright, I am an ignoramus. But it was made clear to me that my presence was not desired because it was thought I could contribute anything intellectually to your discussions, but rather as an historical relic who, moreover, should be invited soon, while he was still around. I must say, having regard to the way I feel at the moment, it wasn't a moment too soon.

The writer, LP Hartley, famously said, "The past is a foreign country, they do things differently there" and that was certainly true of Australia in the late 1950s.

---

[1] Emeritus Professor Leslie Zines is a Visiting Fellow in the Law Program of the Research School of Social Sciences, Australian National University, Australia's most distinguished constitutional scholar, and the author of seminal scholarly works on constitutional law and history.

It seems to me that the most striking feature of the establishment and work of the Copyright Law Review Committee under Sir John Spicer was the pervasive force of what I would call the British Connection, which has been touched upon in relation to earlier periods by the previous speaker. It was, in fact, I believe, an important element still, despite General MacArthur's role in much of Australia's social life at the time, and was to remain that way, with decreasing emphasis perhaps, over the next decade or so.

The Attorney General, Neil O'Sullivan, who was very shortly replaced by Sir Garfield Barwick, and the Secretary of the Attorney General's Department and Solicitor General, Sir Kenneth Bailey, were anxious that the Copyright Law Review Committee should not undertake a lengthy fundamental examination of the social, economic and legal aspects of copyright. That was because it was thought it had already been undertaken by the Gregory Committee in the United Kingdom which led to the enactment of the Copyright Act 1956 of that country.

The first and major term of reference, therefore, was to advise which of the amendments recently made to the law of copyright in the United Kingdom should be incorporated into Australian law. Then, rather incidentally, the Committee was asked to consider what other alterations should be made. The Committee did not feel irked, or hampered, or hemmed-in in any way by the terms of reference. On the contrary, it considered that the approach adopted was desirable. They gave reasons why one should not depart unduly from the British precedent, reasons which would not be regarded as very cogent today.

Emphasis was given to the close connection between the law of the two countries for many years. Also, where a person wished to maintain rights in the United Kingdom, as well as in Australia, in the same work, there was, as the Committee said, "great advantage in being able to rely on legal provisions that were substantially the same in each country."

The Committee also had the view that there was an advantage in being able to rely on the decisions of English courts in order to help interpret our law. Furthermore, it was said, and probably rightly for that period, that text books and articles on copyright would appear more frequently in Britain than in Australia.

It reminds me of an occasion where two years earlier, when I was a post-graduate student at Harvard, I was discussing with my Administrative Law Professor, Louis Jaffe, a topic for a research paper. He suggested I look into Australian and American law relating to jurisdictional and non-jurisdictional issues. I told him that in respect of Australia at that time, most of the law was English. He looked at me with great surprise and said "I had no idea colonialism was so all pervasive".

Ben Atkinson in his history of copyright law, I'm sorry, in his true history of copyright law, (which presumably distinguishes it from the pack of lies that we get elsewhere), has suggested that this desire to follow Britain led the Committee to neglect Australia's national interest in respect of its lack of consideration of the posthumous term of copyright and of the import provisions.

As to the term, the Committee didn't examine the question as a matter of economic self-interest, as the Canadian and New Zealand bodies had done in 1957 and 1959, respectively. For the Spicer Committee, the requirements of the Berne Convention incorporated into British law were of overwhelming importance. The economic interests of Australia as primarily a copyright user, were shortly dismissed in favour of what was described as "justice to the overseas authors".

One of the Committee members, the Reverend Dr Percy Jones, Vice Director of the Conservatory of Music at the University of Melbourne, and Organ Master at St Patrick's Cathedral, was most vigorous on this issue. When I wrote in the report that factors other than the balance of payments were involved, such as justice to overseas authors, those words were largely taken from him. I thought then, and think now, that it was a very simplistic view of justice, and I remember saying I didn't think natural law laid down the life of the author of 50 years as the most just period of copyright, and there was no question of the balancing of conflicting interests.

The report also refers to the United Kingdom as one of the main users of Australian copyright material, and states that Australian authors should receive the same copyright protection as British authors. The assumption is, throughout, that the predominant overseas market for Australian works would be Britain.

The report does not enquire into arguments against the import monopoly provisions which were so prominent, as Ben has told us, in the parliamentary debates of the 1905 Act. I was probably remiss here, I did as I will explain shortly, an enormous amount of background work for this Committee, but one thing I didn't do was to go to the Hansard in relation to the 1905 Act. If I had, and I had placed that material before the Committee, it is quite possible that they would have considered it to a greater extent, although whether it would have changed their view is another question. But I do not recall that anyone noted the provisions, or any strong submissions were made to the Committee on the matter.

It may be that some more consideration would have been given to it had the Committee known of the recent misfortune of Sir Kenneth Bailey. He returned from a conference in New York with a record of the latest New York musical hit, *My Fair Lady*. To his great embarrassment and confusion, he discovered that he had smuggled in a prohibited import. He told a small group of us. I rang my colleague, the Director General of Customs and told him the full story. "What should I do?" he asked. His colleague, apparently, told him to do nothing, but to go away and sin no more. I think actually, he said he would get in touch with the copyright owners, who no doubt said much the same thing.

One issue which Australia had no need to worry about for more than 40 years was constitutional power. Before 1968, Australian copyright law was governed by the Imperial Copyright Act of 1911. It operated throughout the Empire but in the case of the self governing dominions, it applied only if each dominion Parliament decided it should apply with or without modifications. Nevertheless, once applied, it applied as imperial law.

In adopting the 1912 Act, the Parliament was not applying its constitutional powers, it was applied by virtue of a provision of the 1911 Act. So, the issue of what is the extent of the copyright power, or any other power didn't arise because the Act applied by virtue of paramount force. So it's not true to say, as I think Ben said in his overheads, that the 1912 Act incorporated the British provisions. It "applied" the British provisions and applied them as British or imperial law.

But once, of course, Australia decided to bring its own Act, or to change that law, then the question of constitutional power of course arises.

The orthodox view is that the words of the Constitution have the meaning that they had when the Constitution was enacted, a view which has been very strongly opposed by the gentlemen sitting in the front there.[2] This raised questions whether copyrights under section 51(18) covered the rights in gramophone records and in TV broadcasts looking back to 1900. The particular problem with the broadcast was that unlike copyrights existing in 1900, it was not in any permanent form, but was a fleeting image. The Committee, sensibly enough, decided not to explore those questions. They did point out that broadcasting power could perhaps be of assistance.

Nevertheless, lack of constitutional power was given as a reason, and sometimes "the" reason, for not recommending protected rights in certain areas. It was the reason for denying protection to an artist's moral right, although I think most of the Committee thought of this as a rather strange continental motion, and to the performer's right, and similarly in relation to the protection of sporting spectacles, apart from the offence created by the Broadcasting Act.

The wider scope given today to the external affairs power, and other powers, and the somewhat broader approach to constitutional interpretation, with Justice Heydon dissenting, would be relevant if the Committee were inquiring today.

Another feature of the 1950s, as far as I was concerned, was that there seemed to be no people around who had any deep knowledge of copyright law, or any interest in the theory of copyright law. That applied to all members of the Committee and to its Secretary. Nobody was teaching copyright law, or, indeed, any intellectual property law. When I was informed by Sir Kenneth Bailey that I was to be Secretary of the

---

[2] A reference to the Hon Michael Kirby, whose opinions on constitutional power, expressed in judgments, were not identical to those of Professor Zines.

Committee, I spent the next two or three weeks reading Copinger and Skone James on Copyright – I think the 9th Edition – from cover to cover. I then started on the minutes of the international conferences beginning with that of the Berne Convention, armed with my knowledge of high school French and a French/English dictionary.

None of the Committee members had any greater knowledge of the subject. Whether there were any copyright experts in Australia then, or academics in the subject, they did not, if I remember rightly, bring themselves to our attention, or make submissions.

One is only to look at the size and vitality of this gathering to realise how much Australia totally differs from that foreign country 50 years ago.

Thank you.

3

THE COPYRIGHT ACT 1968: ITS PASSING AND ACHIEVEMENTS

Professor Adrian Sterling [1]

INTRODUCTION

I hope you will allow me to begin by giving some biographical details to show how it is that I come to be here today and to have the pleasure and privilege of addressing you.

After graduating and being admitted to the Bar in Sydney, I went to England and was called to the English Bar. By a strange chance I took up work in 1954 with IFPI, the international organisation representing the record industry in legal matters. So I came to specialise in national, regional and international copyright law: I stayed with IFPI till 1974, when I returned to the Bar in London, eventually in 1992 entering academia to teach international copyright law in the University of London, where I still teach this subject.

When at this Conference I look at the Australian Copyright Act, I see it from two perspectives: firstly as regards my participation in the debates on the 1967 Copyright Bill, and secondly from the point of view of a copyright lawyer having spent over 50 years working in the field of international copyright. So I start with a description of some of the events which occurred during the debates on the Bill in 1967–1968, then give general summaries of how I see the achievements of the Act, and of Australia in the copyright field generally. In another paper, I describe some of the challenges facing copyright as I see them.

May I say that it gives me particular pleasure to give this address in Old Parliament House, where so much Australian history has taken place, where I came in 1967/1968

---

[1] LL.B. (Sydney, 1948); Bar of New South Wales (1949); Bar of England and Wales (1953). Professorial Fellow, Queen Mary Intellectual Property Research Institute, Queen Mary, University of London, Visiting Professor, King's College, University of London. Professor Sterling is one of Australia's most distinguished copyright law scholars, and the author of the leading reference work *World Copyright Law,* Sweet & Maxwell, 2008 (3rd edition), a unique compendium of the international law of copyright. © J.A.L. Sterling 2009.

to make representations on the Copyright Bill, and which calls to mind friends and colleagues I met then.

PART I: THE PASSING OF THE ACT

Background to the 1968 Act

As indicated by previous speakers, Australian copyright law grew as a branch of the copyright tree planted in the UK in 1710 with the passing of the first copyright law, the Act 8 Anne c.19. Following the 1710 Act a number of Acts extending the scope, duration etc. of copyright were passed in the 18th and 19th Centuries in the UK, culminating in consolidation and formulation of a comprehensive copyright law in the UK Copyright Act 1911, which by one legislative means or another extended or was applied throughout the British Empire as it then was.

Soon after Federation in 1901, Australia adopted its first Copyright Act (1905). This incorporated provisions of UK copyright legislation (not at that stage consolidated), and introduced a number of fresh concepts in approaches to copyright law.[2] Following the passing of the UK Copyright Act, 1911, the Australian Copyright Act 1912 was passed, broadly following the provisions of the UK Act. The UK pattern of preliminary recommendations by a Copyright Committee[3], followed by publication of a Bill was reflected in Australia by the Report of the Spicer Committee 1959, followed by the presentation of the Copyright Bill 1967. The 1967 Bill led to intense debate and a political crisis (see below) but the Bill as amended passed into law in 1968, coming into force in 1969.

At the international level, the Berne Convention sets the copyright standard for the world. The original text of the Berne Convention (1886) was revised at Conferences in 1908, 1928 and 1948. The 1948 text was the most recent version of the Convention prior to the passing of the 1968 Act in Australia, and (as had all previous texts) the Convention dealt with author's rights, but not with the related rights of performers, phonogram producers or broadcasting organisations. After 1948, in accordance with resolutions ("*voeux*") adopted at the 1948 Revision Conference, studies began for the creation of a separate Convention dealing with these related rights.

So it was that in 1961, the Diplomatic Conference for the adoption of a Convention for the Protection of Performers, Producers of Phonograms and Broadcasting

---

[2] For history of Australian copyright legislation, with detailed description of the political and legal background to the 1968 Act, see Benedict Atkinson, *The True History of Copyright 1905–2005: the Australian experience* (Sydney University Press, 2007).

[3] Report of the Copyright Committees 1909 (Gorell Report), 1952 (Gregory Report 1952 (UK) Report) and 1955 (Whitford Report).

Organisations took place in Rome, 10–26 October. Some 40 States (among them Australia) sent delegates to the Conference, Australia being represented by Mr. Clive Weston of the Commonwealth Department of Labour and National Service. International and non-governmental organisations were also represented. I was fortunate to be present at the Conference as a member of the delegation of one of the non-governmental organisations (IFPI).

While the rights of record producers and broadcasters to authorise the reproduction etc. of their phonograms and broadcasts were recognised without opposition, there were two main controversial issues at the Rome Conference, namely the rights of performers to control the subsequent uses of their performances (whether in sound recordings of films) and the question whether performers and phonogram producers should have the right to receive remuneration for the broadcasting and public performance of their sound recordings.[4]

In the event, the Rome Convention provided (1) that the protection provided for performers shall include the possibility of preventing certain acts of broadcasting, fixation etc. of their live performances (Article 7), and (2) the right of performers and phonogram producers to receive remuneration for broadcasting and public performances of sound recordings; this right was voted into the Convention (Article 12) at the Plenary Meeting on 25 October, 20 votes for, 8 votes against and 9 abstentions.[5]

Among the countries voting for Article 12 were the UK and Australia. Australia's vote did not represent mere passive following of the UK, as I know from my discussions with Mr. Weston at the Conference. Australia was entirely free to decide on which way to vote on each issue, and indeed I had no idea of how Mr. Weston would vote until the crucial votes were taken on 25 October. Australia's acceptance of the principle of Article 12 was to have relevance in the debates on the 1967 Bill.

---

[4] For general description of the provisions of the Rome Convention, see J.A.L. Sterling *World Copyright Law* (3rd edition, Sweet & Maxwell, 2008) ("WCL") Chapter 20, and for the eventual outcome of the dispute on the question of performers' rights in films (Articles 7 and 19 of the Convention) see WCL para.20.09(1). The dispute concerning performers' rights in their filmed performances was not finally resolved in 1961. It continues today (cf the lack of consensus necessary to adopt the WIPO draft Treaty on Protection of Audiovisual Performances at the WIPO Diplomatic Conference in 2002).

[5] Article 12 permits Contracting States to make reservations on the acceptance or exercise of the right. See also B below.

The need for new legislation

The United Kingdom had updated its Copyright Act 1911 in 1956. Then in Australia followed the Spicer Committee 1959, and its recommendations.[6] In 1967, a Copyright Bill for legislation to replace the Australian 1912 Copyright Act was published by the Commonwealth Attorney General. The Bill completely overhauled the copyright law and introduced new provisions, not all related to the solutions adopted in the UK. In this section I wish to deal only with one crucial issue in the debates, concerning one provision of the Bill.

A crucial issue and its resolution: the record performing right

The debates on the Bill leading to the adoption of the UK Copyright Act 1911 were preceded by the Report of the Committee on the Law of Copyright Report 1909 ("Gorell Committee").[7] Submissions to the Gorell Committee on behalf of producers of sound recordings ("record producers") included the following passage:

> [We desire recognition of] copyright protection for the artistic and manipulative skill employed in the creation of the phonogram, subject, in the case of copyright works, to the rights of the original author ... We claim that a two-fold copyright protection should be accorded to the phonogram, on precisely the same lines as the Convention accords protection to the cinematograph ...[8]

The Gorell Committee reported:

> The Committee think that protection should be afforded by legislation to the manufacturers of discs, cylinders, rolls and other mechanical devices, necessary to be used in the course of producing sounds, against piracy of these objects or their reproduction, either by means of direct copies or by means of copies produced by sound or otherwise. The grounds for this recommendation are that, as was pointed out in the evidence which has been placed before the Committee, these discs and other records are only produced at considerable expenditure by payments to artists to perform, so as to record the song, etc., and by the expenditure of a considerable amount of ingenuity and art in the making up of these records; and that therefore

---

[6] Report of the Committee appointed by the Attorney-General of the Commonwealth of Australia to consider what alterations are desirable in the Copyright Law of the Commonwealth 1959 ("Spicer Committee Report").

[7] Report of the Committee on the Law of Copyright, Dec.1909, Cmnd 4976, Parliamentary Papers 1910, Vol.21.

[8] Gorell Committee Report, pg.44.

the manufacturers are, in effect, producing works which are to a certain extent new and original, and into which the reproduction of the author's part has only entered to the extent of giving the original basis of production. Therefore, the Committee regard this as one of the things which can be subject of the copyright and further recommend that public performances by means of pirate copies of these records should also be treated as an infringement of the rights of the manufacturer.[9]

Reflecting the recommendation of the Committee, the UK Copyright Act 1911 provided as follows in s.19(1):

Copyright shall subsist in records perforated rolls and other contrivances by means of which sounds may be mechanically reproduced in like manner as if such contrivances were musical works …

Following the increased use of records for purposes of public performances in cafés, theatres etc. and in broadcasting, in 1933 the Gramophone Company Limited, in order to confirm the ambit of the copyright granted by s19(1), to took a test case against a restaurant company (Cawardine) in whose premises a Gramophone Company record of a musical work[10] had been played in public. Mr. Justice Maugham upheld the plaintiff's claim that the copyright accorded to the record under s19(1) of the 1911 Act subsisted independently of the author's copyright (if any) in the recorded work, and embraced all the attributes of copyright under the 1911 Act, including the public performance right.[11]

On the basis of the decision in *Cawardine,* the UK record industry founded Phonographic Performance Ltd, for the exercise of the record performing right recognised under the 1911 Act, and licensing of such use of records in public places and broadcasting was then commenced.

After the revision of the Berne Convention in 1948, the UK Government decided it was appropriate to consider revision of the 1911 Act, and set up the Committee on the Law of Copyright (Gregory Committee). The Committee's Report was presented in 1952, and recommended the retention of the record performing right. [12]

---

[9] For discussion of the Committee's recommendation see J.A.L. Sterling "*Intellectual Property Rights in Sound Recordings, Film and Video*", (Sweet & Maxwell, 1992, para.6.21).

[10] Overture to *The Black Domino* by Auber (died 1871) (out of copyright).

[11] *Gramophone Co. Ltd. v. Stephan Cawardine and Co.* [1934] 1 Ch.450. The judgement was not appealed. For further description of the case and the history of the record (phonogram) performing right and its recognition in national, international and regional law, see WCL paras 90.01 – 90.15.

[12] Report of the Committee on the Law of Copyright Oct. 1952 (Cmnd 8662, Parliamentary Papers 1951–52, Vol.9), para.184.

When the Copyright Bill 1955 was presented in the House of Lords, two members of the Upper Chamber declared their determined opposition to the retention of the record performing right in the new legislation. "This right got in by a side-wind", thundered Lord Jowett, supported by Lord Lucas of Chilworth, "and we are determined to see its abolition".

Some months of intense lobbying by the record industry and broadcasting interests then followed.[13] In the event the right was retained in section 12 of the Copyright Act 1956 (and still remains in the current legislation, the Copyright, Designs and Patents Act 1988, sections 16(1)(d), 20).

The campaign for the international recognition of the record performing right had as above described come to fruition with the recognition of the right in Article 12 of the Rome Convention.

The scene shifts to Australia. The Spicer Committee Report 1959, having considered the various arguments and the history of the recognition and exercise of the right, recommended the retention of the right.[14] When a new Copyright Bill was being prepared in Australia, the indications were that the matter would be hotly contested in the debates on the forthcoming Bill. Accordingly in February 1967, I (then Deputy Director General of IFPI) was at the request of the Australian record industry association sent to Australia to assist the association in its campaign for the retention of the record performing right. Throughout my visits to Australia in this connection, I was in close consultation and full agreement with the association on all decisions and steps to be taken.

As a first step, I sought a meeting with the Minister in charge of the Bill, Nigel Bowen Q.C., as he then was. He received me courteously in his Chambers in Macquarie Street, Sydney. I began by saying that this was not a political, but a legal issue and spoke of the history and exercise of the record performing right. When I had finished I expected some searching questions, even, I hoped, some tiny indication of the Attorney-General's view. But Nigel Bowen simply said "Now I will hear the other side. Good morning". A great lawyer.

Later, in February 1967, I went to Canberra with the industry representatives and had extensive meetings with Lindsay Curtis, the Attorney-General's officer responsible for dealing with matters connected with the proposed legislation. Lindsay was the perfect civil servant, courteous, receptive and impartial, and more than that, highly intelligent, an excellent draftsman and blessed with a warm personality and a great sense of humour. There was much drafting of submissions and exchange of views, not only

---

[13] Then Assistant to the Director General of IFPI, I took part in 1955/1956 in the making of representations to Parliament on the issue.

[14] See Spicer Committee Report para.260, and for extensive review of the question, paras 228–264.

about this issue, but also on the issue of the conditions applying in respect of the compulsory licence to make sound recordings.[15] I then returned to the UK.

In May 1967, the Attorney General published the Copyright Bill. The record performing right was retained. A fierce controversy broke out. The Government of the day was a coalition of the Liberal Party and the Country Party. The radio stations opposed retention of the right – but the unexpected development was that the small country radio stations providing programs to lonely homesteads and farms of settlements in the outback went to their Country Party MPs and said that payment of royalties for the broadcasting of records would mean that in many cases they would have to terminate their programmes, removing the services and the entertainment to large numbers of persons in the country areas. While the Liberal Party wished to retain the right, the Country Party opposed the right's retention, and said it would leave the Government if the Liberals insisted on retaining the right. This would have meant an election, and thus the issue had created a political crisis.

At the invitation of the Australian record industry I returned to Australia in October 1967. After meetings with the industry I went to Canberra and the Attorney-General received me in his rooms here in Old Parliament House. The first thing he said was "Mr. Sterling, you told me this was not a political issue and now the Government is about to fall because of it". I made such apology as one could in such circumstances. "You had better stay here in Canberra and see my people in my Department", said Mr. Bowen. That was all: we did not speak again.

I settled down in the old Hotel Canberra near Parliament House and commenced a series of meetings with Lindsay Curtis and industry representatives.[16] I did not meet

---

[15] Two of my fellow students from Sydney University Law School (Class of '48) who were in Parliament in 1967, were T.E.F. (Tom) Hughes and Lionel Murphy. I went to see them (separately) and asked for their support of the record performing right. Tom Hughes (Liberal Party) said he would support the right, as did the Liberal Party. Lionel Murphy (Labor Party) said "But what are you doing for the little man?" by which he meant the rank and file performers in bands and orchestras. I said I would do what I could to encourage the Australian record industry to support participation for performers in royalties paid for the record performing right, and he said on that basis he would support the right.

[16] The old Hotel Canberra was then a modest building, one might say redolent of the charm of colonial days, in the dining room of which Members of Parliament were often seen, and where, it was said, the political future of Australia was forged in, it was hoped, confidential conversations. Walking in the sylvan surrounds to Parliament House each morning, one had to be on the alert, as magpies were constantly attacking passersby and it was reported that Parliamentarians had been issued with pop-guns to ward off avian attacks. Two vignettes, both of Prime Ministers, which stay in my mind from visits to Parliament House in 1967/1968, were the dapper figure of Harold Holt as he made a statement to the Chamber and departed from the front bench (at which some of us will be privileged to sit at this Conference) with a sprightly step that reflected his athletic attributes, always to be

any representatives of those opposed to the retention of the right. The pattern was that we would meet Lindsay Curtis and put a proposal on behalf of the industry. Lindsay would convey this to the "other side" and we would meet again in a few days to consider the reply: this process continued for some weeks.

Finally, it was announced that the Government would amend the Bill to specify, *inter alia*, the general rules on the maximum royalties payable for broadcasting of records by commercial and non-commercial stations. Thus the matter was resolved, and the right was retained in the 1968 Copyright Act and remains there still, with the provisions on maximum royalties (ss 85, 152), the right now being embraced in the right of communicating the sound recording to the public. It is understood that there are now moves for the deletion of the maximum royalty provisions on the basis of changed circumstances, technological developments etc.

The campaign in Australia did not end the national battles for the recognition of the right. The same dispute between the industry and the broadcasters arose again in Canada in 1970 – on that occasion with victory for the broadcasters, as Mr. Trudeau's Government voted in the Canadian Parliament for the retrospective abolition of the right (after the Canadian record industry's successful case before the Canadian Copyright Tribunal in which the Tribunal fixed tariffs for the exercise of the right).[17] Twenty-eight years later the Canadian Parliament voted for the re-instatement of the right.[18] In the United States, the right has been recognised (after long debates) in the US Copyright Act (s106(6)) limited to public performance by means of digital audio transmissions, and debates still continue for the extension of the right.[19]

In sum, the record performing right has been recognised in the majority of national copyright laws (estimated as those of approximately 100 counties), at the international level in the Rome Convention 1961, and in the WIPO Performances and Phonograms Treaty 1996, and at the regional level in the Cartagena Agreement 1969 (founding

---

associated with his memorable departure, and the courtesy with which John Gorton greeted me as I passed him early one morning in the entrance hall (though I was totally unknown to him).

[17] The main argument used by those opposed to the recognition of the right in Canada in 1970 was not based on legal or equitable grounds, but on an allegation (unsubstantiated, and vigorously denied by the Canadian industry and performers) that the royalties for exercise of the right would go to the United States.

[18] I have been asked by the editors of this publication to record personal memories of the events here related, so I mention that on the cold December night in 1970 when I left the Canadian Parliament building after the abolition vote to fly back to London, I purchased at the departure airport a bottle of Champagne which I vowed to open when the right was re-instated, something I was able to do twenty eight years later.

[19] For details see WCL paras 90.03 – 90.15.

Parties Bolivia, Colombia, Ecuador, Peru and Venezuela) and in the European Community Rental and Related Rights Directive, as consolidated in 2006.

The history of copyright contains many examples of the influence of personalities. In Australia in 1967/1968, possibly determinative was the decision of John Sturman, then General Manager of the Australasian Performing Right Association (APRA), in deciding APRA's role in the dispute concerning the record performing right. In those days, the "cake theory" was much supported by those in author's right circles. The argument ran that broadcasters and other users could only pay a certain amount for the use of protected material, and if record producers and performers were to have a share, there would be less of the cake for beneficiaries of author's rights. It would have been entirely understandable if John Sturman had taken the same view. When I met him in Sydney in February 1967, however, he said "You have your problems. We have ours. You argue your case and we will argue ours. I will remain neutral on this issue".

John Sturman's attitude was of critical importance, and I am glad to have this opportunity to recognise that.

PART II: ACHIEVEMENTS OF THE 1968 ACT

General

Seen from the international point of view, the 1968 Act is remarkable for its detail and its length: some 600 pages, the longest Copyright Act in the world, as far as I know. A number of provisions of the Act offer precisely described solutions to a number of challenges posed to modern copyright by technological and other developments: some of these provisions are mentioned in B-D below. In addition, it should be mentioned that from the overall point of view, Australia has made distinctive contributions to copyright law and learning, both in the past, and today as regards the continuing development of copyright law in the world context (see E below).

Provisions on moral rights

Amendments to the 1968 Act in 2006 contained some 87 sections relating to moral rights, constituting, as far as I know, the most extensive and detailed legislation on these rights in any copyright law. While the granting of moral rights of attribution and integrity for authors and performers follows the provisions of the Berne Convention and the WIPO Performances and Phonograms Treaty 1996, the provisions go into great detail as to what constitutes infringement, what remedies are available etc. Here I wish to mention one aspect of these provisions which has attracted international attention, particularly in common law countries, namely the provisions on defences against claims of infringement of moral rights:[20] these provisions introduce a concept of "reasonableness" as a defence in relation to allegedly infringing acts.

Thus, as regards the attribution right, there is no infringement if in the particular case the defendant establishes that it was reasonable in all the circumstances not to identify the author. Section 195AR(2) provides that in determining such reasonableness a number of factors are to be taken into account, which include (besides factors relating to the nature of the work, and the purpose, manner and context in which the work is used) any practice in, or contained in a voluntary code of practice in, the industry in which the work is used, or any difficulty or expense that would have been incurred as a result of identifying the author. There is a similar "reasonableness" defence as regards alleged infringement of the integrity right where the defendant establishes that it was reasonable in all the circumstances to subject the work to the treatment of which complaint is made (s195AS). There are also "reasonableness" defences as regards alleged infringement of performer's moral rights (ss195AXD, 195AXE).

The abovementioned defences concerning practices, and difficulty and expense of identification, are, it is believed, unique to the 1968 Act. They are, in the international context, important for international study in the context of the exercise of moral rights, not only generally, but particularly as regards use of protected material in online communication.

The fair dealing provisions

Section 41A of the 1968 Act, introduced by amendments adopted in 2006, provides that a fair dealing with a literary, dramatic, musical or artistic work, or with an adaptation of a literary, dramatic or musical work (or an audiovisual item (section 103AA)), does not constitute an infringement of copyright in the work (or item) if it is for the purpose of parody or satire.

There are apparently no similar provisions in copyright legislation of other common law countries providing that fair dealing for the purpose of parody or satire does not constitute infringement: in these other countries a defence on the basis of parody or satire lies under the general fair dealing (or in the US, fair use) rules.[21]

---

[20] Ss 195AR (author's attribution right), 195AS (author's integrity right), 195AXD (performer's attribution right) and 195AXE (performer's integrity right).

[21] In the UK a proposal for a fair dealing exception regarding caricature, parody or pastiche is contained in the Gowers Review of Intellectual Property 2006, Recommendation 12. In some civil law countries (eg, Belgium, France) there are specific legislative provisions for parody, but in other civil law countries defences are under general provisions or limitations. See WCL para.13.22.

Space and format shifting

The 1968 Act, as amended in 2006, contains detailed provisions regarding exceptions from copyright infringement in respect of space shifting (section 109A) and format shifting (sections 43C, 47J, 110AA).[22]

I do not know of any legislation in any other country dealing specifically and in detail with space and format shifting, as in the Australian Copyright Act.

PART III: AUSTRALIA'S ACHIEVEMENTS IN COPYRIGHT: AN INTERNATIONAL PERSPECTIVE

Judicial achievements

Here are some of the Australian cases which have attracted international interest, particularly in common law countries: references to them will be found both in court decisions in other jurisdictions, and in Government and other reports and studies on current issues in copyright.

Australasian Performing Right Assn. Ltd. (APRA) v. 3DB Broadcasting Co. Pty Ltd[23] [recognition of record performing right]

Bulun Bulun and anor v R & T Textiles Pty Ltd[24] [protection of traditional knowledge: concept of application of principles of confidential information to sacred tribal knowledge]

Gutnick v. Dow Jones & Co. Inc[25] [private international law: allegedly defamatory material on US website, accessed in Victoria: defamation law of Victoria applicable]

IceTV Pty Ltd v Nine Network Australia Pty Ltd[26] [analysis of concept of originality]

Moorhouse v University of New South Wales [27] [principles applying in assessing liability for authorising infringement of copyright]

---

[22] See WCL para.10.05. Recommendation 8 of the abovementioned UK Gowers Review proposes introduction of a limited private copying exception for format shifting for works published after the law comes into effect.

[23] [1929] VLR. 107; 35 A.L.R. 109; WCL, para.90.02.

[24] [1998] FCA 1082.

[25] [2001] VSC. 305; [2002] H.C.A. 56 (HC); WCL, para.3.31.

[26] [2009] HCA 14 (HC).

[27] (1975) 133 CLR. 1; 49 ALJR. 267; 6 ALR. 193; [1976] RPC 151 (HC); WCL, para.13.10.

Rank Film Prodn. Ltd v Dodds[28] [hotel rooms: liability for unauthorised viewing in hotel rooms of TV programs containing material protected by copyright]

Telstra Corpn. Ltd v Australasian Performing Right Association Ltd[29] [liability for unauthorised provision of protected material in "music on hold" service for telephone subscribers]

Telstra Corpn. Ltd v Desktop Marketing Systems Pty Ltd [30] [labour as criterion of originality]

Universal Music Australia Pty Ltd v Cooper[31] [infringing authorisation through linking to sites hosting unauthorised copies of protected material]

Universal Music Australia Pty Ltd v. Sharman Licence Holdings Ltd[32] [infringing authorisation of unauthorised file sharing]

In this connection special mention should be made of the World Trade Organisation Dispute Settlement Body Panel Report on section 110(5) of the United States Copyright Act. This Report on the interpretation of the "three step test" laid down in Article 13 of the WTO Agreement on Trade Related Aspects of Intellectual Property (TRIPS) has made a major contribution to the appreciation and application of this fundamental provision of the TRIPS Agreement throughout the world. The Chairman of the Panel was Hon. I.F. Sheppard, formerly President of the Copyright Tribunal established under the Copyright Act 1968.[33]

Academic achievements

Australia has produced a number of academics internationally recognised for the contribution of their writings and teaching of the theory and practice of copyright. The doyen of this group is Professor W.R. Cornish. Among publications of

---

[28] [1983] 2 NSWLR 553; 2 I.P.R. 113 (NSW SC, 1984); WCL, para.9.10; (*cf Rafael Hoteles SL*, Case C306/05, [2007] E.C.D.R. 2 (European Ct of Justice)).

[29] (1995) 31 I.P.R. 289 (Fed.Ct.); (1997) 71 A.L.J.R. 1312; 146 A.L.R. 649; [1997] HCA 41 (HC).

[30] [2001] FCA 814 (Fed.Ct.); [2002] FCAFC 112; [2002] 55 I.P.R. 1 (Full Fed. Ct, 2002); WCL, para.7.16. Cf. *Telstra v APRA* supra.

[31] [2006] FCAFC 187 (Full Court, Fed. Ct); WCL, para.13.53.

[32] [2005] FCA 1242; [2006] FCA 1 (Fed. Ct); WCL, para.13.53.

[33] Panel Report on United States Copyright Act, s110(5) (Hon. IF Sheppard, AO, QC, A.V. Guarion, CL Guada) 15 June 2000, ref WT/DS160/R: in WTO Dispute Settlement Reports, (Cambridge University Press, 2008). See also WCL para10.14.

international renown by Australian academics are those of Professor Cornish,[34] and of Professor Brian Fitzgerald[35], and the classic text of Professor Sam Ricketson *The Berne Convention for the Protection of Literary and Artistic Works 1886–1986*[36], with its second edition, *International Copyright and Neighbouring Rights: The Berne Convention and Beyond* (with Professor J.C. Ginsburg)[37], and in the Australian context Professor James Lahore's *Intellectual Property in Australia – Copyright.* [38] Recent publications of international interest include Dr. Elizabeth Adeney's *The Moral Rights of Authors and Performers: an International and Comparative Analysis*[39], and (with J. Davis) Dr. Tanya Aplin's *Intellectual Property Law: Text, Cases and Materials*[40] and numerous learned articles by Professor Peter Drahos and others, as well as the historical survey of Benedict Atkinson above mentioned.

Organisational achievements

The Australian Copyright Council and the Copyright Society of Australia promote research projects, and hold seminars, and generally provide information on copyright, available for Governments, academics and practitioners, and the public generally, with up to date and detailed studies on the background to, and recent developments concerning, copyright law in Australia, also covering regional and international developments: the online availability of this material being particularly valuable. Organisations representing authors and other copyright owners in Australia have long been established and continue to develop and play their part, not only in the administration of copyright, but also in contributing to studies on copyright reform.

Achievements in the communication area: worldlii and austlii

The World Legal Information Institute was established on the initiative and continues under the direction of Professor Graham Greenleaf of the University of New South Wales. The Institute provides access to over 800 databases in over 120 countries and territories via the Free Access to Law Movement, embracing Legal Information Institutes in Asia, Australasia, Canada, the Commonwealth, Hong Kong, New

---

[34] See e.g. Cornish, W. R., Llewelyn, D., *Intellectual Property: Patents, Copyright, Trademarks and Allied Rights* (6th ed., Sweet & Maxwell, 2007).

[35] See e.g. Fitzgerald, B., Gao, F., O'Brien, D., Shi, S.X., eds *Copyright Law, Digital Content and the internet in the Asia-Pacific* (Sydney University Press, 2008).

[36] Centre for Commercial Law Studies, Queen Mary College, Kluwer, 1987.

[37] Oxford University Press, 2006.

[38] Sydney, Butterworths, looseleaf 1977.

[39] Oxford University Press, 2006.

[40] Oxford University Press, 2009.

Zealand, Pacific Islands, Southern Africa, United Kingdom and Ireland and the USA, also Droit Francophone and regional sites including Europe (European Union and European Community legislation, European Court of Justice reports etc.), Caribbean, Middle East etc., together with other material (law journals, law reform etc.), forming compendious and convenient access to legal materials throughout the world. For ease of navigation, and breadth of comprehensive coverage the service is as far as I know unrivalled.

CONCLUSION

Australia has achieved legislative, judicial, academic and other accomplishments of world renown in the field of copyright. It is my hope that Australia will continue to give to the world the benefit of its expertise in this field, for the benefit of all peoples. I believe that this is the time, in collaboration with New Zealand, for Australia to provide new initiatives in the Asian Pacific area, as described in my other material submitted to this Conference.

4

THE FRANKI COMMITTEE (1976 REPORT) AND STATUTORY LICENSING

John Gilchrist [1]

INTRODUCTION

The Franki Committee reported in 1976 on a new technological means of disseminating information. It was tasked:

> To examine the question of the reprographic reproduction of works protected by copyright in Australia and to recommend any alterations to the Australian copyright law and any other measures it may consider necessary to effect a proper balance of interest between owners of copyright and users of copyright material in respect of reprographic reproduction. The term 'reprographic reproduction' includes any system or technique by which facsimile reproductions are made in any size or form. [2]

The Committee made over 30 recommendations for reform of the *Copyright Act*. I propose to concentrate on the two most significant ones. Both recommendations raise 21st century issues and illustrate the perennial problem in finding an equitable balance of interests in the law between owners of copyright and users of copyright material in response to technological change.

---

[1] John Gilchrist is Senior Lecturer in Law, Faculty of Law, University of Canberra. He was Secretary of the Copyright Law Committee on Reprographic Reproduction (the Franki Committee) and as an officer of the Australian Attorney-General's Department was heavily involved in the development of the Copyright Amendment Act 1980 (Cth) (No 154 of 1980) which implemented many of the Franki Committee recommendations. John has a particular interest in publishing and the early history of copyright and has researched and published in this area.

[2] Australia. *Report of the Copyright Law Committee on Reprographic Reproduction* (October 1976) Introduction 1.01.

THEMES OF THE REPORT

The Report of the Committee contains a number of themes which still resonate as copyright policy concerns today.

- One was the Committee's concern for the free flow of information. To quote from Section 1 of the Report "Australia is geographically isolated from the major centres of scientific and industrial research and the vast area of the Australian continent raises special problems in relation to the dissemination of information, particularly in the remoter parts".[3]

  There are a quite a number of references in the Report to the public interest in ensuring the free flow of information for education and research and for the scientific, technical and social development in Australia.[4]

- The second concern was that Australia was (and still is) a substantial importer of copyright material and it should be hesitant in adopting a radical solution to the problem of a kind that is unlikely to find widespread acceptance amongst member countries of the multi-lateral copyright conventions.[5]

- The third concern of the Committee was that its recommendations should be consistent with Australia's international convention obligations and not divorced from what might be called "world standards" so far as the balance of the rights of the copyright owner and interests of the user were concerned.[6]

- And finally it was not only concerned with the question to what extent should copyright owners benefit from the use of the new technology (reprography) on the grounds of principle, but to what extent it was practical for them to do so.[7]

The concern about the free flow of information was and is a concern to Australia and has gained momentum worldwide. Over the last decade it has gained momentum and we now use the term "access to information" to describe it. At the time of the Franki Committee's deliberations there was a strong public criticism about the effect of the British Publishers Marketing Agreement, which was to carve up most of the English speaking world between British and American publishers, with the result that countries like Australia were deprived of access to cheaper American editions of

---

[3] Ibid, 1.37.

[4] Ibid, 1.02, 1.40, 1.51, 4.06, 6.40, 7.07.

[5] Ibid, 1.35,

[6] Ibid, 1.27.

[7] Ibid, 1.19–20, 1.35–37, 2.53.

works. This problem was also aggravated by the slowness of British publishers in producing cheaper paperback editions of works in comparison with their American counterparts.

While action initiated by the US Justice Department in 1976 led to a consent decree that prohibited American publishers from engaging in market allocation with British publishers,[8] this issue has resonated until the present day despite changes in publisher practice and some changes to the *Copyright Act* relaxing commercial import barriers. These concerns about difficulties of access swayed the Franki Committee. Within the Report there were a number of recommendations that sought to respond to complaints about the unavailability of texts in Australia and the unreliability of delivery when ordered from overseas. In a number of their recommendations the Committee provided for wider copying rights using the formula "where a work cannot be obtained within a reasonable time at a normal commercial price".[9]

I now turn to the two most significant recommendations of the Franki Committee – the clarification of the fair dealing provision (s 40) and the statutory licence scheme for the multiple copying of copyright works which became s 53B of the *Copyright Act* and is now embodied in Division 2 of Part VB of the Act (s 135ZJ and 135ZL).

THE FRANKI COMMITTEE RECOMMENDATIONS

A Clarification of fair dealing for private use (s 40)

The Australian Copyright Council Ltd had made submissions to the Franki Committee that all copying should be remunerated upon the basis that authors should receive a royalty for each copy page made of any work within copyright. In Britain the Whitford Committee also reached a similar view by concluding that all reprography be remunerated and that fair dealing be confined to hand or typewritten copies.[10] The Franki Committee took the view that as a matter of principle a measure of copying – by reprographic or other means – should be permitted without remuneration. It did so after examining the laws of other countries – to examine using their term 'world standards' – and the requirements of the copyright conventions.

At one stage in the Committee's deliberations it appeared that the fair dealing provision for research or private study would undergo only very modest reform,

---

[8] *United States v Addison-Wesley Publishing Co* CCH 1976–2, Trade Cases 70.640.

[9] *Report of the Copyright Law Committee on Reprographic Reproduction* (October 1976) 2.60, 3.19, 4.20, 6.58.

[10] United Kingdom. *Report of the Committee to consider the Law on Copyright and Designs* (the Whitford Committee) Cmnd 6732 (1977) [291].

despite widely expressed criticism from many who made submissions – from copyright owners to users – that the provision was too vague and uncertain in practice.

The Committee recommended clarifying the section by inserting a list of factors to be taken into account in determining what constitutes a fair dealing, which was derived from a similar list in the then US Copyright Bill's provision of fair use. But this was hardly a radical step since the factors listed were supported by case law.

The further step was to recommend a deeming provision. That is, certain copying for research or study was deemed to be a fair dealing, namely the making of a single copy of a periodical article or a reasonable portion (10% or one chapter, whichever was the greater) of another published work.[11]

I did not have a vote on the Committee but was encouraged by the Chairman to participate in discussions and I had a hand in persuading the Committee to suggest a reform that would respond to a widely held view about the vagueness of the provision in its practical operation. When confronted by a clear problem, it seemed important not to shy away from its resolution. The clarification of section 40 still stands, and I am pleased to say has since been enhanced to deal with other media.

Two members of the Committee recommended that the fair dealing provision should be extended to cover private and personal use (following the laws of many civil law countries) rather than limit the provision to the rather more scholarly pursuits of research and study.[12] This recommendation was not adopted by the Government, although in practice I did not see this as a dramatic change to the operation of the provision, simply because the recommendation was still limited by the notion of fair dealing, which did not govern the concept of personal or private use adopted in civil law countries.

What the legislative reform of section 40 of the *Copyright Act* did was to clarify the rights of users of copyright material and recognise in particular the practical needs of users of informational literature, particularly periodicals.

B Statutory licence scheme for the multiple copying of copyright works by educational establishments.

The second significant recommendation – the major reform of the Franki Committee – was the legislative enactment of a licence scheme for the multiple copying of copyright works.

---

[11] Australia. *Report of the Copyright Law Committee on Reprographic Reproduction* (October 1976) 2.60.

[12] Ibid, 2.67.

The scheme provided for a statutory licence permitting an educational establishment to make multiple copies of parts of a work and in some cases of whole works for distribution to students, subject to recording the copying taking place under the scheme and an obligation to pay an appropriate royalty if demanded by the copyright owner or the owner's agent within a prescribed time.

The Committee said it was conscious that the idea of a statutory licence would not appeal to some copyright owners who would regard it as a derogation from their rights under the *Copyright Act* but felt the public interest in education and need for access to works in educational establishments justified this approach. It did not consider it would breach the provisions of the Berne Convention and Article 9 dealing with the right of reproduction.

1. Authors of literary and artistic works protected by this Convention shall have the exclusive right of authorizing the reproduction of these works, in any manner or form.

2. It shall be a matter for legislation in the countries of the Union to permit the reproduction of such works in certain special cases, provided that such reproduction does not conflict with a normal exploitation of the work and does not unreasonably prejudice the legitimate interests of the author.

3. Any sound or visual recording shall be considered as a reproduction for the purposes of this Convention.[13]

The Committee considered a total coverage of copyright owners in the scheme was practically important for users but that ultimately voluntary licensing by owners may provide a more attractive option to educational establishments. That of course has come about. The Copyright Agency Ltd has a well-established voluntary sampling system outside the operation of the statutory scheme.

When the Franki Committee made its recommendations there were only three schemes operating or proposed in the world. All in non-English speaking countries.[14] Legislative effect had been given to a licensing scheme in the Netherlands and the Swiss were proposing a similar scheme. The Swedish scheme was a voluntary agreement between the Swedish Government and 17 Swedish organisations including

---

[13] Australia. *Report of the Copyright Law Committee on Reprographic Reproduction* (October 1976) 10.06 and at World Intellectual Property Organisation, *Berne Convention for the Protection of Literary and Artistic Works* (1886 as revised) www.wipo.int/treaties/en/ip/berne/trtdocs_wo001.html at 12 August 2009, and *Berne Convention (Paris text 1971)* www.law.cornell.edu/treaties/berne/overview.html at 12 August 2009.

[14] Australia. *Report of the Copyright Law Committee on Reprographic Reproduction* (October 1976) 6.33

the Association of Swedish Authors and the Swedish Publishers Association and was limited to government schools.

In particular the substance of the agreement proceeded on the basis that the various organizations could be expected to represent 95% of the copyright owners whose works were likely to be copied.[15] These were works in the Swedish language. At the time in Australia no voluntary arrangement could have guaranteed that level of coverage security for users.

REFLECTION AND CONCLUSION

The Copyright Amendment Act 1980 (No 154 of 1980) embodied the Government's response to the Franki Committee's Report. It was not a complete legislative implementation of its recommendations. The recommendations have been characterised accurately as tending to favour the interests of users of copyright material as against the interests of copyright owners. But the Government did not adopt some unremunerated copying recommendations. One example is that the Committee recommended that a library of a non-profit educational establishment be permitted to make up to 6 temporary or ephemeral copies of a copyright work provided it had not been separately published or if it had been, copies of it could not be obtained within a reasonable time at a normal commercial price. That would have legitimised the so-called 'reserve stack' copying which had been a practice of those libraries for some time.

The Franki Committee took the view that the entitlement of an educational establishment to make multiple copies of a work under its statutory licence scheme was to be addition to whatever might be done under its recommendations on fair dealing and "reserve stack" copying. Case law since the *Copyright Amendment Act 1980* came into force suggests that the multiple copying licence has reduced reliance on fair dealing in so far as copying could be said to fall within the "teaching purposes" (now "educational purposes") of the statutory licence (*Re Haines and Director General of Education of New South Wales v Copyright Agency Ltd*[16] and *Copyright Agency Ltd v Charles Sturt University (No 2).*[17]

Overall the Committees recommendations constituted a response to what was perceived to be a strong public interest in accessing works particularly in the informational category. They were however mindful of the fact that the rate of change

---

[15] Ibid, 11.29–42.

[16] [1982] FCA 137 (22 July 1982).

[17] [2001] FCA 1145 (24 August 2001).

in technology was great and thought it desirable to examine the state of the law at regular intervals.

The Franki Committee's recommendations were expanded to include institutions assisting handicapped readers and the scheme established by the *Copyright Amendment Act 1980* was among the first in the English speaking world. Statutory licensing was since been further expanded under Part VB of the *Copyright Act*. One significant change adopted in the *Copyright Amendment Act 1980* was the introduction of a host of offence provisions to ensure adherence to the statutory scheme. This was a significant step in the use of criminal sanctions to underpin this private property right. On reflection I consider there were too many.

The use of offence provisions to outlaw commercial activities in breach of copyright is defensible in most circumstances, but questionable when the criminal sanctions are aimed at the recording and retention of records by public institutions fulfilling an educational need and aimed at both individuals and the institutions which employ them. Another option may have been to give legislative power to enable a court to award additional damages (punitive or aggravated) for infringement of copyright in circumstances of some breaches such as the making of a record that is false or misleading in a material particular. As a matter of policy criminal offence provisions should be used cautiously in the underpinning of personal property rights.

5

A BRIEF PERSPECTIVE: THE HISTORY OF COPYRIGHT IN NEW ZEALAND

Professor Susy Frankel [1]

INTRODUCTORY REMARKS

I wanted to thank the Ngunnawal people for their welcome this morning. We from New Zealand believe in thanking the traditional owners, and in fact, in New Zealand, the real owners of the land. I see that Ruth has actually left so I hope that's passed on.

The Attorney General did mention the Copyright Tribunal, this morning and Ben also mentioned that in his talk. I did want to briefly mention it and I hope at some stage during this day and a half (I chair the New Zealand Copyright Tribunal) that we can return to the modern role of the Copyright Tribunal.

Just to put an issue out there for you to think about, the modern role of the Copyright Tribunal might be a fast track mechanism that actually involves some due process, as opposed to those fast track mechanisms like notice and take down, where due process is arguably missing. So I say that provocatively. Not because I think tribunals are the answer, but it's certainly worth discussing.

I do want to thank Brian and Ben for organising the Conference. I'm not going to say much about them in the interest of keeping to time, but I am eternally grateful to Brian

---

[1] Faculty of Law, Victoria University of Wellington, susy.frankel@vuw.ac.nz. Professor Susy Frankel teaches, researches and publishes on various aspects of copyright, trade marks and patents, and international trade. She is co-director of the New Zealand Centre of International Economic Law, and co-author of *Intellectual Property in New Zealand*. She is a Hearings Officer for the Intellectual Property Office of New Zealand and a neutral arbitrator and mediator for the World Intellectual Property Organization Arbitration and Mediation Center. She is consultant expert to the Waitangi Tribunal on the WAI 262 claim.

as an academic who is one of the Australians, and there are a few of them, who are aware that New Zealand is on the map. I say this facetiously of course.

I'd like to pay a personal tribute to Adrian Sterling. He was one of my teachers. In fact, I took a course at Queen Mary the first year that Adrian and Gerald Dworkin[2] offered the international copyright course. And in trueness to his statement about the role of authors, he took the class on a field trip. Among many places, we went to Keats's house, just to see copyright in action. He was never so blunt as to point out that we were in an author's house but the message filtered through. Thank you, Adrian and Caroline, for taking us there.

I want to add that I think copyright freedom is also about cultural freedom. If we reduce everything to economics, life is a bit sad. My father's an economist. I'm a lawyer – need we say more. It's about culture. It's about dynamic culture and it's also about cultural independence. More on that tomorrow perhaps.

Having said it's about culture, I'm now going to ironically turn to the price of cars. It was not until the price of cars became excessively beyond the reach of the average person in New Zealand that New Zealand changed its copyright law considerably from that of Britain. Through much of the 19th and 20th Centuries, New Zealand's copyright law was a replica of Britain's copyright law. The 1994 New Zealand Act saw some differences to that of the UK law, but for the most part, those differences did not signal any radical policy changes.

So why did the price of cars achieve this first major separation from UK law? Many of you will realise it's because New Zealand protects industrial design through copyright. There is a Registered Designs Act but the primary form of industrial design protection is copyright.

PROVENANCE OF NEW ZEALAND COPYRIGHT LAW

The history of copyright law in New Zealand unsurprisingly reflects New Zealand's history as a colony of England. New Zealand's modern copyright law draws heavily on United Kingdom legislation and cases from that jurisdiction are relied on and often followed in judgments of New Zealand courts. For most of the 20th century New Zealand copyright law was very similar to United Kingdom copyright law. Despite these close ties to United Kingdom copyright law, some significant differences can be found in New Zealand's law both before the 20th century and in the 21st century.

---

[2] Emeritus Professor of Law, King's College, University of London.

COPYRIGHT LAW BEFORE THE 1913 ACT

The 18th ordinance enacted in New Zealand, after the signing of the Treaty of Waitangi[3], was the Copyright Ordinance 1842.[4] The passing of that law was something that the Governor of the day seemed to note as occurring early in the colony's life.[5] The ordinance provided:[6]

> An Ordinance to secure the Copyright of Printed Books to the Authors thereof.

> WHEREAS it is desirable that the copyright of books should be secured by law to the authors thereof:

> BE IT ENACTED by the Governor of New Zealand, with the advice and consent of the Legislative Council thereof, as follows:

> 1. The author of any book which shall hereafter be printed and published, and his assignees, shall have the sole liberty of printing and reprinting such book for the full term of twenty-eight years to commence from the day of first publishing the same, and also, if the author shall be living at the end of that period, for the residue of his natural life.

> 2. If any person shall during the period or periods aforesaid print reprint or import, or cause to be printed re-printed or imported, any such book without the consent in writing of the author or assignee of the copyright thereof, or shall, knowing the same to have been so printed reprinted or imported without such consent as aforesaid, sell publish or expose for sale, or cause to be sold published or exposed for sale, or have in his possession for sale, any such books without such consent as aforesaid, every such person shall be liable to an action at the suit of the author or assignee, in which action double costs of suit shall be allowed, and shall also, upon a verdict being given against him in such action as aforesaid, forfeit and pay

---

[3] The Treaty of Waitangi of 1840 was signed between Maori and the British Crown. The treaty has three articles, one of which allowed the British to make laws for New Zealand. For a discussion of the history of the treaty see Claudia Orange *The Treaty of Waitangi* (Bridget Williams Books, Wellington, 1987)

[4] See Jeremy Finn "Particularism versus uniformity: factors shaping the development of Australasian intellectual property law in the nineteenth century" (2000) 6 Australian Journal of Legal History 113.

[5] See McLay, Geoff, "New Zealand and the Imperial Copyright Tradition" (June 29, 2010). Essays on 1911 Imperial Copyright Act, Forthcoming. Available at ssrn.com/abstract=1719679

[6] See Victoria University, New Zealand's Lost cases, www.victoria.ac.nz/law/nzlostcases/5_Vict_18.pdf For a discussion of the ordinance see" New Zealand and the Imperial Copyright Tradition", Ibid.

the sum of fifty pounds to the use of Her Majesty, her heirs and successors, for the public uses of the Colony and the support of the Government thereof.

The main impetus for the ordinance seems to have been to protect a forthcoming dictionary of Maori grammar.[7] The work in question had been written by the Reverend Maunsell's, who was a significant figure in the Maori church. That New Zealand should enact a copyright law for such a purpose is telling of the nature of New Zealand at the time and foreshadows what is today one of the biggest challenges of all of New Zealand intellectual property law.

Today New Zealand is a country which is poised to consider how much to protect traditional knowledge, known to Maori as matauranga Maori, as it relates to works akin to copyright and other intellectual property rights. Whether laws protecting matauranga Maori in some way will be enacted will depend on the recommendations, and government action based on those recommendations, arising from a forthcoming Waitangi Tribunal report. The Waitangi Tribunal hears claims brought by Maori pursuant to the Treaty of Waitangi.

The report relating to protection of Maori traditional knowledge and related issues arises from a claim brought by Maori against the Crown about New Zealand's flora and fauna and to the use of Matauranga Maori.[8] New Zealand already has trade mark laws which take account of some Maori interests.[9] If New Zealand law, in the future, creates greater protection of Maori interests in intellectual property or related laws, New Zealand law will be quite different from that of the United Kingdom or Australia.

COPYRIGHT LAW IN NEW ZEALAND FOR MOST OF THE 20TH CENTURY

For most of the 20th century New Zealand's copyright law was the same as English law. The Copyright Act 1913 adopted the United Kingdom Act of 1911 and the subsequent Acts in New Zealand of 1962 and 1994 were substantively based on the United Kingdom 1956 and 1988 Act respectively. Some points of difference from the

---

[7] Letter Hobson to Colonial Office (29 March 1842), Alexander Turnbull Library (ATL), CO 209/14, cited in "New Zealand and the Imperial Copyright Tradition", Ibid.

[8] This is known as the WAI 262 claim. The author of this is advisor to the Waitangi Tribunal on intellectual property issues relating to that claim.

[9] Trade Marks Act 2002, s17(6)(ii). See also Susy Frankel "Third-Party Rights as a Violation of Indigenous Cultural Property – A New Statutory Safeguard" (2005), *Journal of World Intellectual Property* (8)1:83–98.

United Kingdom Acts can be found in the New Zealand Acts, but the differences are not substantive policy differences.

In some ways this is hardly surprising, after all the United Kingdom law of 1911 was framed as part of an effort to secure copyright laws as consistent as possible in all of the Empire, so as to protect British works abroad. The law reform followed the Imperial Copyright Conference in which some agreement with the colonies was reached.[10] Sherman and Bentley summarise the goals of the British 1911 reform:[11]

> The law at the time, which was "incomplete and often obscure", was governed by no fewer than twenty two Acts of Parliament, passed at different times betwen1735 and 1906; and to those should be added a mass of Colonial legislation, frequently following blindly the worst precedents of English law... the new Copyright Bill ... makes a clean sweep of all of these enactments and proposes to set up in their place a homogenous code of copyright law on sound and generous lines'.

Thus, New Zealand's law of 1913 reflected this homogenous code which spread across the Empire as far an in as much detail as the British could persuade colonial legislatures to do. New Zealand was quite obedient in this respect.

It was not until the price of cars became excessively beyond the reach of the average person in New Zealand that New Zealand changed its copyright law considerably from that of the United Kingdom and the imperial copyright tradition.

So why did the price of cars motivate a major change of direction from United Kingdom law? New Zealand's copyright law includes, in the scope of its subject matter the protection of industrial design.[12] Drawings and models, which lie behind the design and eventual production of motor vehicles, are protected copyright works in New Zealand. There is a Designs Act, which registers some designs, but the primary form of industrial design protection is copyright.[13] Thus, copyright law could used to prevent the importation of cars made in out of New Zealand.

THE PRICE OF CARS

In the 1980's New Zealand progressively instituted a free market and deregulated economy. As a result of that economic policy New Zealand stopped manufacturing

---

[10] See Brad Sherman and Lionel Bentley, *The Making of Intellectual Property Law* (Cambridge University Press, 1999), 136.

[11] Ibid, page 128 fn 119, citing Copyright Law Reform (1910) 216 Quarterly Review 482.

[12] Copyright Act 1994, section 14 includes artistic works, defined in section 2 to broadly include drawings and prototype models of processes of industrial design,

[13] Design Act 1953.

goods which could be more cheaply made elsewhere. One of the sectors most radically affected in the early years of this economic policy was car assembly. Major car manufacturers, including Ford, Mitsubishi and Toyota, closed their New Zealand assembly operations. There was and is no comparative advantage in car assembly in New Zealand. But, New Zealanders do drive cars and they drive cars long distances. New Zealand may have only 4 million people on a small land mass compared to Australia, but New Zealand is a slightly larger land mass than the United Kingdom. Not assembling cars locally meant they were imported and this in turn resulted in cars being expensive.

The solution to escalating car prices was to allow the parallel importation of cars, which would eventually come primarily from Japan and Korea. But the appointed New Zealand distributors, of the car manufacturers, used copyright law to make sure that cheaper imports entered New Zealand. The price of cars then provided the political motivation to change copyright law and allow parallel importing of all copyright products including films, sound recordings and computer programs.

Since allowing parallel importing, New Zealand has tweaked the law to make parallel importing a balance between the interests of New Zealand consumers and copyright owners. For example, a copyright owner of a film for instance has a nine month exclusive window to make the film available in New Zealand before parallel imports are permitted.[14] Also, when there is a dispute over whether parallel imported goods are legitimate or otherwise the burden of proof is on the importer to show there is not an infringing copy.[15] Usually the burden of proof would be on the party alleging infringement.

COPYRIGHT LAWS FOR THE BENEFIT NEW ZEALAND

Since the 21st century began, when it comes to enacting intellectual property laws, New Zealand policymakers have been conscious that copyright and other intellectual property laws should be for New Zealand's benefit. All intellectual property reform, in the last decade has, at the policy and Bill stages, included statements that one of the purposes of the relevant law reform is for the benefit of New Zealanders and New Zealand's economic benefit. Whether this is, in fact, true in substance is debatable, but the policy of intellectual property laws for local benefit is a good starting point.

The most recent copyright policy debate was focused digital copyright protection and culminated in the Copyright (New Technologies) Amendment Act 2008. There are many difference of detail between New Zealand's digital copyright laws and those of

---

[14] Copyright Act 1994, s35(3)

[15] Copyright Act 1994, s 35.

the United Kingdom, European Union or United States approach. One key difference, for example, is that technological protection measures are only protected where they prevent copying rather than access to copyright works.[16]

New Zealand does have copyright law that is different in some respects from other common law countries. Those laws are based on a common standard, which is no longer determined by United Kingdom law, but by international agreements, including the TRIPS Agreement.[17] Sometimes little differences in legislation can create bad outcomes because often there is no case law to test those little differences. The law then becomes uncertain and users of copyright works such as librarians, educators or authors themselves, don't quite know what is legitimate and what is infringing. However, major differences that can be achieved within international frameworks on the grounds of local policy interests are important. Parallel importing is one of those.

New Zealand may well end up having less copyright freedom once it strikes a trade deal with the United States.[18] Even though small, New Zealand it has experienced trade negotiators. Keeping parallel importing of copyright goods will be an important goal for these trade negotiations because of the obvious and proven benefit for New Zealand consumers.

---

[16] Copyright Act 1994, s226A.

[17] Agreement on Trade-Related Aspects of Intellectual Property Rights, Annex 1C *of* Marrakesh Agreement Establishing the World Trade Organization, Apr. 15, 1994, 33 I.L.M. 1197, 1198 (1994).

[18] New Zealand is currently negotiating with the United States for the United States to join what is known as the P4 agreement. P4 is a free trade agreement between New Zealand, Singapore, Chile and Brunei. The expanded negotiations are known as the Trans-Pacific partnership and include the United States, Australia and Vietnam. For a discussion of intellectual property in these negotiations see Susy Frankel "Intellectual Property and the Trans-Pacific Partnership" in Jane Kelsey (ed) *No Ordinary Deal: Unmasking Free Trade and the Trans-Pacific Partnership Agreement* (Bridget Williams Books, 2010) forthcoming.

6

"WE ARE ALL DEVELOPING COUNTRIES": CANADA AND INTERNATIONAL COPYRIGHT HISTORY: FAULT LINES IN THE MAP OF INTERNATIONAL COPYRIGHT

Dr Sara Bannerman[1]

"Canada consents to enter Copyright Convention."[2] These six words, sent by Canada's Prime Minister in reply to the British government's inquiries as to the willingness of the colonial governments to enter the *Berne Convention*, masked domestic tension that surrounded the issue of copyright in Canada. Canada would follow Britain into the *Berne Convention* but Canada, as a British dominion and, eventually, a middle power, would have a very different story from other, more familiar, copyright histories. Canada's path crossed hidden fault lines that would later appear in the political map of international copyright.

Current mappings of the politics of international copyright – alignments that classify the various copyright interest groups – tend to mask the tensions within these categories. Such categories and classifications have a powerful ability to mask tensions, to organize, to mobilize, and to shape the history of copyright.

In this paper I will make three arguments, drawing on the historical experience of Canada with the *Berne Convention* between 1886, when the *Berne Convention* was founded, and 1971, its last revision. First, Canada, though aligned with the most powerful countries on issues of international copyright, has a unique and important history with international copyright that is very different from the histories of the major powers. Second, for many middle powers, the *Berne Convention* was a symbol of

---

[1] B.Mus., MA, PhD, SSHRC Postdoctoral fellow, Centre for Governance of Knowledge and Development, Regulatory Institutions Network, College of Asia and the Pacific, Australian National University.
[2] Sir R. Herbert to Sir J. Pincefort, 12 June 1886. *Switzerland No. 2: Further Correspondence Respecting the Formation of an International Copyright Union*; John Lowe. Memorandum. 9 February 1889. RG13 A-2 Vol. 2361 File 1912–1424 Part 4. Library and Archives Canada.

progress in international law, and a hallmark of a civilized country. Canada has aligned with the major powers on issues of international copyright. Though this alignment has not always comfortable, it stems in part from a desire to be associated with ideas of progress and civilization, and to be aligned with one's largest trading partners. Third, I ask, what contribution do middle powers make to the international copyright system today?

I

CANADA'S COPYRIGHT HISTORY IS DIFFERENT FROM THOSE OF THE MAJOR POWERS

Canada's historical experience with the *Berne Convention* has been very different from the experiences of the major powers. Like many of today's middle powers, Canada signed on to the international copyright treaty in 1886 not as an independent country but as a British colony. Canada had no foreign affairs institutions or diplomats and was not directly represented at the founding meetings of the convention.

Economically, unlike France or Great Britain, nineteenth-century Canada, like many other colonies, stood to gain little from the new international regime; Canada's copyright industry was almost non-existent.

In 1886 just 574 copyrights were registered in Canada, and, since Canadian authors had almost no international recognition, few Canadian authors would benefit from the internationally expanded copyright protection that would come about through Canada's participation in the *Berne Convention*.[3]

Competitively, the *Berne Convention* put Canada at a disadvantage. Canadian printing and publishing was in competition with the printers and publishers of the United States – a country that did not yet recognize international copyright. American publishers could reprint the works of foreign authors without permission and without any legal requirement to pay royalties to foreign authors. Canadian publishers, under the *Berne Convention*, would not have this freedom.

As a result, the Canadian printing and publishing industry suffered, affecting authors as well.[4] Although the industry was expanding – by 1881 the number of people employed in the industry had almost doubled since 1771, and over the next ten years

---

[3] Canada. *The Canada Year Book: Statistical Abstract and Record for the Year 1886*, 270, www66.statcan.gc.ca/u?/eng,17565; George L. Parker, "The Evolution of Publishing in Canada" In *History of the Book in Canada*, eds. Patricia Fleming, Yvan Lamonde and Fiona A. Black, Vol. 2 (Toronto: University of Toronto Press, 2004), 17–26.

[4] William Kirby to John A. Macdonald, 24 March 1885. In Prime Minister Macdonald fonds (MG26 A), pages 61277 to 61281. Library and Archives Canada.

employment in the industry would grow by 30%[5] – it was also seen to be struggling. Novelist and journalist William Kirby argued, in an 1885 letter to Canadian Prime Minister Macdonald, that his concern was "not primarily to secure copyright to Canadian authors – they have plenty of that," but to "give our publishing industries such fair play and protections as they might obtain or the trade will become extinct in Canada."[6]

Nineteenth-century Canada's strides towards independence from Britain in foreign affairs were slow and gradual. By 1886 there was an increasing trend for Canada to send representatives to international negotiations, and it was established that British colonies were to be consulted on matters of international treaties.[7] However, consultation with Canada and the other British colonies, in the case of the initial negotiations for the *Berne Convention*, was minimal, and no Canadian representative accompanied the British delegation at the founding meetings of the *Berne Convention*. On 9 September, the British delegates signed the *Berne Convention*, making the following declaration:

> Plenipotentiaries of Her Britannica Majesty state that the accession of Great Britain to the Convention for the protection of literary and artistic works comprises the United Kingdom of Great Britain and Ireland, and all the Colonies and Foreign possessions of Her Britannica Majesty.

At the same time, they reserve to the Government of Her Britannic Majesty the power of announcing at any time the separate denunciation of the Convention by one or several of the following Colonies or possessions in the manner provided for by Article XX of the Convention, namely: India, the Dominion of Canada, Newfoundland, the Cape, Natal, New South Wales, Victoria, Queensland, Tasmania, South Australia, Western Australia, and New Zealand.[8]

There was a conflict at the root of Canada's position as a party, under Britain, to the new convention – one that would disturb and threaten the new Union. While the

---

[5] Éric Leroux, "Printers: From Shop to Industry" In *History of the Book in Canada*, eds. Patricia Fleming, Yvan Lamonde and Fiona A. Black, Vol. 2 (Toronto: University of Toronto Press, 2004), 75–87.Canada. *Census of Canada, 1870–71*, Volume 3, Table LV – Summary of Industrial Establishments, by Provinces.

[6] William Kirby to John A. Macdonald, 24 March 1885. In Prime Minister Macdonald fonds (MG26 A), pages 61277 to 61281. Library and Archives Canada.

[7] David M. L. Farr, *The Colonial Office and Canada, 1867–1887* (Toronto: University of Toronto Press, 1955), 234–235.

[8] Francis Adams and J.H.G Bergne to the Earl of Iddelsleigh. *Report on the Third International Copyright Conference at Berne.* 10 September 1886. In RG6 A3 Vol. 214 File "Copyright Conference at Berne, 1886." Library and Archives Canada. Emphasis added.

Canadian government moved to make Canada a part of a copyright system that was being portrayed as the advancement of civilization, there were also significant differences between Canada and the countries that initiated the Berne Convention. Great Britain, France, Italy, Spain, Switzerland and Germany housed major publishers with interests in publishing in foreign countries, while Canada was a net copyright importer. They were highly developed, and Canada was still developing. They had a flourishing literary culture; Canada did not.

The differences between Canada and the lead countries in the movement to establish the *Berne Convention* only grew wider. Although Canada had agreed to join Berne, by 1889 there were strong arguments that Canada should control its own copyright law, independently from Britain, and denounce the *Berne Convention*. Canada's decision to join the Berne Union would soon be called an act of "profound...almost criminal – negligence" on the part of Canadian politicians, because the principles of the international agreement were out of step with what many Canadian interest groups at the time were calling for.[9] Canada, shortly after joining the *Berne Convention* in 1886, reversed position; for years following Canada's initial accession, Canada would attempt unsuccessfully to denounce the agreement.

Canadian Minister of Justice John Thompson, who came to see the *Berne Convention* as being highly disadvantageous to Canadian interests, felt that the convention allowed foreign copyright holders to gain a monopoly on publishing their works in the Canadian market, causing Canadian printers and publishers to lose out. The benefits that Canadian copyright holders received under the *Berne Convention* did not equal, in Thompson's view, the harm caused to Canadian printing and publishing industry:

> the condition of the publishing interest in Canada was made worse by the Berne Convention...The monopoly which was, in former years, complained of in regard to British copyright holders is now to be complained of, not only as regards British copyright holders, but as to the same class in all countries included in the Berne Copyright Union. Canada is made a close market for their benefit, and the single compensation given by the convention for a market of five millions of reading people is the possible benefit to the Canadian author...[who has been described as] "belonging rather to the future than to the present."[10]

[9] John Ross Robertson quoted in Ron Poulton, *The Paper Tyrant: John Ross Robertson of the Toronto Telegram* (Toronto: Clarke, Irwin, 1971), 107.

[10] John Thompson to Governor General in Council, 1892, 7. RG13 A-2 Vol. 85 File 892–217. Library and Archives Canada.

Thompson also felt that the terms of the *Berne Convention* largely favoured densely populated and highly urbanized countries such as those in Europe, but that such terms were unsuited to relatively less developed countries like Canada:

> The Berne Convention had in view considerations of society which are widely different from those prevailing in Canada. In Europe the reading population in the various countries is comparatively dense; – in Canada, a population considerably less than that of London is dispersed over an area nearly as large as that of Europe. In the cities of Europe, especially in Great Britain, the reading public is largely supplied from the libraries, while, in Canada, as a general rule, he who reads must buy. In European countries the reading class forms but a fraction of the whole population, while in Canada it comprises nearly the whole population.[11]

Opposition to the agreement from printers, publishers, and related industries grew and mobilized. As a result, a Canadian copyright act was unanimously passed in 1889 containing domestic printing requirements and a compulsory licensing system that were not compatible with the *Berne Convention*.[12]

The Copyright Act of 1889 contained domestic printing requirements that were disallowed under the *Berne Convention*, which did not allow member states to require any formality as a condition of copyright.[13] The new act required *first or simultaneous* printing and publishing in Canada – that is, printing and publishing in Canada within one month of publication or production elsewhere.[14] Works that were not first printed and published in Canada or printed and published in Canada within a month of their publication or production elsewhere would not be eligible for the protections provided by Canadian copyright.

The Copyright Act of 1889 went further. The failure to meet the domestic printing and publishing requirements of the act would have opened the way for the grant of compulsory licenses to reprint the work in Canada without permission of the copyright owner under compulsory licensing provisions. These compulsory licensing provisions, designed to make access to books more affordable in Canada, and to enable Canadian printers and publishers to better compete with the Americans, who

---

[11] Ibid.

[12] 52 Vict, c 29.

[13] *Convention Concerning the Creation of an International Union for the Protection of Literary and Artistic Works* (*Berne Convention*), 9 September 1886. Berne: Office of the International Union for the Protection of Literary and Artistic Works, 1886, Article 2.

[14] "such work shall be printed and published or produced in Canada, or reprinted and republished or reproduced in Canada, within one month after publication or production elsewhere." 52 Vict. c. 29, article 1.

did not yet recognize international copyright, were also seen to be incompatible with the *Berne Convention*. Therefore Canadian Parliament, in a unanimous decision, requested denunciation of the Berne Convention.[15]

The British, who had ultimate control both of Canadian legislation and Canadian foreign affairs, refused to let the Canadian act enter into force, and refused to allow Canada to denounce the *Berne Convention*. The British government was loathe to allow Canada to abandon the *Berne Convention*, as denunciation would break up the system of copyright uniformity throughout the British Empire. It infuriated some members of the British government that a colony such as Canada might threaten to break up the Berne Union. Henry Bergne, who had been a British delegate to the early meetings creating the *Berne Convention*, wrote:

> An International Union has only just been accomplished, with great difficulty, and on principles which commend themselves to the civilized world. To this, Great Britain and all her Colonies are parties, with the express and unanimous consent of the latter. Is a British colony, like Canada, for the sake of their infinitesimal interest in the publishing business, or for the supposed benefit of Canadian readers, to be the first to withdraw, and so to raise a hand to destroy the Union, which comprises a population of four or five hundred millions?[16]

Bergne and others feared that if Canada were to withdraw from the *Berne Convention*, other countries would follow. A British committee studying the matter wrote that if "the interests of publishers or printers were allowed to prevail over those of authors, the lead given to Canada would not improbably be followed by other colonies, and thus the whole system of Imperial copyright would be broken up."[17]

Denunciation, the British Secretary of State for the Colonies Lord Knutsford informed Canada's Governor General in 1890, would be unnecessary since the 1889 act contravening the *Berne Convention* would not receive the necessary approval from

---

[15] Great Britain. *Report of the Departmental Representatives Appointed to Consider the Canadian Copyright Act of 1889*. E 1701. London:n.p., 1892. Prime Minister Abbott fonds (MG26 C), Vol. 5 File: Copyright. Lord Stanley of Preston to Lord Lord Knutsford, 16 and 17 August 1889, Great Britain. *Correspondence on the Subject of the Law of Copyright in Canada*, C. 7783. London: George Edward Eyre and William Spotiswoode, 1893. In RG13 A-2 Vol. 2361 File 1912–1494 Part II. Library and Archives Canada.

[16] National Archives of Britain. Foreign Office fonds 881/5989. As quoted in Seville, *The Internationalisation of Copyright Law: Books, Buccaneers and the Black Flag in the Nineteenth Century*, 118.

[17] *Report of the Departmental Representatives Appointed to Consider the Canadian Copyright Act of 1889*, 19.

Britain.[18] British imperial power was used to forcefully keep Canada in the Berne Convention.

Thompson, who became Canada's fourth Prime Minister in 1892, was furious at this refusal to recognize Canadian copyright sovereignty. He wrote long letters to the Imperial government; he refused to meet with British representatives who came to negotiate on the issue, and finally he went to London to negotiate on, among other things, the copyright issue.[19] At Windsor Castle on December 12 1894, Prime Minister Thompson died of a heart attack. His body was returned home to Canada in a boat with the sides painted black, and the dream of Canadian copyright sovereignty – and a copyright that differed from the norms of the Berne Convention – was never realized.[20]

The histories of copyright that focus on major powers such as England, France, and the United States tell a story about copyright that is very different from Canada's story. It is often assumed that Canadian copyright history has been uneventful, and that Canada's association with the *Berne Convention* has been uncontentious and unproblematic. However, the Canadian history stands as a reminder that the international copyright system was built and held together by imperial power. The Canadian history reminds us of the power struggles and conflicts that were part of the Union's history from the very beginning.

It would not be long before Canada's course in international copyright would once again change direction. Following World War I, perceptions of Canada and its place in the world shifted; Canada's participation in the Great War meant that Canada now viewed itself as an independent participant in international affairs, and there were feelings that the rebellious copyright policies of the past might tend to make Canada an "outsider in the general community of nations."[21] At the same time, Britain began to loosen its grip on the handlebars of Canadian copyright and, with the Canadian *Copyright Act* of 1924 Canada, under Britain, moved to implement the *Berne Convention*.

---

[18] Lord Knutsford to Lord Stanley of Preston, 25 March 1890, *Correspondence on the Subject of the Law of Copyright in Canada*, C. 7783.

[19] See for example John Thompson to Governor General in Council, 1892. In RG13 A-2 Vol. 85 File 892–217. Library and Archives Canada; Lord Knutsford to Lord Stanley of Preston, 30 Jun 1892. In *Correspondence on the Subject of the Law of Copyright in Canada*, C. 7783; "The Copyright Question," *The Globe*, 11 December 1894.

[20] P. B. Waite, *The Man from Halifax: Sir John Thompson, Prime Minister* (Toronto: Toronto University Press, 1984), 425 and 429.

[21] Canada. House of Commons, *Debates of the House of Commons, Fifth Session – Thirteenth Parliament 11–12 George V., 1921*, Vol. CXLVI (Ottawa: F.A. Acland, 1921), 3833.

II

CANADA'S ALIGNMENT WITH MAJOR POWERS ON ISSUES OF INTERNATIONAL COPYRIGHT HAS NOT ALWAYS BEEN EASY

Canada used its copyright policies to gain status – to project an image of Canada as a "civilized country". Although other alignments were considered, and Canada in the 1960s and 1970s took particular note of its commonalities with the "developing" countries, generally Canada has aligned with the more powerful countries – afraid that if the country took any other route, the country would be considered as "an outlaw among the copyright nations of the world,"[22] an "outsider in the general community of nations,"[23] and a "non-harmonious and non-musical instrument" within the concert of nations.[24]

Today, Canada is aligned, as a part of Group B, with the United States and the other industrialized countries. This was not always the case; Canada also has a history of copyright conflict with the US. In the nineteenth century, Canada was used as the back door to Berne protection for American authors who, by publishing in Canada, received protection throughout the Berne Union.[25] This led to a dispute between the two countries, with Canada refusing for some time to grant to Americans Canadian copyright protection.[26] Later, Canada's 1924 *Copyright Act* contained special provisions that sought to retaliate for the US manufacturing clause.[27] Disputes continued over the manufacturing clause but were mitigated when both countries signed the *Universal Copyright Convention* in 1952. Canada's copyright relationship with the US was never easy, and its association with the major powers has not been unproblematic.

Canada's acquiescence to the norms embedded in the *Berne Convention*, and the country's alignment with the major powers on international copyright issues, had much to do with the association between the Berne norms of international copyright

---

[22] F.C.T. O'Hara to W.M. Dickson, 2 June 1919. RG20 Vol. 91 File 22655 Vol. 1.

[23] Canada. House of Commons, *Debates of the House of Commons, Fifth Session – Thirteenth Parliament 11–12 George V., 1921*, Vol. CXLVI (Ottawa: F.A. Acland, 1921), 3833.

[24] Canada. House of Commons, *Debates of the House of Commons, Third Session – Sixteenth Parliament 21–22 George V., 1931*, Vol. I, 1931 (Ottawa: F.A. Acland, 1931), 2309.

[25] Gordon Roper, "Mark Twain and His Canadian Publishers," *Papers of the Bibliographical Society of Canada*, no. 5 (1966).

[26] Draft memo from Ministers of Justice and Agriculture to the Governor General in Council. Undated. RG13 A-2 Vol. 2361 File 1912–1494 Part I. John Lowe. Memorandum. 23 May 1892. RG13 A-2 Vol. 2361 File 1912–1494 Part I.

[27] 11–12 Geo. V, c. 24 and 13–14 Geo. V, c. 10.

and ideas of progress and civilization. For many, the *Berne Convention* symbolized the forward march of international law, civilization, and progress.[28] Progress has, as Shanin points out, gone by various names: 'modernization', 'development', 'growth', 'civilization'.[29] According to Shanin, this vision of progress portrays:

> all societies … advancing naturally and consistently "up", on a root from poverty, barbarism, despotism and ignorance to riches, civilization, democracy and rationality, the highest expression of which is science. This is also an irreversible movement from an endless diversity of particularities, wasteful of human energies and economic resources, to a world unified and simplified into the most rational arrangement. It is therefore a movement from badness to goodness and from mindlessness to knowledge, which gave this message its ethical promise, its optimism and its reformist "punch".[30]

The world has thus been classified according to particular systems and ideas of progress – some societies and peoples as "developed", others as "underdeveloped" – and some in the middle.[31] These ideas have their own power alongside material realities; because of its powerful ability to organize, to mobilize, and to legitimize the actions of powerful interests and states.

Escobar shows that the discourse of development, beginning in the 1950s, became universally accepted and omnipresent.[32] The discourse of development, according to Escobar, constructs the "developing" world through conceptual maps, categories, and social practices.[33] The discourse and categories of development have been powerful not only in constructing the "developing" world; they have also been influential in

---

[28] Bently and Sherman point out that "In most standard histories, the signing of Berne signifies the point in time when national regimes regulating the protection of literary and artistic property came to recognize one another and to provide reciprocal protection. The emergence of the Berne Convention is also seen as the point at which the ramshackle and disorganized collection of bilateral treaties inevitably gave way to the rationality of a multilateral regime that established common standards of copyright protection." Lionel Bently and Brad Sherman, "Great Britain and the Signing of the Berne Convention in 1886," *Journal of the Copyright Society of the USA* 48, no. 3 (2001), 311.

[29] Teodor Shanin, "The Idea of Progress" In *The Post-Development Reader*, eds. Majid Rahnema and Victoria Bawtree (London: Zed Books, 1997), 66.

[30] Ibid, 65.

[31] Ibid, 68.

[32] Arturo Escobar, *Encountering Development: The Making and Unmaking of the Third World* (Princeton, N.J.: Princeton University Press, 1995).

[33] Ibid, 10–11.

creating conceptualizations of the "developed" world and the copyright policies and positions acceptable for "developed" countries.

Just as nineteenth-century Canadian politicians grappled to identify the copyright policies most appropriate to the leading British colony and to a "civilized nation", paddling within a sea of discourse largely generated by the international interests that had encouraged the creation of the Berne Union, Canadian officials in the early 1970s struggled to find a position on international copyright that encompassed Canada's position as a net copyright importer, similar in that sense to developing countries, and an industrialized country aligned with some of the biggest copyright exporters. The weight of categorization, of commonsense notions of the type of country Canada was, played a significant role in the determination of what copyright policies Canada took.

The year 1967 marked a crisis in international copyright. Newly independent countries, beginning in the 1960s, raised important questions about whether the Berne system of international copyright was appropriate to developing countries who were importers, rather than exporters, of copyright materials and for whom international copyright created a net outflow of payments. They noted the lack of availability and high price of copyright materials, and wished to see a copyright system that would do more to solve these problems.

They called for major changes to the *Berne Convention* that would allow for the compulsory licensing of works to make foreign works available at affordable prices in developing countries. This led to the failure of the 1967 revision of the *Berne Convention*, with both developing and developed countries unhappy with the compromise that was reached.[34] This crisis in the Berne Union prompted fears that either the core countries or the developing countries might withdraw *en masse* from the Union.[35]

Scepticism about the appropriateness of the *Berne Convention* to countries at various stages of development also appeared in Canada. Beginning in the 1950s, doubts were raised about whether Canada had been "well advised" in joining the *Berne Convention*. The 1957 Royal Commission on Patents, Copyright, Trade Marks and Industrial Designs took the view that the *Berne Convention* represented a European approach to copyright, granting high levels of copyright and placing the rights of authors in the forefront. The Commission suggested that a more American approach--with a utilitarian view of copyright that understood copyright as serving the public interest

---

[34] *Records of the Intellectual Property Conference of Stockholm June 11 to July 14, 1967.* Geneva: World Intellectual Property Organization, 1971. See also Sam Ricketson and Jane Ginsburg, *International Copyright and Neighbouring Rights: The Berne Convention and Beyond*, 2nd ed. (London: Oxford University Press, 2006)

[35] Ibid, 914–915.

above the interests of authors--might be more suitable to Canada as a net copyright importer.

The Commission reported: "It may be that, in becoming a party to the Berlin Revision of the Berne Convention in 1923, Canada was not too well advised. Apart from Haiti and Brazil no nations in the Western Hemisphere are members of the Berne Union..."[36]

In the 1960s, following the Royal Commission's report, Canada attended fewer meetings related to the Convention and its revisions, and refused to sign or implement the revision of 1967. Many countries refused to ratify that revision due to its controversial provisions for developing countries. Canada's refusal was for different reasons; Canada's prime objection was not with the provisions for developing countries; rather, Canada's Secretary of State for External Affairs questioned whether Canada's participation in the *Berne Convention*, and the high levels of copyright protection granted under the convention, was in the national interest:

> Successive revisions of the Berne Convention have progressively extended the monopoly rights of copyright holders. The current revisions suggested for the [1967] Stockholm conference are intended to extend these rights still further. Unfortunately, this raises the question of the cost in relation to the value of present copyright legislation as a device for encouraging creativity in Canada before the Economic Council's report is available. An important consideration in the study of this matter is the fact that as much as 90% of the total cost (about $8 million) of copyright to the public in Canada is accounted for by the protection given foreign works. In turn, compensation to Canadian authors by way of payments from overseas to Canada is minimal. That raises the fundamental question of whether protection of the kind Canada is committed to by adhering to the Berne Union is in the national interest.[37]

The Secretary therefore recommended to Cabinet that Canada should refrain from supporting any proposed revision to the *Berne Convention* that would reduce the government's flexibility of action.[38] Canada did not sign the revised *Berne Convention* of 1967.[39]

---

[36] Canada. Royal Commission on Patents, Copyright, Trade Marks and Industrial Designs. *Report on Copyright*. (Ottawa: Supply and Services Canada, 1957): 18.

[37] Secretary of State for External Affairs. Letter to Secretary of State for Dominion Affairs, 16 February, 1928. In RG25 G-1 Vol. 1260 File 218 Part I. Library and Archives Canada.

[38] Ibid.

[39] *Records of the Intellectual Property Conference of Stockholm June 11 to July 14, 1967*. Geneva: World Intellectual Property Organization, 1971.

At the same time, the crisis that resulted from the 1967 conference in Stockholm sparked a new resolve that Canada should become a more influential and active player within the Berne Union. Some Canadian government officials hoped that the discourse of development now being established within the Berne Union, having been absent when former colonies like Canada joined the Union, might be translated to apply to Canada.

A government committee, formed in 1969 to assist in the formulation of Canada's position in response to the crisis in international copyright, recommended an adaptation of the definition of 'developing country' such that Canada might benefit from concessions made to developing countries under the *Berne Convention*.[40] The committee argued that, "Canada's position is somewhat analogous to that of developing countries when compared to countries with higher exports of copyright material."[41] A Memorandum to Cabinet explained:

> Although Canada is undoubtedly a "developing country" in so far as copyright is concerned (because of the large import imbalance of trade in copyrighted material), nevertheless it is not so considered by the two Conventions. A "developing country" under U.N. definition is considered a country which has an average per capita income per year of $U.S. 300 or less. In my view [Minister of Consumer and Corporate Affairs, Stanley Basford], any country with a very large export-import imbalance in copyrighted materials should be entitled, like the developing countries, to maintain a somewhat lower level of international copyright protection.[42]

The Memo to Cabinet recommended, "That the Canadian delegation suggest to the Joint Study Group that, in so far as international copyright is concerned, the definition of a "developing country" should not be based on per capita income, but on a substantial import imbalance of trade in copyrighted material."[43]

The reformulation of the concept of "developing country" in such a way as to include Canada was absolutely radical. Such a precedent might have opened the door to a variety of definitions of developing countries based on the balance of trade in different areas, making possible a cascade of unexpected country coalitions and policy alignments unthinkable under the existing categorizations. It is unsurprising that an

---

[40] See generally RG25 Vol. 10902 File 55-19-1-ICC Pt 1-1. Library and Archives Canada.

[41] Canadian Statement to the Joint Study Group. RG25 Vol. 10902 File 55-19-1-ICC Pt 1-1. Library and Archives Canada.

[42] Memorandum to Cabinet re participation by Canada in a Joint Study Group Established by the Berne Union and the Universal Copyright Convention, September 1969. RG25 Vol. 10902 File 55-19-1-ICC Pt 1-1. Library and Archives Canada.

[43] Ibid.

idea so radical and so different from the regimes of representation and the practices of categorization that were being inscribed in international institutions at the time did not go far; a note on file called this aspect of the committee's recommendation "utter nonsense":

> Efforts to claim Canada is a "developing country"… are usually greeted with derision. We have the 3rd highest per capita income in the world and this is partly due to our importation of capital and know-how.[44]

The idea that provisions for developing countries should apply to Canada conflicted with the established discourse that by now placed Canada as a middle power, associated with industrialized countries.

Canadian copyright policymakers in the late 1960s and early 1970s nevertheless felt that that international copyright, as implemented under the *Berne Convention*, primarily responded to the interests of the copyright-exporting nations. A 1977 report by Andrew A. Keyes and Claude Brunet in 1977 concluded that:

> the fully developed nations, largely exporters of copyright material, have a stronger voice in international copyright conventions, and a tendency has existed over the past half century for developing countries, including Canada, to accept too readily proffered solutions in copyright matters that do not reflect their economic positions.[45]

As a result of such perceptions, Canada attempted to form a coalition of 'intermediate' countries who were not officially "developing" countries, but who were net copyright importers. Canadian government officials envisioned that Canada might "for the first time… play a leading role in shaping the course of international copyright by fostering and leading a block of countries with interests similar to Canada." Officials felt that this coalition "could conceivably control a certain balance of power, given active participation."[46]

Canada hoped, through this vehicle, to press for major structural change to the international copyright system that would allow different countries--including net-copyright importers like Canada--to adhere to different levels of copyright protection,

---

[44] Ibid.

[45] Andrew A Keyes and Claude Brunet. *Copyright in Canada: Proposals for a Revision of the Law.* Ottawa: Consumer and Corporate Affairs Canada, 1977: 234.

[46] Canadian Delegation to Meetings of the Intergovernmental Copyright Committee of the Universal Copyright Convention and the Permanent Committee of the Berne Union.*Report of the Canadian delegation: Meetings of the Intergovernmental Copyright Committee of the Universal Copyright Convention and the Permanent Committee of the Berne Union, Paris, December 15–19, 1969.* Ottawa, Library and Archives Canada, RG19 Vol. 5168 File 8510-6785-3 pt 4.

according to domestic circumstances.[47] However, this initiative to redraw the political map of international copyright failed due to Canada's inability to attract sufficient support, and due to fears that such a stance would affect Canada's relations with countries like the United States, the United Kingdom and France.[48]

In an effort to resolve the crisis of 1967, simultaneous diplomatic conferences were held in 1971 to come to a more workable compromise and to revise both the *Berne Convention* and the *Universal Copyright Convention* in a way that would unify, and prevent the breakup, of the international copyright system.[49] Its radical initiatives having failed, Canada supported the revision process and aligned itself generally with the major powers. Adopting a middle power image, Canada portrayed itself at the 1971 diplomatic conference to revise the *Universal Copyright Convention* not as a developing country, but as "both developed and developing", an intermediary that understood the needs of both developing and "developed" countries:

> The delegate of Canada emphasized the great interest of his government in the problems of international copyright and the work of the Conference. This special interest arises from a combination of factors, including the existence within Canada of dual languages and cultures, and the problems of reconciling copyright protection and technological innovations in a country of immense size.[50]

Canada portrayed itself as a middle power leader: a country in a unique situation that allowed it to understand the positions of all sides:

> Finally, Canada thought, in cultural matters, that it was half-way between industrialized and developing countries, which enabled it to understand the

---

[47] Canadian Delegation to the Extraordinary Joint Session of the Permanent Committee of the Berne Union and the Inter-Governmental Committee of the Universal Copyright Convention. *Report of the Canadian delegation on the extraordinary joint session of the Permanent Committee of the Berne Union and the Inter-Governmental Committee of the Universal Copyright Convention, Paris, February 3 to 7, 1969.* RG25 Vol. 10902 File 55-19-1-ICC Pt 1-1.

[48] Ibid. and Canadian Delegation to the Washington Meeting, *Memorandum to the Minister: Report of the Canadian delegation at the Washington meeting, September 29–October 3/1969*, 10 October 1969: 2 and 4. Ottawa, Library and Archives Canada, RG19 Vol. 5574 File 8510–C785–1 Part 2.

[49] *Records of the Conference for Revision of the Universal Copyright Convention, Unesco House, Paris, 5 to 24 July 1971.* Paris: Unesco, 1973; *Records of the Diplomatic Conference for the Revision of the Berne Convention (Paris, July 5 to 24, 1971).* Geneva: World Intellectual Property Organization, 1974.

[50] *Records of the Conference for Revision of the Universal Copyright Convention*, Unesco House, Paris, 5 to 24 July 1971, 62.

problems of both and to foresee perhaps the possibility of reconciling the interests at stake.[51]

Canada, however, did not sign the 1971 revision, and a rhetorical hint of Canada's rethinking of the map of international copyright remained; the Canadian delegation declared, "We are all developing countries."[52]

The 1971 conferences resulted in revised texts of the *Berne Convention* and the *Universal Copyright Convention* that were widely accepted. At the same time, the crisis of 1967 had shown that copyright revision would no longer be easy. Following the 1971 agreement, no further major revisions have been attempted. The 1971 text of the *Berne Convention* is still in force today, and formal country groupings, established under the UN system, have solidified political alignments on international copyright. Under this system, Canada is aligned as a part of Group B, the group of the most powerful countries.[53]

III

WHAT CONTRIBUTION DO MIDDLE POWERS MAKE TO THE INTERNATIONAL COPYRIGHT SYSTEM TODAY?

Mark Neufeld argues, drawing on Gramsci's concept of hegemony, that the middle power language that portrays Canada as an honest broker is used by dominant groups to advance and legitimise Canadian foreign policy and the existing international order. However, he also argues that the language of middlepowermanship has come to be used by dissident groups who, beginning in the late sixties and early seventies, recast the idea of a "middle power" "to signify the influence enjoyed by a country like Canada, and the potential such influence offers to effect radical progressive change in terms of disarmament, economic development and wealth re-distribution, environmental policy and democratization of the foreign policy-making process."[54]

Countries like Brazil, Argentina, and India are still pushing for changes in the international copyright system, and some would argue that Canada should play a part

---

[51] Ibid, 105.

[52] Canadian delegate to the Conference for Revision of the *Universal Copyright Convention*, Paris, July 1971. *Records of the Conference for Revision of the Universal Copyright Convention, Unesco House, Paris, 5 to 24 July 1971* (Paris: Unesco, 1973), 62 and 105.

[53] Karl P. Sauvant. *The Group of 77: Evolution, Structure, Organization.* (New York: Oceana Publications, 1981).

[54] Mark Neufeld, "Hegemony and Foreign Policy Analysis: The Case of Canada as Middle Power" In *Readings in Canadian Foreign Policy: Classic Debates and New Ideas*, eds. Duane Bratt and Christopher J. Kukucha (New York: Oxford University Press, 2006), 94–107.

in advocating for progressive change. A 2004 proposal to WIPO's General Assembly from a group of developing nations (*Proposal By Argentina And Brazil for the Establishment of a Development Agenda For WIPO*) raised issue with both the basic assumption that intellectual property protection contributes positively to international development, and WIPO's core mandate, which is "to promote the protection of intellectual property throughout the world through cooperation among States."[55]

This proposal sparked a series of high-profile international meetings at WIPO in which WIPO's mandate, impartiality, transparency, and core activities, as well as intellectual property's contribution to international development, were broadly questioned. The meetings resulted in an agenda, approved by all member states, intended to make WIPO more transparent and responsive to the needs of developing countries. However, some of the original key proposals made by developing countries, such as a treaty on access to knowledge and an organizational restructuring at WIPO, were not included in the final agenda.

In the discussions, Canada was aligned with the Group B of industrialized countries that opposed such radical proposals.[56] Similarly, in discussions surrounding a World Blind Union proposal for a narrower treaty aimed at rectifying current shortages of accessible works for the visually impaired, Canada has been aligned with the major powers who have been hesitant to commit to a treaty, preferring other non-binding approaches.[57] Canada's emphasis during the discussions has been on the importance

---

[55] World Intellectual Property Organization. *Convention Establishing the World Intellectual Property Organization, signed at Stockholm on July 14, 1967 and as amended on September 28, 1979.*

[56] Sara Bannerman, "The Development Agenda at WIPO: Where is Canada?" Chapter 10 in *Innovation, Science and Environment: Canadian Policies and Performance 2008–2009.* Edited by Glen Toner. (Montreal: Published for the School of Public Policy and Administration, Carleton University by McGill-Queen's University Press, 2008).

[57] World Intellectual Property Organization, Meeting documents: Standing Committee on Copyright and Related Rights: twentieth session, June 2010, www.wipo.int/meetings/en/details.jsp?meeting_id=20200; Catherine Saez. "High expectations this week for progress on exceptions and limitations at WIPO," in Intellectual Property Watch, 22 June 2010, www.ip-watch.org/weblog/2010/06/22/high-expectations-this-week-for-progress-on-exceptions-and-limitations-at-wipo/; Catherine Saez, "No decision on WIPO treaty for blind persons misses 'golden opportunity'," in Intellectual Property Watch, 30 June 2010, www.ip-watch.org/weblog/2010/06/26/no-decision-on-wipo-treaty-for-blind-misses-%E2%80%98golden-opportunity%E2%80%99/

of maintaining flexibility within any international instrument (whether binding or non-binding) for a variety of domestic approaches to ensuring access.[58]

Since the 1970s Canada has been aligned with the major powers. In 1984 the Department of Consumer and Corporate Affairs and the Department of Communications jointly prepared the paper *From Gutenberg to Telidon: a White Paper on Copyright*, issued as part of a public consultation on copyright reform, and set down the path that Canada would follow:

> Since Canadian creators receive national treatment protection in [countries that are Canada's major trading partners and who belong to one or both of the major copyright conventions], they benefit from Canada's participation in these conventions. The government intends that Canada's international obligations be met in the spirit as well as in the letter of the law.[59]

This philosophy has generally guided Canadian participation in international copyright agreements since 1984. As in 1928, when Canadian delegates were instructed to support any proposals that seemed likely to meet general approval of the governments represented, "particularly those of the leading countries, such as Great Britain, Italy and France"[60], Canada today adopts the view that it must align on important issues with its largest trading partners.

Canada is now, more than ever before, an active participant in the coalition of most powerful copyright exporters on matters of international copyright. Objections to and scepticism surrounding the appropriateness of Canada's participation in the *Berne Convention* have been replaced with this Canadian version of a trade-based approach to international copyright. Support for counter-hegemonic projects has been held at bay by a vision of a Canada associated with the major powers.

Change in international copyright is not impossible. Other countries like India, South Africa, Brazil and Argentina have been successfully enrolled by domestic and transnational interests to advocate change within the international copyright system; room for exceptions, such as the 1971 Appendix to the *Berne Convention*, which, though labelled "unworkable", has been achieved; and copyright treaties that would advocate greater access to knowledge are even now being considered.

---

[58] Douglas George, *Presentation by Mr. Douglas George*, 13 July 2009,
www.wipo.int/meetings/en/2009/vip_ge/presentations/george_douglas.html.

[59] Canada, Department of Communications and Department of Consumer and Corporate Affairs, *From Gutenberg to Telidon: A White Paper on Copyright: Proposals for the Revision of the Canadian Copyright Act* (Ottawa: Department of Consumer and Corporate Affairs and Department of Communications, 1984): 4.

[60] Fernand Rinfret. *Instructions to the Canadian Delegates to the Rome Conference on Copyright.* 25 April 1928. RG25 Vol. 1490 File 1827–278 Part I.

Such initiatives and visions press against the great weight of inscribed associations, norms, expertise, authority, institutions, and resources of a Union that has been in place since 1886. Such initiatives and visions are based in a hope that the regime of international copyright might be transformed, might overcome the exclusions of its past, and might embed this overcoming at the core of its ongoing practices. It is only by forming an awareness of the material and discursive structures of international copyright – an awareness that is formed by examining the historical experiences of weaker countries and groups as well as the views of the stronger ones – that such a transformative commitment can be made.

7

CONCLUDING COMMENTS: THE COPYRIGHT ACT 1968 FORTY YEARS ON

Professor Sam Ricketson[1]

It seems such a short time, but, in the forty years since it came into operation, the *Copyright Act 1968* has moved from being a rather peripheral enactment which was really only known to the few initiated in its mysteries to a sizable[2] piece of legislation that lies at the centre of so much of our daily economic, social and cultural life. Ignored, reviled, admired or sanctified (it all depends where one is standing), it is a legislative achievement whose mid-life anniversary is well worth celebrating today.

Indeed, real life and architectural analogies readily come to mind when one considers the *Copyright Act 1968* in all its present day, much-amended, glory. Take real life first. If one remembers that it began its life as a relatively sleek and well muscled Act (although still more fully developed than its even slimmer 1911 and 1905 ancestors), it remained thus for well over a decade, but then gained steady accretions of muscle and flesh, with some nine substantive sets of amendments since 1980 that have now turned it into a bloated and blurred version of its original self.

Middle age is not treating the Act kindly, particularly when one considers the lateral extensions that have occurred, with the journey between some provisions that were previously simply numerical now requiring a clamber, several times over, through all the letters of the alphabet (just try going now from ss 131 to 133, and finding some 46

---

[1] Professor Sam Ricketson is Professor of Law, Melbourne Law School, and Barrister, Victoria. He is one of Australia's most famous and highly regarded specialists in intellectual property law, the world's leading authority on the history and interpretation of the Berne Convention, and internationally renowned expert on international copyright law. He is the author of *The Berne Convention for the Protection of Literary and Artistic Works: 1886–1986,* Kluwer, 1987, and (with Jane Ginsburg), *International Copyright and Neighbouring Rights: The Berne Convention and Beyond,* Oxford University Press, 2005 (2nd ed). Professor Ricketson is the author of numerous other leading works and texts on intellectual property law.

[2] The adjective "monster" came first to mind, but this would be to ignore the far greater claims of our taxation, social security and corporations legislation to such a descriptor.

pages of intervening provisions from s 131A to s 132C; the trip from s 135 to s 136 is even more demanding, with some 102 pages of intervening text, beginning at s 135AA and ending at s 135ZZZE). Middle aged sag assumes a rather disconcerting image when one sees these alphabetical folds of legislative fat flowing over a now invisible waistline down to the ground.

The metaphor should not be taken too far. It is all too easy to point to complex and wordy provisions, and rush to judgment as to their utility. Very often, however, they do mean something quite precise from the perspective of particular addressees, and represent delicate compromises that have been made between competing interests and policies (this is certainly true of the educational provisions in Parts VA and VB). Furthermore, some valiant attempts at slimming down have been made, although the difficulties involved should not be underestimated. In this regard, the simplification proposals of the former Copyright Law Review Committee (the "CLRC") should be remembered.

These embodied a new and original scheme of classification of subject matter and rights,[3] as well as an extensive streamlining of exceptions and limitations.[4] The difficulty, of course, lies in proposing such a radical weight loss program, when so many other issues, such as the internet and the digital agenda, were also clamouring for attention. Legislators and policymakers, perhaps, may be forgiven for not taking up the reformist programme offered them by the CLRC. A good piece of management advice might be, "never let the immediate crowd out the important", but this is a nostrum that is usually impossible to act upon when developments occur at such a frantic pace, and appear to call for urgent and immediate attention.

Architectural metaphors, however, may offer a more rewarding insight into the 1968 Act and its achievements. The UK Whitford Committee in 1977 offered such a view when it described the development of UK copyright laws up to the time of the *Copyright Act 1956* (UK) in the following terms:

> 15. The first Copyright Act was enacted in 1710 (8 Anne c 19) and dealt only with books. This Act may be likened to a modest Queen Anne house to which there has since been Georgian, Victorian, Edwardian and finally Elizabethan additions, each adding embellishments in the style of the times …[5]

---

[3] Copyright Law Review Committee, *Simplification of the Copyright Act 1968, Part 2: Categorisation of Subject Matter and Exclusive Rights, and Other Issues* (February 1999)

[4] Copyright Law Review Committee, *Simplification of the Copyright Act 1968, Part 1: Exceptions to the Exclusive Rights of Copyright Owners* (September 1998).

[5] *Copyright and Designs Law: Report of the Committee to consider the Law on Copyright and Damages* (Cmd 6732, HMSO 1977) ("Whitford Committee"), paras 15 and 16.

In the case of the 1968 Act, one may not want to pause too long in contemplating the exterior (a very bland 60's glass and concrete construction), or the internal fittings (the language and terminology of the legislative draftspersons is frequently dark and obscure). However, the layout of rooms is not without some coherence, even elegance. It is certainly instructive. Consider the following:

- The ante-rooms and reception rooms: a rather cluttered cloakroom area (full of definitions and interpretations in Part II), leading to more spacious galleries with clearly defined sections for works and their exclusive rights, connecting factors, term of protection, and provisions on infringement (Part III, Divisions 1 and 2). The first time visitor can stroll through these and gain a reasonable understanding of what is contained in the rest of the building.

- A parallel set of smaller reception rooms running along on the side for subject-matter other than works, with clearly defined alcoves for each specific subject-matter (Part IV, Divisions 2 to 6). The rooms likewise are reasonably accessible to the first time visitor.

- Smaller rooms running off the side of each of the larger reception rooms: this, however, is where things start to become confusing. Some of the rooms are crowded, but still relatively accessible and possible to navigate, at least in some parts (for example, the fair dealing provisions in Part III, Division 3, and Part IV, Division 6, and the artistic work exceptions in Part III, Division 7); others are lined with further series of compartments that are nonetheless reasonably easy to locate and are relatively self-contained (for example, the computer program exceptions in Part III, Division 4A); others again have some rather timeworn but familiar items of furniture where the "industry players" will have little difficulty (such as the provisions dealing with the recording of musical works in Part III, Division 6). But there are some rooms that are really quite dangerous to enter, either because they are so crowded that one needs an expert guide to find one's way through (such as the library and archives provisions in Part III, Division 5) or because they have some nasty hidden traps that no amount of amending legislation has ever quite managed to remove (for example, the designs/copyright overlap provisions in Part III, Division 8). None of these rooms, however, are very comfortable for the first time entrant.

- The large entertaining rooms that adjoin the reception areas, once reasonably welcoming, have also become steadily more cluttered:
    o The remedies hall (Part V), once clearly laid out and easy to walk through, has now had some complicated extensions made to it, for example, the technological circumvention measures, electronic rights management and safe harbour annexes (Divisions 2AA and

2A), to say nothing of the particularly hazardous and bristling basement area under the hall, where the criminal offence and penalty provisions (Division 5) are now filed away neatly for ready deployment.

- o The statutory licence halls (Parts VA,-VC), while complex in their appointments, are more readily justifiable, in that few will enter here unless they (a) are one of the affected parties, such as an educational institution or a collecting society, and (b) will almost invariably be accompanied by a skilled guide (in-house counsel, legal adviser, and the like). The same is true of the rambling Division 6 passageway which deals with the Copyright Tribunal. There is really no need for any member of the general public to wander down these halls and passage ways, although clearer signs, such as "Administration – only authorised personnel to enter", might be helpful here.

- There are some discreet (and discrete) rear rooms where entry will only be required for very specific purposes, such as Crown use (Part VII), or where the only appreciative audience will be lawyers and no one else will ever need to enter (I refer here to the transitional and miscellaneous sections in Divisions X and XI).

- Finally, there are some large structures that really sit to the rear or side of the building, although there are some narrow connecting doors, often hard to find, that provide a linkage back to the main structure: moral rights (of two distinct kinds in Division IX) and performers' rights (Part XIA). It might be tempting to liken these to conservatories, and the plants to be found inside are certainly exotic, at least so far as Australian copyright law traditions are concerned. They are fragile and delicately framed, and readily cut down.

It is all too easy to flog a metaphor too far, but the above serves to illustrate the large and sprawling structure and scope of the *Copyright Act 1968*. To return to our earlier metaphor, the Act is a complex organism, but is not an invertebrate: there is still an identifiable and recognizable spine running through it and providing it with a semblance of sense and organisation. The above metaphors also enable the making of some larger points:

1. Simplification, while desirable at one level, is not a goal in itself: so long as the relevant provisions are accessible and meaningful to those who must deal with them, it is of little consequence that they are not comprehensible to the rest of us (if we never have to use them). There are horses for courses: it may be defensible for the provisions of Parts VA and VB to rejoice in their present complexity if they nonetheless provide clear pathways for the relevant parties to track their way through and to achieve some acceptable resolution. Complexity, on the other

hand, may be unforgivable in the case of sections of more general application: for example, do we need over 40 pages of text to give effect to moral rights provisions that are comprehended within a few lines of text in the relevant international conventions?[6]

2.   Some complexity is also understandable (and hence forgivable) as an index of human failing. The parallel importation provisions, for example, reflect the deep public policy divisions that have arisen, and continue to arise, over this difficult question, particularly in relation to books. Complex procedures and timelines simply embody the results of the uneasy compromises that have been reached here, and reflect the lack of resolution applying at the policy level.

3.   Nowhere is this complexity and policy division more exposed than in the case of exceptions and limitations: the proliferation and dissemination of these throughout the Act underlines sharply the need for some kind of simplification or streamlining, even perhaps the adoption of a single, flexible, open-ended, omnibus fair use provision, as suggested by the CLRC over a decade ago. But while this might reduce the Act significantly in length, would it really achieve its goals of clarity and simplicity, other than to displace the work of negotiation and compromise on the part of legislators, lobbyists and officials to the courts? In the long term, this may well mean more expense and time, and less comprehensive solutions. Matters that are unlitigated may simply lead to holes in protection where no one benefits.

4.   Some of the causes of the more recent legislative bloat in the 1968 Act come from external sources, rather than being the direct fault of our legislators and policy makers. While we have sought diligently, perhaps too much so in the case of performers' moral rights, to give effect to our international obligations under the *Berne Convention*, the *WCT* and the *WPPT*, we have had some other things forced upon us in the form of the *Australia-US Free Trade Agreement*, with its bewildering series of provisions that seek to transplant and replicate US legislative provisions Down Under. Such deals are always fraught with difficulty, even where there might be the expectation of longer term benefits in other areas that have nothing to do with copyright, such as beef and primary products. So far as the *Copyright Act 1968* is concerned, this has recently added significantly to its bulk and complexity.

5.   For all its defects, the 1968 Act has still had its admirers in other places, for example, in Singapore[7] and Malaysia[8] where it has provided a model for local law

---

[6] *Berne Convention for the Protection of Literary and Artistic Works*, art 6bis, and the *WIPO Performances and Phonograms Treaty*, art 5.

[7] *Copyright Act 1987* (Singapore), Chap 63.

making. This may suggest that the floor layout still remain usable, even if there is too much furniture cluttering up some of the rooms and annexes. In terms of legislative export, we should seek to build upon this experience and improve the product.

The speakers in the present session have each provided fascinating insights into the history and development of this significant piece of private legislation.

Ben Atkinson has highlighted some of the important pre-history, going back to the 1911 Act and the even more interesting legislative predecessor, the *Copyright Act 1905* which was the first truly national copyright enactment in Australia.

Two other speakers, Leslie Zines and John Gilchrist, have drawn attention to two particularly important stages in the early life of the 1968 Act: its beginnings and the work of the Spicer Committee, and the first significant response to technological development, in the form of photocopying and the Franki Committee review.

Each of these inquiries was considerably more reflective and extensive than anything we have seen in more recent history. Spicer, indeed, was pre-computers and long before the advent of the networked environment; copyright in those days was seen as rather peripheral, of concern only to those involved in the "soft areas" of the arts: music, theatre, and publishing. Nonetheless, there were significant commercial interests involved, in particular those of broadcasters and sound recording companies, while the concerns of educationalists and libraries were also beginning to be voiced. Nonetheless, nearly nine years elapsed before the 1968 Act was finally passed (although Adrian Sterling tells a revealing story of some of the lobbying on the part of the record industry that preceded this).

Once passed, however, the new Act seemed to slumber in its slips for a decade or so, while the importance of one particular new form of technology – the photocopier – was pursued in the courts,[9] and then ultimately became the focus of the next significant review by the Franki Committee. After this, the floodgates of regular review and amendment were opened up, and this has remained a continuous torrent. Copyright in this latter period moved much more to the centre of things, although perhaps without the time, care and resources that were possible in the case of the Spicer and Franki reports.

Sara Bannerman and Susy Frankel provide interesting perspectives from the outside. Both Canada and New Zealand, despite their common colonial backgrounds with

---

[8] *Copyright Act 1987* ((Malaysia).

[9] See, in particular, *UNSW v Moorhouse* (1975) 133 CLR 1, and see further S Ricketson and D Catterns, "Of vice-chancellors and authors: *UNSW v Moorhouse*" in Andrew T Kenyon, Megan Richardson and Sam Ricketson (eds), *Landmarks in Australian Intellectual Property Law*, Cambridge University Press, Melbourne, 2009, pp 97–109.

Australia, have different copyright histories, marked by a measure of independent initiative not present in our own. Even at an early stage, Canada was unhappy with the application of the Berne Convention to it (Bannerman's account of the visit of the Canadian premier, Sir John Thomson's visit to Windsor to seek permission to denounce it is similar to the much later, and successful, effort by the Australian prime minister, James Scullin, to secure the appointment of Sir Isaac Isaacs as the first Australian-born governor general), and the notion of Canada as a developing country and "copyright middle power" is an appealing one for Australia to aspire to, in seeking to establish its own international copyright identity.

Susy Frankel, in the case of New Zealand, points to one particular instance of decisive independence, in the case of parallel importation prohibitions. There are others: for example, the recommendations of the Dalgleish Committee in relation to the question of term (New Zealand, unlike Australia, saw little advantage for it in the adoption of the 50 year *post auctorem* term of protection).[10]

In all, this has been a fascinating and event-filled forty years of copyright history in Australia, and one that will clearly merit further investigation of its internal workings by historians such as Ben Atkinson. The onset of early middle age suggests that some weight loss may be in order, but the relevance and centrality of the Act to our national economic, social and cultural life can be doubted no longer.

---

[10] *The Report of the Copyright Committee* (NZ, 1959), par 41. Note also similar reservations that were expressed by the equivalent Canadian inquiry: *The Report on Copyright of the Canadian Royal Commission on Patents, Copyright, Trade Marks and Industrial Designs* (1957). See further Ricketson and Creswell, *The Law of Intellectual Property: Copyright, Designs and Confidential Information,* Thomson LBC, 3rd ed 2006, [6.75].

PART TWO

THE UNITED STATES OF COPYRIGHT

ETHICS, REALITY AND REMIX

8

REMARKS INTRODUCING KEYNOTE SPEAKER PROFESSOR LAWRENCE LESSIG

The Hon Michael Kirby

Ladies and gentlemen and Professor Lessig, we are very lucky to meet on this day in this wonderful building and to have had such a fantastic session this morning. I mean, I missed the first couple of speakers because I had to attend an Australia Day Council Breakfast in Sydney (which is one of those awful American traditions that seems to be spreading to our country) and then came down here, but I came in time to hear the tremendous talk given by Professor Zines and also by Professor Sterling and I think we were very fortunate to have heard their input.

I knew all of those people – I knew Sir John Spicer – I appeared before him as a young barrister quite often when he was the Chief Judge of the Commonwealth Industrial Court. He was a very fine and very temperate judge and he had some very angry judges who would sit with him. I attended his funeral in Toorak and he was a very fine and intelligent man. I knew Sir Nigel Bowen – he was my Chief Judge when I was appointed to the Federal Court of Australia and he was a considerable intellectual property lawyer. And I knew Bob Franki, just as Franki, who was a very courteous (and as John Gilchrist and I were saying) a very dignified person who if he gave his word, that was it. And I was very glad to hear a tribute paid to Lindsay Curtis who was truly one of the most fantastic officers of the Commonwealth that I ever worked with.

When I was appointed Chair of the Law Reform Commission back in 1975, Lindsay was the officer of the Commonwealth Attorney General's Department who worked with me and he was truly a brilliant man and a really hard worker. He helped to get the Law Reform Commission established. He helped to get the Administrative Review Council established. He himself worked with John Ewen in drafting the *Administrative Decisions Judicial Review Act* (the ADJR Act) which is one of the most influential statutes of the Commonwealth in bringing the rule of law to a reality in our country.

His daughter is Lyndal Curtis, whose name you would have heard quite often on the ABC. She contacted me recently to say would I record something for her children so that they would know what a magnificent person Lindsay was, who died too young? So I'll tell her of what was said about him today, because we should remember these wonderful civil servants who give their all, and are anonymous, but they are really very influential in our nation.

Now, two little comments, if I may, just very briefly before we get into the business of this session. Number one, I would say to Ben Atkinson, don't change your script about the source of the constitutional power in relation to the original, or the second Copyright Act. Though the imperial rulers of Australia no doubt thought that all the colonial parliament out there in Australia was doing was implementing their will.

There is an alternative theory which has gained force during the course of the last century, that of the sovereignty of the people of Australia being the source of the Constitution, and their having voted in the referenda for it, that the source of the power of the Federal Parliament to do anything lay in the sovereignty of the people of Australia, and in the constitutional document of this country, and that therefore, in incorporating the imperial Act, they were doing what they thought was appropriate for the people of Australia, and the sovereignty of Australia.

Ben, you can put a footnote – I will let you put a footnote. There is an alternative theory about the source of the imperial statute in Australia, but don't ever give away, ever – ever give away the sovereignty of the people of Australia.

Now the second point is, when I walked in, did you see this? I was sitting down humbly and quietly after my address this morning, and Leslie Zines said "some judges in this country, a minority view, take the view that the Constitution is a living document", and then pointed at me! Now, if you look at what judges actually do in the High Court – if you look at what they did on the meaning of the word "jury" – I mean they didn't go back and say "well only men can sit in juries in federal trials, only people of property can sit in juries" – they updated it. Was that originalism?

If you also look at *Sue v Hill* [1] about a subject of the Queen, there is no doubt that in 1900, a subject of the Queen would have been a subject of the Queen, and that would have been it, and therefore, by saying, well, this was a subject of the Queen in the United Kingdom and that [therefore] she was disqualified from being a member of the Parliament of the Commonwealth, then that was not an originalist view. This is a debate they have in the United States – I'm telling you Professor Lessig, we have it here, and there are some who adhere to the view that you have got to go back to that original text. They don't actually have to have 1776 dictionaries in this country, only 1900, but it's not what they do, and therefore, we've got to keep our eye on what is actually done. I didn't want that to pass. I just want you to have the benefit of my views on that.

---

[1] [1999] HCA 30. Hill, a dual citizen of Australia and the United Kingdom, won election to the Australian Senate, and a voter challenged her election on the grounds that, under section 44(i) of the Constitution, a "subject or citizen" of a "foreign power" is not entitled to stand for Parliament. The High Court found that the United Kingdom is, under s.44(i), a "foreign power".

It was fantastic to hear Adrian Sterling in his tribute to Lindsay Curtis. Telling of Attorney General Bowen. Telling that this was legal, not political. I hope no-one in the room believes any of this is legal, not political. And saying the motto of this Conference – I took a note – tremblingly I wrote down "easy access with easy licensing". I would suggest there may be an alternative theory, and I think this might be closer to the view of our speaker.

This is, "easy access with justifiable licensing", because there is a question as to what is the justifiability of licence. See, we don't want lots of easy licensing for unjustifiable purposes. We want easy, maybe easy technical, licensing, but only in circumstances where there is a true public interest, and I thought that that was the whole purpose of this conference to be talking about thinking again, conceptually and freshly, about what is the purpose of intellectual property law, and copyright law in particular. I really found the session this morning terrific.

Now, this afternoon, we have one of the great gurus of the intellectual property law world, Professor Lessig of Stanford, previously at Harvard and at Chicago, the great universities of the United States of America, the writer of all of those books that you know. I was the first to quote him in the High Court of Australia in an extended footnote, and also, I quoted Brian Fitzgerald. That's why he loves me, just because I quoted him. What wonderful leaders we have here with Sam Ricketson and really fantastic people who think through and look deeper at these issues.

I had the privilege to go to a conference at King's College in London and the keynote speaker was Lawrence Lessig, and he came along and he really conveyed two really original ideas to my mind and did it very, very clearly, as he will now do today.

The first was the idea of code, and how we are talking about a very important issue which has puzzled me since my law reform days. In this age of rapid technology and changes in biotechnology, information technology, and so on, how can a parliament keep up? The somewhat sobering news that Lawrence Lessig brought was, well, in part, that that is a question that has been bypassed, because now, often with information technology, and the multinational corporations that control it, the law is effectively embedded in the technology, and the local legislature is not always capable of changing how it works. The universality of the technology, which is what Professor Sterling was talking about, is really controlled by this phenomenon, and "code" is his word for it. I thought that was a really important point.

Professor Lessig really gave a fantastic presentation of the ideas that he has to the conference in London and I'm sure he is going to do so again today. So, without further ado, I would invite Professor Lessig to come forward, and to present, and then we are going to have an interaction afterwards, so that there will be a real dialogue at this meeting.

9

"CULTURE WARS": GETTING TO PEACE

Professor Lawrence Lessig [1]

KEYNOTE ADDRESS

I start with some stories and then an observation on the way to an argument about what we should do about "The Culture Wars".

The first story

A long time ago in a place far away (Europe), the elite spoke Latin while the masses spoke "vulgar" languages (English, French and Germany). The elite ignored the masses. The masses ignored the elite.

The second story

In 1927, Huxley, wrote this:

> In the days before machinery men and women who wanted to amuse themselves were compelled, in their humble way, to be artists. Now they sit still and permit professionals to entertain them by the aid of machinery. It is

---

[1] Professor Lawrence Lessig is Director of the Edmund J Safra Foundation Center for Ethics at Harvard University, a Professor of Law at Harvard Law School and former Professor of Law at Stanford Law School. He is a founder of the Creative Commons organisation, which enables copyright holders to license their work online for primarily non-commercial purposes, and Change Congress, an organisation dedicated to changing the system that requires members of Congress to solicit private donations in order to fund election campaigns. Professor Lessig is perhaps the world's most famous exponent, and critic, of copyright policy in the United States. He has written seminal works on information policy, focusing on the social and economic effect of government regulation of the use of digital communications technology. He has written several seminal works, including *Code and Other Laws of Cyberspace* (1999) and *Remix: Making Art and Commerce Thrive in the Hybrid Economy* (2008).

difficult to believe that general artistic culture can flourish in this atmosphere of passivity.[2]

John Philip Souza had uttered that very same idea about two decades before. Souza was testifying at the United States Capitol about what he called "the talking machines." As he said:

> These talking machines are going to ruin the artistic development of music in this country. When I was a boy … in front of every house in the summer evenings you would find young people together singing the songs of the day or the old songs. Today you hear these infernal machines going night and day. We will not have a vocal chord left. The vocal chords will be eliminated by a process of evolution, as was the tail of man when he came from the ape.

This is a picture: the picture of young people singing the songs of the day or the old songs. It is a picture of culture that we might call, using modern computer terminology, a kind of "read-write" culture. It's a culture where people participate in the creation and re-creation of their culture. In this sense it is read-write.

Souza's fear was that we would lose the capacity to engage in this read-write culture because of these "infernal machines". They would take it away – displace it – and in its place we would have the opposite of read-write culture, what could call, using modern computer terminology, a kind of "read-only" culture. A culture where creativity was consumed, but the consumer was not a creator; a culture, which was top-down, where the "vocal chords" of the millions of ordinary people have been lost.

If you look back at the 20th century, at least in what we call the "developed world", it is very hard not to conclude that John Philip Souza was right. Never before in the history of culture had its production become as concentrated. Never before had it become professionalised. Never before had the ordinary people's creativity been effectively displaced and displaced for precisely the reasons that Souza spoke of because of these "infernal machines". The 20th Century was the century of read only culture, and it stands against a background of read-write culture from the beginning of man.

Why was it like this? The answer is technical, or at least largely technical. This was the age of broadcasting and vinyl. It produced a culture that could do little more than passively consume. It enabled efficient consumption, thus "reading", but inefficient production, at least by ordinary people, thus "writing." It was an age wired for mass reading; it was an age that discouraged mass writing.

---

[2] Huxley, Aldous, *The Doors of Perception* Harper & Bros, 1954.

The third story

In 1919, the United States voted itself dry. By a constitutional amendment, the nation launched a war against an obvious evil: the dependence upon intoxicating liquors. This was a war waged first by the progressives of the era, people who thought they could use law to make man better.

A decade later, this war was largely failing. The police found it increasing difficult to stop the illegal trade of intoxicating liquor. They therefore adopted new techniques to fight back. One such technology was the wiretap. And in a case involving Roy Olmstead and other defendants,[3] the Supreme Court had to consider whether this technique, the wiretap, was legal.

To answer that question, the Supreme Court looked at our Constitution — in particular to the Fourth Amendment. That Amendment reads:

> The right of the people to be secure in their persons, houses, papers, and effects, against unreasonable searches and seizures, shall not be violated, and no Warrants shall issue, but upon probable cause, supported by Oath or affirmation, and particularly describing the place to be searched, and the persons or things to be seized.

The question the Court had to answer was whether police attaching a wiretap to the telephones of Roy Olmstead and his associates, without any judicial authorisation, violated this prescription against "unreasonable searches and seizures".

The Chief Justice of the Supreme Court, former President William Howard Taft, looked at the objectives of the Fourth Amendment. These, he held, were to protect against "trespassing." Wiretapping, however didn't necessarily involve any trespass. There was no need to enter the apartment of Mr Olmstead to tap his phones. The police just needed to attach an alligator clip to the telephone wire once it left the apartment. Since there was no trespass, Taft held, there could be no violation of the Fourth Amendment. And thus was there no constitutional proscription against the government tapping telephones in the United States until the Court reversed itself until 1968.

More important than the opinion of the Court was a critical dissent by Justice Louis Brandeis. There was a principle at stake here, Brandeis wrote. That principle

---

[3] *Olmstead v United States* 277 US 438 (1928). The Supreme Court considered whether police wiretapping of the telephone of a bootlegger, Roy Olmstead, violated rights of privacy and against self-incrimination protected by the fourth and fifth amendments of the Constitution. The Court upheld Olmstead's conviction for bootlegging and he served a four year prison sentence.

was to protect against a certain kind of invasion. It was, in other words, to protect "privacy." But how you protect privacy is a function of technology. Citing an earlier case, Brandeis wrote, "time works changes" in those technologies. And thus the objective of the Court must be to translate old protections into a new context.

Brandeis lost, and the wiretap won. But by 1933, the war against intoxicating liquor had been deemed a failure. Increasing costs — the rise in organised crime, the fall in civil rights — and vanishing benefits — everyone drank, Prohibition notwithstanding — led the country to realise that perhaps costs outweighed the benefits. In 1933, Prohibition was ended and peace was declared by a constitutional amendment that repealed the constitutional amendment that had banned the sale of intoxicating liquors.

But the important point to recognise here was that what was repealed was not the aim to fight dependence on alcohol. All that was "repealed" was the idea of using war, or this metaphorical war, as a means to fight that dependence on intoxicating alcohol

Observations

Think about the idea of "writing". Writing is a quintessentially democratic activity. I don't mean that we vote upon what you are allowed to write. I mean instead that we expect everyone to have the capacity to write. Indeed, we teach our children how to write, and we measure the quality of their education on the basis of how well they write.

Why is it that we teach our kids how to write? I can understand why we teach them how to write in 1st grade to 8th grade, when they learn the basics to understand how to use words to communicate. But why do we waste our time teaching them to write from about 9th grade to college? Why do we tell them they have to write essays on Shakespeare or Hemingway or worse still, Proust? Why would anybody force their children into this activity? What do they expect to gain, because I can assure you, as a Professor who reads the writing of many students, that the vast majority of this writing is just "crap". So why do we do it?

The answer is obvious, but we should remark it nonetheless. We all understand that we learn something in the act of writing even if what we write is no good. We learn, if nothing else, respect for just how hard this creativity is, and we learn the value of the ability to engage in that creativity.

Now within this democratic activity of writing, think about a particular activity called "quoting." I had a friend in college who wrote essays that were essentially the stringing together, in the most elaborate and artistic way, of quotes that he had gathered from other writing, in order to make a point that was the point of his essay. He always got the very highest grades for that writing. He took it for granted that he could take, and use, and build upon, other people's writing, without permission from anyone — at least so long as he cited the original source accurately.

So long as you cite, we believe you can take and build upon anybody's work. Indeed, imagine what it would be like the other way round, imagine having to ask permission before you quoted someone's work. Imagine how absurd it would be for my friend to call the Hemingway estate to ask for permission to quote Hemingway in his college essay. Imagine how absurd it would be, and then you would understand how you too believe writing and quoting are an essentially democratic form of expression. Democratic in the sense that we all take for granted the right to take, and use, other people's work freely.

Argument

Think about writing or creating in a digital age. What should the freedom to write, or the freedom to quote, or the freedom to remix, in a digital age be?

In answering that question, notice the parallels with the stories that I told you.

As with the fight over Prohibition, right now in the United States, we are engaged in a war, the copyright wars, war which my friend, the late Jack Valenti, Head of the Motion Picture Association of America, used to refer to as his own "terrorist" war, where the terrorists in this war are our children.

As with the fight Souza was engaged in, this war is inspired by artists and an industry terrified that changes in technology will effect a radical change in how culture gets made.

And as with the war that led to prohibition, there is a fundamental question about these copyright wars that we need to raise: are the costs of this war greater than the benefits?

To answer that last question — in my view, the critical question — we have to think first about the benefits of copyright.

Copyright is a solution to a particular kind of problem. In my view, it is an essential solution to an unavoidable problem. Without the restriction on speech that copyright is, we would, paradoxically, have less speech. Copyright limits freedom, the freedom to unreservedly copy other people's work, or compete with the original creator of creative work, in order to inspire more free speech.

We limit this freedom — through regulation — to give creators the incentive they need to create more free speech. But as with privacy, the right regulation is going to be a function of the technology of the time. As technology changes, the architecture of the right regulation will change as well. What made sense in one period will make no sense in another. Instead, we need to adjust the architecture of regulation, so the same value protected before in a different context can be protected now in the new context.

With copyright, what would that right regulation look like today?

I believe with Souza that we need to distinguish between the amateur and the professional, but recognise that we need a copyright system that encourages both. We need the incentives for the professional, but also freedom for the amateur.

How could we achieve that?

If we watch the evolution of digital technologies, we can begin to see how the law could cope with both.

Think of this evolution in two stages: The first stage begins around 2000. In this stage, digital technologies simply extend the read only culture from our past. Technologies that make it massively efficient to get and consume culture created elsewhere: Apple is the poster child of this vision of culture, with its iTunes music store, allowing you for 99 cents to download any song you want to your iPod (and only to your iPod), and in the United States, at least mark yourself as cool. This is the vision my colleague, Paul Goldstein, spoke of when he described the "celestial jukebox" — enabling you at any time, whenever you want, to access any culture you want.[4] This is a critically important model for providing and supporting culture, facilitating an enormous diversity of culture, and the spread and support for culture. But it is just one model of culture supported by digital technology.

The second stage in this evolution begins around 2004. It is a revival of the read-write culture from our past. The poster child for this image of culture is Wikipedia, and the enormous energy directed to that project. But I want to talk here about a slice of that culture that is distinct from Wikipedia — what I call "remix".

Some examples will make the idea clear.

In the context of music: Everyone knows the *White Album*, created by the Beatles. That album inspired the *Black Album*, created by Jay-Z. That then inspired DJ Danger Mouse to produce the *Grey Album*. Four years later, Girl Talk sets the

---

[4] Paul Goldstein published *Copyright's Highway: From Gutenberg to the Celestial Jukebox* (Stanford University Press) in 2003.

standard, mixing together hundreds of songs to produce a single album, *Feed the Animals*.

In the context of film: In 2004, the film Tarnation made its debut at Cannes. It was said by the BBC to "wow Cannes." This was made with $218: A kid took video that he had shot through his whole life, and using an iMac given to him by a friend, remixed it in a way to wow Cannes and win the 2004 Los Angeles Film Festival.

Or finally, in the context of politics: Consider Will.I.Am's work, taking the words of Obama and mixing them with music. Or still my favourite, think about the work of Johan Soderberg, mixing images of George Bush and Tony Blair, with the song, Endless Love.[5]

This is remix. But these are still examples of creativity which is in some way broadcast, though by using the Internet.

More interesting is the way that this platform has become a platform for communities to remix the work of other communities. You Tube has become the best example of this. Take, for example, *Superman Day Parade*, or *Superman Retires*, which mixes cartoon footage of a mature Superman, Wonderwoman, Birdman, Mr T and others, and dubs dialogue that involves Mr T challenging "old man" Superman to a fight, and propositioning Wonderwoman. This video inspired a Simpsons remix on You Tube, which inspired a Bambi remix video.

Or one final example from You Tube: a performance of the Canon in D Major by Johann Pachelbel by Funtwo: This arrangement has been seen by more than 60 million people across the world, and more interestingly, it has inspired thousands of replications and remixes.

These remixes are conversations. They are the modern equivalent of what Souza was speaking of when he romanticised young people singing the songs of the day, or the old songs. But instead of gathering on the corner, or the back lawn, now people from around the world use this digital platform to engage in a form of read-write creativity, powerful and original and (to anyone who will listen), inspirational.

The importance in this has nothing to do with the particular technique: for the techniques have been available since the beginning of film or recorded music. The importance is that the technique has been democratised. It is the fact that anybody with access to a $1500 computer can make sounds and images that remix the

---

[5] Soderberg remixed audiovisual material to create a 2003 video of George Bush and Tony Blair ostensibly serenading each other with the words of *Endless Love*, the duet performed by Lionel Richie and Diana Ross. Posted on You Tube in 2007 the video became a viral sensation.

culture around him or her and spread them broadly in ways that speak more powerfully to a younger generation than any words could.

And here then is the key linking back to my first story.

This is "writing" in the 21st century. It is not the "writing" that most of us do. Most of us write with words and sentences — this essay, for example. But that sort of "writing" in the 21st century will be the equivalent of Latin in the Middle Ages. Writing with images, sounds and video in the 21st century is the writing of the "vulgar." They engage in it and if we ignore it, they, the vulgar, ignore us.

Yet here's the problem with this new way of writing: The norms and law from the 20th century, as applied to this "writing" in the 21st century, are different. The norms that we apply to media are different from the norms we apply to text. With respect to text, the freedom to quote is taken for granted. With media, the norms assume you need permission first.

Why did these norms develop and support such a difference in freedom? Again, the reason is technical. If you look at the architecture of copyright law, and the architecture of digital technologies, the reasons are clear. The architecture of copyright law triggers its regulation on the production of something called a "copy." The architecture of digital technology says every single time you use culture you produce a copy. This is a radical change in the scope and reach of copyright law, for copyright law never purported to regulate every use of culture.

Think about this point in the context of a book. Many uses of a book are simply unregulated by the law. To read a book is not a fair use of the book. It is a free use of the book, because to read a book is not to produce a copy. To give someone a book is not a fair use of the book, it is a free use of the book, because again, to give someone a book is not to produce a copy. To sell a book under the American copyright scheme is specifically exempted from the reach of the copyright owner because to sell a book is not to produce a copy. To sleep on a book is in no jurisdiction anywhere in the world a copyright relevant use of the book, because to sleep on a book is not to produce a copy.

These unregulated uses are balanced by a set of important regulated uses, regulated so as to create the incentives necessary for authors to create great new works. To publish a book you need permission from the copyright owner because that monopoly right is deemed essential to create the incentive in some authors to create great new works.

And then in the American tradition, there is a slim sliver of exemptions from copyright law called fair use: uses which would have otherwise been regulated by the law, but which the law says are to remain free to encourage creativity or critique to build upon older work.

This balance between unregulated, regulated and fair uses gets radically changed when digital technologies are brought into the mix. Because now, every use produces a copy, and thus now, the balance between regulated and unregulated uses gets radically changed. Merely because the platform through which we get access to our culture has changed, the presumptive reach of copyright law has changed, thus rendering this read-write material presumptively illegal under the regime we inherit from the 20th century.

No one in any legislative body ever thought about this. There was no *Act To Massively Regulate Every Creative Activity Act* — anywhere. This is instead the unintended consequence of the interaction between these two architectures of regulation, copyright law and digital technologies.

This unintended consequence is what I think of as Problem 1 in the copyright wars. Law is out of sync with technology, and just as before with the Fourth Amendment, in my view, that law needs to be updated. Just as the Fourth Amendment needed to be updated to take account of new technologies, copyright law needs to be updated to take account of these new technologies.

Problem 2 is what people refer to as piracy, or peer-to-peer "piracy." Here however, we must link to prohibitions. This is a war of prohibition, and this law of prohibition, like most wars of prohibition, has not worked, if by worked we mean reduced the "bad" behaviour. We have learned that kids who share files don't read opinions of the United States Supreme Court. Here is a map of peer-to-peer file sharing in the United States. Here is the point where the Supreme Court declared this activity illegal, but we still see no drop off in the behaviour of peer-to-peer file sharing. Instead of reducing the bad behaviour, all this war has done is render a generation of criminals. This is Problem 2, a technology out of sync with the law, and just as with the Fourth Amendment, copyright needs an update to take care of this misapplication as well.

What we should do?

Abolitionism is growing among the denizens of digital culture. Copyright, in their view, may have been needed for a couple of hundred years. We don't need it anymore. Other techniques (business models) and other technologies (digital rights management) provide all the "protection" creators need, on this view. Anything more is simply unnecessary government regulation.

I am not an abolitionist. But I do believe abolitionism will grow unless we find a way to update the law of copyright to better take into account new technology. We need a series of changes in law. I am going to outline two here.

First: the law has to give up its obsession with the "copy." The idea of a law being triggered upon reproduction in the digital age is insane. Instead the law needs to focus on meaningful activities. "Copying," in a digital age, is not meaning, meaningful.

"Meaningful" in turn should be determined by the function of use. If we distinguish between copying and remixing, and between professionals and amateurs, we get something like this matrix.

	Copies	Remix
Professionals	Copyright	
Amateurs		

The presumption of copyright law today is that all of this is regulated in the same way. Professional or amateur, copies or remix: it's the same law that gets triggered. The first point to recognize: Never has the law of copyright purported to reach this broadly, and it makes no sense for the law to reach that broadly now.

	Copies	Remix
Professionals	Copyright	
Amateurs		

Instead of course the law has to regulate efficiently here with professionals controlling the distribution of copies of their work. For if it doesn't regulate efficiently here, then we can't create the incentives that some professionals need to create their work.

	Copies	Remix
Professionals	Copyright	
Amateurs		Free

But equally clearly, amateurs remixing culture should be free of the regulation of copyright law. There should be a simple clear directive that this activity should be set free of any regulation, without needing a lawyer to provide an opinion that such use is "fair."

	Copies	Remix
Professionals	Copyright	Mixed
Amateurs	Mixed	Free

In the middle, we have two harder cases — instances where the law has some important role in restricting use, but where that restriction must be balanced with important freedoms. Amateurs distributing copies of work should, to some degree, be privileged (I should be free to share my favourite song with my brother), but in some sense controlled (I should not be free to share my favourite song with my 10,000 best friends). Likewise, professionals involved in remix need the freedom to remix without requiring the permission of every copyright owner, but plainly, some derivative work is rightly owned by the copyright holder.

This map of reform is essentially libertarian. I am arguing for a fundamental deregulation of a significant space of our culture, and for focusing the regulation of copyright law in those areas where it can do some good. If we need regulation here, that regulation should at least demonstrate its necessity. Too much regulation is allowed to pass without any such demonstration.

Second: We need a change of law in the context of peer-to-peer piracy. We need to recognise that this decade-long war has been a failure. Some respond to failed wars by waging an ever more vicious campaign against the enemy. My response is to sue for peace, and find a better way to achieve the objectives of the war. The objectives of this war are to compensate creators for the exploitation of their work. We can provide that compensation without waging war against our kids.

For the last decade, many of us here have been bouncing around from hearing many decent proposals to address this fundamental problem, compulsory licenses to the voluntary collective licenses that the Electronic Frontier Foundation has proposed. All of these proposals seek to compensate the artist for the exploitation of her work without also breaking the Internet.

When we reflect on these proposals, here's the point I want you to see: if we had enacted any one of these proposals into law one decade ago, the world today would be very different, in very tangible ways:

1. Artists would have more money. The current campaign to sue peer-to-peer "pirates" has given nothing of value to artists. When students are sued by the RIAA in America, artists get nothing from those lawsuits. Instead, the money simply funds further lawsuits, which means, the money simply goes to the lawyers. Whatever copyright law is for, it is not to provide a full employment act for lawyers.

2. Businesses would have enjoyed more competition and more opportunity for innovation. If the rules had been clearer at the start of this last decade, then more companies than Apple could have stepped in to figure out how to exploit this opportunity for spreading culture more broadly.

3. And certainly most important by a mile: If we had enacted these proposals a decade ago, we would not have raised a generation of "criminals." As it is, we have millions of kids who have spent the last decade engaging in activities that they are told is criminal, but that in their own head seems as sensible as any behaviour that any normal person who "gets it" engages in. That creates a dissonance. That dissonance is a cost. It is a tax on their soul, as it alienates them from doing what's right.

When you weigh these different factors — profit to record companies on one side, and gains to artists, business, and the souls of our kids on the other — I suggest the cost of this war to this generation is high enough to force us to adopt a different way to secure the promise of copyright in the 21st century.

In Europe we see this battle being fought in a very distinctive way. In France, we have recently seen the consideration of a 3- Strikes proposal, which basically says "Violate copyright law three times and your ISP has an obligation to kick you off the internet." By contrast, Germany is now considering the Green Party's proposal of a cultural "flat rate," under which everyone pays a given amount in exchange for legalising non-commercial peer-to-peer sharing of copyrighted material.

That contrast, in my view, frames the contrast of choices that we are facing around the world. The 3-Strikes proposal is the American response to hopeless wars — waging an ever more effective war against the enemy. The German cultural flat rate is a response that recognises that this war of prohibition has failed, and that we need a different way to secure the objectives of copyright: to ensure copyright owners get compensated for the use of their work.

Australia and New Zealand have an enormously important role to play in that debate. Of course, New Zealand has recently considered and rejected the 3-Strike proposal and at least is speaking about a fundamental reconsideration about the way copyright law regulates in the 21st century. There is also here in Australia, a significant question about the way copyright law will regulate in the future.

My plea to you today is that you recognise the leadership you could play in this debate, and that you direct that leadership not to figuring out ever more fancy weapons to use against our kids, but to push all of us, and especially those of us in the United States, towards a position of sanity and sensibility for copyright in the 21st century.

*   *   *

I had the opportunity to speak at a conference at the Association of the Bar of the City of New York. The conference was held in a beautiful room, with luxurious red velvet curtains and a plush red carpet. The aim of the conference was to explain to creators how they could comply with the law of copyright, and how they could rely upon the law of fair use.

The law of fair use offers four factors that must be weighed by a judge before the judge can conclude that a particular use was "fair." The lawyers organising the event decided that they would ask four lawyers to speak for 15 minutes each on each of the four factors — on the theory, I take it, that at the end of the hour the audience would be educated about fair use, and could go forward and create consistent with the law.

As I sat there and looked out at the audience, it wasn't an understanding that I saw. It was total confusion. That confusion then led me to a day-dream about the event, and about its purpose.

Because as I looked around the room, I kept asking myself what that room remind me of. And eventually, it dawned on me. As a college student, I had spent a lot of time travelling throughout Eastern Europe and the Soviet Union. That room, I realised, reminded me of the soviet parliament. And that led me to ask:

When was it in the history of the Soviet system when you could have convinced the Soviets that their system had failed? 1976 was too early, as it was puttering along okay in 1976. 1989 was too late: If you didn't get it by 1989, you were never going to get it. So when was it, between 1976 and 1989, that you could have convinced them that the system had failed and, more importantly, what could you have said to these Soviets to convince them that the ideology that they had romanticised had crashed and burned, and to continue with the Soviet system was to betray a certain kind of insanity.

Because, as I listen to lawyers insist that "nothing had changed," and that "the same rules should apply," and that "it is the pirates who are the deviants," I recognised that it is we, lawyers, who are insane.

This existing system of copyright could never work in the digital age. Either it will force kids to stop creating, or it will force upon the system a revolution. In my view, both options are not acceptable.

Extremism invites extremism in response. And the extremism of the rights holders today has created the extremism of abolitionism. I think both extremes are wrong. Thus in this war, I am Gorbachev, not Yeltsin: an old communist who's trying to preserve this old system in a new time against extremisms from both sides. Extremisms that would destroy the system of copyright that we have inherited.

Some of you might not care about destroying the system of copyright. So then allow me one final plea: We have to recognise this: We can't kill this form of creativity; we can only criminalise it. There is no way we can stop our kids from engaging in this form of creativity; we can only drive their creativity underground. We can't make them passive; we can only make them "pirates." The question we have to ask is, is that any good? In my country, kids live in an age of prohibition, constantly living their life against the law. We need to recognise: that life is corrosive, and corrupting to the rule of law, at least the rule of law in a democracy.

That is a cost of this war. In my view, it is large enough to say that our first moral obligation must be to find a way to stop this war. Now.

Thank you very much.

10

QUESTIONS AND ANSWERS FOLLOWING PROFESSOR LESSIG'S ADDRESS MODERATED BY THE HON MICHAEL KIRBY

THE HON MICHAEL KIRBY

Could I say that I left hanging in the air the second point that Lawrence taught in a very different lecture that he gave in London, but it is relevant, and I would like to ask him about it, and that was the lesson you taught about the difficulty of securing change because of the corruption of our political system by reason of the intermeshing of politics with reform.

In a week's time, I go to New York for a meeting with the Council on Foreign Relations,[1] and the UNAIDS Global Reference Panel,[2] which is relating to how, in the new Obama world, we adjust our response to the AIDS epidemic, given that President George W. Bush tripled the funding of AIDS assistance, which was a very good thing, but [in a way] designed to exclude the United Nations and the UN AIDS machinery – as some have sometimes unkindly said, because of the very large resources that were paid into his electoral funds by the pharmaceutical industry.

And I think it would be helpful, you have given us as it were, if I dare use this expression, the road map, but we really have got to know, does the road map lead anywhere given the intermeshing of industry and politics and the funding of politics in all of our countries?

PROFESSOR LESSIG

Yes, it's a great question, because in fact as some of you know, about a year ago I said that I was shifting my academic work away from these questions of free culture and balance in copyright to focus on what I call this problem of institutional corruption

---

[1] The Council on Foreign Relations is a non-profit think-tank based in New York City, the mission of which is to improve understanding of the 'world and the foreign policy choices facing the US and other countries.'

[2] UNAIDS Global Reference Panel on HIV/AIDS and Human Rights.

which is not the problem, of say, Rod Blagojevich, who was the Governor who tried to sell a Senate seat for money, or Randy Duke Cunningham, who would sell defence contracts in exchange for kick-backs to himself.

Not that kind of corruption, but instead the kind of corruption which is endemic in the American political system, where politicians spend between 30% and 70% of their time raising money to get back to Congress, and therefore become enormously sensitive to the wishes of those who provide the greatest amount of funding. I think this is a central part of the problem, fixing that problem.

And it's not, as you said, just an American problem. Take for example, the situation of the democracy gap that exists in Europe right now. The EU recently has been considering the question of whether to extend the term of copyrights for recordings. The recording term was 50 years. This of course was an issue at the centre of my work, because we began our organising around the Sonny Bono Copyright Term Extension Act, which extended the term of existing copyrights by 20 years in the United States. The EU wanted to extend the recording term from 50 years to 95 years.

And when that was being considered in the United States, we brought a challenge, when it was being considered as legislation, and then we brought a legal challenge to it once it was enacted, challenging the constitutionality of this extension. The extension challenge was supported by a brief that was signed by about 17 economists including five Nobel Prize winners including such lefty liberals as Milton Friedman, oh I'm sorry, wait, he's a right wing Nobel Prize-winning economist.

Milton Friedman said he would only sign this brief if it argued that there could be no public good that would come from extending an existing copyright, and if the term "no-brainer" was in the brief somewhere, so clear was it, that this could serve no public interest. When Europe was considering the same issue, a whole bunch of respected institutions around Europe considered the question.

Gowers ran a Commission in Britain about intellectual property generally, and concluded that it could "never make sense to extend the term of an existing copyright". In Holland, there was an equivalent study by a very respected intellectual property centre that made a similar conclusion about how this could not serve the public interest at all. Yet just last month, the EU voted to extend the term of existing copyrights for recordings, again, solely because the industry has such an enormous influence on policy makers. They acted independently of what makes good sense from a public policy perspective.

Now, you know, when I changed my work, there was this moment, this ah-ha moment, that kind of showed me that I wasn't as smart as I thought I was, because I should have figured this out a long time ago. But the ah-ha moment was watching Al Gore give his speech about global warming, and one of my closest friends was the director of his film, *An Inconvenient Truth*, so I got to follow him around and watch him give this speech a bunch of times. But one of the points that Gore makes, less so in the film, more in his actual speech, is that the very same dynamic that I am complaining about in the context of intellectual property, has lead the United States to make it impossible for them to address the question of global warming.

Even today, with Barack Obama as President, and the Democrats controlling both Houses of Congress, I would predict there is a 57% to 60% chance that this Congress will not be able to enact global warming legislation because 12 Democrats could not afford to vote against the oil or coal industries, and continue to raise the money they need to get back to Congress.[3]

The ah-ha moment was recognising, wait a minute, it's not just esoteric questions like copyright where this corrupting influence is driving bad policy. Absolutely every single fundamental public policy question America faces, including the most important questions, global warming, health care, the financing systems, are stopped because of exactly this corruption.

My view was that unless we find a way to deal with that, we won't be able to deal with copyright, or global warming, or any of these other issues either, and so, yes of course, I am sceptical that we can address these issues before we address the others. But what we can do is at least make it obvious to people who have the principles of copyright in their heart, that really are genuine scholars, or lawyers, focused on what copyright should be about. It is at least possible for us to get those people to recognise what is good policy and if we can't get policy makers to implement it, at least we can get the profession to recognise it. And that, I think, is an enormously important first step, that at least gets us towards the place where policy makers can be shamed into doing what we all recognise is the right thing.

THE HON MICHAEL KIRBY

Some of those comments would have caused ah-ha moments to us in Australia because we have certain similar issues as in the United States. Now Brian can we have five minutes for a few questions? Oh, we've got eight minutes.

Ok, short questions or comments. Yes – and if you wish to identify where you are from.

---

[3] In 2009, 12 Democrats on the House of Representatives' energy subcommittee, all from auto-manufacturing, or coal or oil producing states, wavered on voting for President Obama's climate change bill. The bill stalled in the Senate in 2010.

BRIANNA LAW FROM WIKIMEDIA AUSTRALIA

In your talk about how copyright law might be reformed, you make a distinction between amateurs and professionals, and I wonder if with digital reproduction lowering the cost of producing and disseminating works, is that still meaningful and how can we define that?

PROFESSOR LESSIG

Yes, it's absolutely true that the line between amateurs and professionals is going to be a hard one to draw. But just because we lawyers are very good at turning any black and white distinction into grey, indeed that is how we are trained, that is why we are paid so much money, we can turn black and white into grey, we should recognise that there are radically different reasons that people create.

Some people create for the money and they should be respected because they are great creators, they are trying to be a professional, they are trying to make their creativity, make it so they are free to create.

But there are other people, the original meaning of the word amateur, who create for the love of their creating, not for the money. And when they engage in that act, what they are doing has nothing to do with money, and indeed, if you introduced money into the mix, it would change the kind of creativity. You from Wikimedia know this very well. Wikipedians are people who create access to knowledge because they want to share that knowledge. If Jimmy Wales[4] were to institute a system of paying editors for editing Wikipedia entries, I think the quality of the editing would go down because people participate in that economy of creativity for the love of what they are doing. And we need to respect that there are those economies that we want to continue. Indeed, everybody wants to continue. Think about the sharing economy of two lovers, right. Introduce money into that economy, you have radically changed the nature of the interaction there, in ways that even conservatives who love the market would say no, no, no, we don't want the market to be functioning there.

The point is to see that we have these different motivations for creativity, and we need to respect them, and have a system that can respect them, even though there are going to be places where it's hard to tell the difference. We need to work hard to figure out how the law needs to negotiate the differences, but still not lose sight of the fact that there are important kinds of creativities on both sides of that line.

---

[4] Co-founder and public face of Wikipedia.

THE HON MICHAEL KIRBY

Adrian Sterling, I've got to give you a fair go now. I think it might be a chance for you to ask a question.

PROFESSOR ADRIAN STERLING

Thank you very much. I'm one of those persons that Professor Lessig referred to as a person with copyright in his heart, and a little while ago, I heard lots of discussion about what Professor Lessig said and how bad for copyright it was, and how terrible it was. So I thought, well perhaps one should look to see what he actually says. So I got a copy of his book, *Remix*, published in October last year by Penguin and read it through and came to the conclusion that I agreed with everything that he said. This afternoon, I've heard him repeat some of that and also bring us up to date, and I still feel the same way.

And I want to make just one or two very quick remarks of how I would suggest one takes into consideration reaching that objective that Professor Lessig has brought before us. No abolition, but compensation for right-owners, and recognition of the rights of the amateur in *Remix,* and so forth.

The first thing is, I would say, I don't think that we need, or should have, a revolution. Revolutions sometimes don't end up where they want to be directed. What we need is an evolution, and I don't believe that evolution can be achieved, which we would all want to, by trying to get international changes to the conventions, which we would need, if we were going to change radically the conditions on exclusive rights of copying, reproduction and communication to the public that are granted by the conventions. We have to remember that in the Berne Convention diplomatic conferences, there must be unanimity of voting to change the Convention. We will not get unanimity on changes of that nature.

Therefore, my suggestion is that the road we follow is to consider what rights are in existence now, and how they should be administered. It's the administration of those rights, rather than changing the rights and I believe firmly that those who administer the rights of authors and others, have it within their power to evolve licensing systems and to evolve ways of administering rights, which will fully meet that matrix which Professor Lessig has showed us. That is, as it were, the free area, the regulated area for payment, and those where there's a cross-over.

I do believe, though, that we need to have everything specified in the sense that it is legitimated. I would like to see the situation reached, where my use of somebody else's work is legitimated either by a licence or by legal provision. But I want to know where I stand and I believe this can be achieved.

There is one area that I think Professor Lessig and all of us need to think about in order to achieve this great objective, which is moral rights. When my work is subject to remix in that unregulated area, what about my moral rights.

Now, we have to recognise that moral rights are under the Convention, so we have to see how we are going to meet that. Thank you.

THE HONOURABLE MICHAEL KIRBY

Ok, moral rights or licensing.

PROFESSOR LESSIG

First, I am grateful to you for doing what I have always thought too few of my opponents have done, which is to actually read what I have said, and to engage in that act of understanding. There has been too little of that, and I take responsibility for inflaming the passions of this, I understand. But my hope is to make peace by understanding, exactly the way that you have done.

Number two, I also agree that evolution is what's important here. As you will remember in my book, I talked about my colleague, Terry Fisher's, proposal for radically changing the way copyright law functions, through basically eliminating the property right character of copyright, and replacing it with a whole system of basically sampling use and compensating on the basis of that. And I say that I don't support that because it is too radical a change. But the German Green Party's proposal for the culture of flat rate is actually backed up with a very careful analysis of how that is consistent with the international conventions, and I think that's the kind of evolution that is needed here.

Finally, I'll confess with respect to moral rights, it might be here that there's the greatest potential for conflict. If there's a point of agreement, I would say it's this. My view is not that we should give up moral rights. Indeed we should encourage respect for moral rights in just the sense that people should identify and criticise people who misuse other people's work. So moral rights, in the sense not just of attribution, but in the sense of maintaining the integrity. The only difference we might have is whether that criticism should be engaged in a court as opposed to in the public sphere.

The principles of free speech from America would tend to say that, if you have an argument about how I'm respecting you, that is an appropriate argument to engage in contexts other than legal jurisdictions. It's kind of an engagement to have in the context of open public discourse. So, I should say, this person has misused that person's work, and we should say, shame on you for doing that, and we should punish you in all of the ways that we punish people without using courts. But the burden of legal jurisdiction here is too great.

Now I understand there is room for disagreement here, and the European traditions are much stronger, and as they have been grafted into Japan and many parts of Asia, much stronger than in the American tradition, but I think this is a source of disagreement where we can genuinely understand each other, and try to make progress.

THE HONOURABLE MICHAEL KIRBY

Can we have one more question? Yes very well, I think this gentleman here.

MARK CALLAGHAN – AMPAL (AUSTRALASIAN MUSIC PUBLISHERS' ASSOCIATION LIMITED)

I was just going to make a couple of comments and like Professor Sterling, I was enthralled with today's presentation. I thought it was a breath of fresh air frankly. I also echo his concerns about moral rights and I think ironically, it could be an area that could be agreed upon perhaps more readily than many others yet it is the most complex. I mean, take your reference to the use of Lionel Richie's song to parody George Bush, I mean, he may genuinely have thought it wasn't funny. I mean, he may be a Bush supporter and, you know, we need to respect that.

I think one point that I would like to make, that I think is relevant to this debate, that doesn't get raised a lot, is that there's an additional difference I think in the context of comparing our modern re-write experience with a historical one, in that much of what goes on in that space in You Tube, and on the net and MySpace is commercialised activity. And I think that's a very different overlay to what has happened in the past. And I think I just wanted to make that comment and say that pirate sites, for example, are commercial activities, whereas they are portrayed as being about sharing, although the people that run the sites are making money.

PROFESSOR LESSIG

Yes, so I mean it is a weird inversion. I can only speak about the law in America here. But if you think about a kid taking some videos, and remixing them, he could be engaging in that activity for purely non-commercial reasons. He uploads it to You Tube and You Tube's use of it, in some sense, is deeply commercial. They are in the business of trying to make money. Yet the law says that what the kid does is illegal. But if You Tube takes the thing down within a certain number of days after having notice of the copyright violation, YouTube is immune from any responsibility. And I think that is exactly backwards.

I think what the kid does, should be completely privileged, a free type of creativity. If it's uploaded to You Tube or the equivalent, then I think it's totally appropriate to say that there should be some, you know, flat rate license or some blanket license that is covering the music that's inside that, that has to be paid for by the commercial service, so that it compensates the artist for the commercial use of their work. Just like a public theatre has a blanket license for songs that are performed in the public theatre, so too in the context of what You Tube is doing. Yet we haven't got to that position at all yet and I think, you know, we certainly need to find a way to get there.

THE HON MICHAEL KIRBY

Brett Cottle – one last question or comment.

BRETT COTTLE CEO AUSTRALASIAN PERFORMING RIGHT ASSOCIATION

Professor, I just wanted to take you back to the map of Europe where you contrasted the French approach to the German approach, and the cultural flat rate being proposed by the Greens in Germany. I don't think you will be surprised to know that the authors' societies are in violent agreement with you about that approach. The problem, of course, is how to get to that solution. It is a very difficult legislative path, and, of course, the people who would be paying the cultural flat rate, would inevitably by the ISPs. My question to you really is, how do you think we can get, by regulation, to that path, to that position.

PROFESSOR LESSIG

Well, it's good to see you again. We had the pleasure of debating in Europe about these questions about a year ago. I think that there are two steps to getting us there. First, we need to have a debate which isn't the debate between three strikes and the culture of flat rate, but a debate that brings more traditional rights' holders into the space that says exactly what you have just said. That we support a move towards this, and lets figure out how to implement it.

Number two, we need some experimentation between jurisdictions. I don't think any of us has a clear sense of what's going to create the right balance between artists and the public, and we need to find some – we need to see something about how it's actually being implemented in different jurisdictions. Now, as you know, as was commented before, that turns out to be pretty hard, because of the uniformity of IP rules enforced by agreements internationally. But I think that if we had a genuine and good faith conversation between the rights' holders, and the community, about this, and allow some diversity in the implementation, we could move towards a system that we begin to recognise as actually achieving those objectives.

One important thing, though, is to bring the whole of the artistic community into this discussion. And I'm sure you are aware there's this extraordinary Heidelberg manifesto that has been created in Germany by a bunch of authors who are absolutely against the internet, they are against anybody having access to their work on the internet, and they have created this huge public outcry against a lot of these changes, because they happen to be the most popular writers. They all happen to all be over the age of 60 too, but the most popular writers in Germany.

And I think there's a great amount of misunderstanding here about what exactly we should be achieving. I think if we found more ways for people like you, and people like me, to stand on a common platform, and point to the kind of answer that would be the right answer, then we can have lots more progress in getting to it than we've had in the last 10 years, I think.

Thank you very much for your attention.

THE HONOURABLE MICHAEL KIRBY

We've already thanked Professor Lessig, but I want to make two little comments in closing.

First, I tried to keep, out of the corner of my eye, an eye on you all, and I noticed you all looking at the text that was coming up, instead of looking at the man who was presenting, and doing it so eloquently. I've learned from having watched Professor Lessig before, it's a whole experience just watching him, instead of watching all the text, though he makes the text very watchable because he puts pictures and other things in there, and you're waiting to see what comes next.

The second thing is, and it won't go away, the issue of a democratic politic and how it copes with this issue. I mean we can have dreams of how one would have radical change, but Adrian put a little bit of a real issue into the mix there. And it's appropriate we should think about that in this House, because when I was young, when I was first the Chairman of the Law Reform Commission, this was the Parliament of Australia. It was a temporary or provisional Parliament House. It was opened in 1927, the Parliament having from the beginning of Federation been in Melbourne, in the Melbourne parliamentary building in Spring Street in Melbourne, and then they moved up here and King George VI as he later became, the Duke of York and his wife, the Duchess of York, later the Queen Mother, came here.

There's a wonderful portrait of it actually in the King's Hall, which shows them arriving, and the troops lined up, most of whom would have fought in Gallipoli and on the Somme, and it is important for us to remember, though we are a small country, we are very very mature democracy. We have the fifth oldest still working constitution in the world and this is the chamber of the fifth oldest continuous constitutional nation in the world. And therefore, when Professor Lessig throws out a challenge to us from his vantage point, and from his tremendous ability to see things conceptually, which is what we wanted him to come and do for us, and what he's done for us, then we've got to take that seriously.

Our Parliament has moved up the hill, but ours is still the fifth oldest Constitution in the world, and the fifth oldest continuous democracy, and this is its House, and we are privileged to sit in this House and to reflect on all of the battles and the democracy that were fought out here. And if you have time, just wander, just cast a glance into the old House of Representatives, green carpet as in the Congress, as in the House of Commons, and into the Senate, where there's red carpet.

And that is the heart of democracy in this nation. So we've really got to think about what we've said, and I think that on top of a magnificent morning of a great cake – what a cake we've had today. A terrific morning of history and of interest and of personalities. We've had this most insightful session and I'd ask you once again to thank Professor Lessig.

PROFESSOR BRIAN FITZGERALD

Well thank you both, I'm not sure which one of you travels more, or which one of you was more passionate about your topic, but all I know is I'm thankful that both of you are here. Tremendous presentation Larry. I know it's a very difficult time, you're moving from Stanford back to Harvard, and you're in the process of doing it, and it's a horrible time to have to travel across the world to a far-flung place like Australia. Thank you very much.

And Michael Kirby, the Honourable Michael Kirby, thank you for coming down in between all of the engagements that you've had yesterday, and today, for what has been truly a memorable session. Thank you.

11

COPYRIGHT AND CREATIVITY

Professor Julie E. Cohen [1]

Thank you all. It is a pleasure to be here. What you are going to hear is not a single paper but rather a condensed version of a couple of book chapters.

What I want to argue today is that copyright law, or at least American copyright law, which is my area of expertise, is premised on a defective model of creativity, and that that deficiency in copyright's model of creativity is a direct consequence of the tools that lawyers and theorists have brought to the task of understanding the creative process.

Legal scholarship is closely aligned with the tradition of liberal political economy, and therefore with the foundational principles on which that tradition rests. So, in particular, liberal theory regards the self as a disembodied abstract being; it treats knowledge as transcendent and existing on a plane separate from and superior to culture; and it treats the self and culture as fundamentally distinct entities. Those commitments exact a very high price when we start talking about copyright, because creativity operates at the interface between self and culture, and plays out in the concrete and materially determined contexts in which people live and interact.

I would like to do three things in my time today. First, I want to critically examine copyright's model of cultural development as it builds from those fundamental assumptions. Then we will take a look at some examples drawn from a variety of art forms and genres, and will use those examples to illustrate an alternative model of cultural development that more closely aligns with how creative people actually work

---

[1] Professor Julie E. Cohen, Professor of Law at Georgetown University Law Center, is one of the leading scholars of copyright and intellectual property law in the United States, with a special interest in the effects of copyright and privacy law and policy on information regulation. She is co-author of *Copyright in a Global Information Economy*, Aspen Law & Business, 2010 (3rd ed) and several scholarly book chapters, articles and essays. Professor Cohen has focused attention on the effect of networked communication and society on the production of culture. She is at present working on a book examining the 'networked self' in the context of copyright law, surveillance, privacy law, and internet architecture.

on a day-to-day basis. Finally, I will say a couple of things about how we might actually proceed to revise copyright law in accordance with that alternative model.

COPYRIGHT'S MODEL OF CREATIVITY

First let's take a look at copyright's implicit model of cultural development. You know, certainly, that copyright scholars don't agree on whether current copyright laws strike the right balance between authors and the public. Some people argue that expanded rights are necessary to counteract the effects of technologies for mass reproduction and redistribution. Others disagree, and argue that to exploit the democratising potential of new digital media technologies, copyright protection should be balanced by a more robust set of exceptions. Earlier today, Professor Lessig characterised those debates as the copyright wars.

Even so, copyright law is premised on a set of assumptions about the relationship between copyright and creativity that most people, on both sides of the debate, generally accept. Legal scholars on both sides of the copyright wars largely assume that copyright supplies incentives for authors to produce creative work, but that the creative process is essentially internal and unknowable. They assume that copyright can strike a satisfactory balance between the needs of authors and the needs of audiences as long as it includes well tailored exceptions for uses of great social importance. They assume that because copyright attaches only to creative expression, and not to underlying ideas, copyright can avoid frustrating future authors. A lot hinges on whether those assumptions are right.

Let's start with authors and the question of where creativity comes from. Legal scholars who advance rights based arguments for copyright have generally described creativity in terms of an individual liberty whose form remains largely unspecified. Sometimes this argument relies on self reporting by artists; when asked about why they create, artists tend to describe a process that is intrinsically unknowable. When legal scholars consider those self reports, however, they also add something. They characterise creative motivation as both intrinsically unknowable and essentially internal: a gift of self, or a 'black box' inside the mind of the author. The belief in creativity's essentially internal aspect does not match the experience that artists describe at all. Artists may not be able to tell us why they create but they can tell us a great deal about the where, what and how of particular creative processes: what they were looking at, what they were reading, what they were listening to, who they were talking to, and so on. Social scientists who study the creative process have found that these things matter a lot.

Economically minded scholars have focused on the marketable by-products of creativity. For scholars of the 'copyright maximalist' persuasion, creative motivation matters only to the extent that we presume it is enhanced by the possibility of an economic reward. The details of why somebody would create this rather than that are irrelevant; market signals will take care of the details. Critics of the maximalist model challenge the argument that copyright always supplies an incentive to produce more creative material. They argue that sometimes creative motivation has no market origins. Even so, they generally agree with the maximalist view that the specifics of creative motivation are irrelevant. As James Boyle puts it, "It is irrelevant that people create, only that they do it". If creativity is not purely internal, if it's a function of what authors were looking at, and reading, and listening to, then the details matter.

What's missing from both rights based and economic accounts of copyright is careful consideration of the complicated interrelationship between authors and their surrounding cultural environments, within which works of artistic expression are created and used. Copyright law is an important factor in that environment, but it is only one factor, and we should want to know more about the other factors in play.

Next, let's consider the ways in which copyright defines and enforces rights in expression. In general, the drafters of copyright law have attempted to define rights that will extend to most commercialization of works of authorship. To shield certain uses, they have defined exceptions and limitations, and in most cases they have tried to define them narrowly. Of particular interest to many copyright scholars, there are almost no exceptions or limitations that cover what Jessica Litman has called "lawful personal use" of copyrighted works. Exceptions and limitations instead tend to be directed at public uses of high social value.

Copyright scholars have different positions on where lines between rights and limitations should be drawn. Generally speaking, though, they tend to agree that markets for copyrighted use are more or less value neutral with respect to copyright's ultimate goal of progress. Put differently, they tend to think relying principally on the market to order uses of copyrighted works allows the forward march of progress to proceed without interference, and without attempting to decide which kinds of progress are best. We can argue about whether or not the market needs to be corrected in particular cases, or whether we need a new exception or limitation, but otherwise we should leave well enough alone.

One may object, first, that that account of progress makes some rather large assumptions about the transcendent nature of knowledge, and the linear forward marching character of progress. Those assumptions don't square with a large and growing body of work in the social sciences that suggest that knowledge and cultural context are much more interrelated. That objection is extremely important, but I don't want to talk about it today.

More concretely, one might object that before we decide just how far rights in creative works ought to extend, we ought to have some idea about how the other side of the progress equation works. Once a creative work is prepared and released, how do audiences interact with it, how do they receive it, what do they do with it? We say that copyright is supposed to promote the dissemination of knowledge and learning, but before we assume that the process is working well, we ought to have some understanding of what users of copyrighted works do with those works, and how and why they do it.

Copyright lawyers have answers to those questions, but the answers turn out to depend on some extraordinarily one-dimensional models of user activities and interests. Sometimes people talk about a particular kind of user, who I will call the economic user, who enters the market for copyrighted content with predetermined tastes in search of the best deal or sometimes in search of a free deal. Copyright rules targeting commercial exploitation and rules about secondary liability for technology providers are designed for that user. They presume that, in general, copyrighted works must be paid for to be enjoyed in any of the ways that the user might want to enjoy them. In the context of those rules, the reasons for wanting to copy or reuse created material are typically deemed unimportant.

At other times, some scholars talk about a different user who I call the romantic user. This person is quite an amazing being whose life is an endless cycle of sophisticated debate about current events, high quality blog posts, discerning quests for the most freedom-enhancing new media technologies, and home production of high quality movies, music, remix culture and open source software. This user's reasons for copying or reusing content are so important that they are typically the reason for creating the exceptions and limitations that I mentioned. In general, though, copyright scholars don't spend a lot of time thinking about the processes by which one would become a romantic user, or by which romantic users come into being.

Now the interesting thing about these models is that copyright scholars have very little idea how these users relate to one another, so little that it sometimes sounds like they are talking about members of different species. But of course they aren't different species or even different people. The economic user and the romantic user are often the same person. We should want to know a lot more about how that person comes to encounter and use cultural products, and to understand his or her own experiences.

Finally, let's consider copyright's end-product, the works within which copyright protection subsists. We all learn on the first or second day of the copyright course that rights subsist only in the words "creative expression", which is fundamentally separable from its underlying ideas. When disentangling the two gets complicated, we tell our students they can approach that problem by using levels of abstraction to separate the ideas from the expressions. The ideas, along with similar entities like processing and functional principles, exist in the public domain, where they are building blocks that anyone may use to construct new creative edifices.

The problem with this theory is that it is just plain wrong. It is created out of whole cloth, based on nothing more than legal theory's assumptions about the relationship between culture and true knowledge. Remember again that legal political theory presumes that knowledge and ideas are abstract and transcendent, separate and distinct from the particulars of the expression that embodies them and the culture that surrounds them. We regard culture as an imperfect bridge to knowledge. We are confident that the repeated iteration of ideas through different modes of expression will lead us to progress, and that granting copyrights in the expression won't frustrate that process.

This model of cultural transmission is unique to intellectual property law. Nobody else thinks about cultural transmission this way. Scholars who study the arts and literature have catalogued an extensive list of imitative activities, including illusion, pastiche and so on, that are central to the ongoing process of culture production. All of those activities require the reuse of expression and proceed on the presumption that idea and expression are fundamentally indistinguishable. For artists positioning themselves relative to the previous generations, and relative to the surrounding culture, ideas and expression cannot be separated.

The part of the story about end-products that deals with the public domain is also very odd, and is so regardless of one's position in the copyright wars. The term "public domain" has pronounced geographic connotations, but we tend to worry about what is in the public domain, rather than where it is. The public domain comes to be seen as a mythical Heisenbergian place that is always accessible everywhere, whether or not that is actually true. There is a vital and enormously important advocacy movement for the public domain that has grown up over the last decade, and sometimes the rhetoric of that movement actually makes this particular problem worse. Its advocates use terms like "enclosure" to describe what is wrong with copyright today, and "commons" to describe what copyright ought to create, and those are geographic terms as well. The discourse of the public domain, which proceeds without acknowledging the geographic assumptions, can operate to minimise the questions of where public domain resources are actually located in real space, relative to the people who need to access them.

To understand the cultural work that copyright does, and the role that it plays in our emerging information society, we need to do better than this. We need to confront and study the interdependencies between self and culture, including the ways that people become authors, the ways that users receive copyrighted works and the way that people use copyrighted works in the real world. And we shouldn't begin that process presuming that copyright's artificial model of the way that culture proceeds is the right model.

A DIFFERENT MODEL OF CULTURAL CREATION

Now for the fun part.[2] Before articulating a different model of cultural production it is useful to look at some real world examples. We are all familiar with the seemingly endless parade of contemporary examples of cultural borrowing. So here are two contemporary examples.

The first is a progression of four slides, beginning with some things that served as inputs but were themselves copyrighted: an obscure Japanese art film, *The Hidden Fortress*, and a very popular American comic book series, *The Adventures of Buck Rogers in the 25th Century*, pieces which were combined in an inspired pastiche by the folks who brought us *Star Wars – Episode IV: A New Hope*. The film *Star Wars – Episode IV: A New Hope* ultimately became an empire of its own, and in turn inspired acts of borrowing and reworking. For example, you can visit www.blamesociety.net to view the adventures of Chad Vader, Lord Vader's little brother, who came into being when somebody asked what if someone with Lord Vader's distinctive physical and personality attributes ran a grocery store in New Jersey. Or, if your tastes run more to being the characters that you have imagined for so long, you can have a Star Wars themed wedding or party instead.

Here's a different example – the lawsuit between the Associated Press and an artist named Shepard Fairey. Fairey created the poster *Hope*, using as a template a photograph taken of Barack Obama by a freelancer for the Associated Press. Why did he do it? Well that was an image of Barack Obama that he could get. It could have been anybody else's copyright photograph, but it happened to be that one. Since Fairey is not personally acquainted with Barack Obama, and wasn't able to get close enough to him to get his own photograph, he had to use somebody's. This image, as transfigured in the portrait, helped to fuel a grass-roots popular movement that gained momentum on the internet, but it has been dignified after the fact as high art. Shepard Fairey's painted portrait of Barack Obama, reproducing the image from the poster, has now been hung in the National Portrait Gallery in Washington, DC. It has also been recycled back into popular culture. If you go to the website www.obamiconme.pastemagazine.com, you can create your own Fairey-style portrait. People have done some amazing things, including some that reference the other cultural example I talked about a moment ago, such as this portrait of Obi Wan Kenobi.

We could go on in this vein for some time, and we could see, ad nauseam, examples of cultural works circulating, recirculating, being remixed and recycled in ways that involve the internet, but I don't want to do that because the point I want to make is that the model of creative practice that these two sets of slides illustrate is much older

---

[2] Professor Cohen's lecture linked to a series of videos and audiovisual slides. Images from her presentation are not included in this book.

than the internet. It turns out that this basic pattern of the movement of culture, of the recycling of images back and forth between mass culture, establishment culture, and popular grass roots culture has existed for a very long time.

Let's look at some other examples. In 1920, photographer Louis Hine, working in the modernist medium of documentary photography, created an image of a nameless worker in a big factory, who became an iconic figure of modernist art. That figure was then recycled into a big budget work of mass culture, Charlie Chaplin's movie *Modern Times*, which involves a nameless worker in a big factory, but in a distinctly non-heroic way. The movie is a comedy of errors. Charlie Chaplin's buffoonish character in the factory where everything goes amiss was then recycled into high art by American painter Larry Rivers, who took mass culture as his subject matter and created portraits of icons of mass culture within the settings in which they gained their prominence. And it's not just the visual arts that work this way. Consider now a musical example. In 1899 Gustav Mahler took a nursery rhyme (*Frere Jacques*, or *Bruder Martin* in the German version) and turned it into the Third Movement of his Symphony No 1.

What can copyright lawyers do with the examples on these slides? Well, we can start by acknowledging that the questions what do users do, and what do authors do, are really the same question. Everyone is a user of cultural works first and an author second, so we can start by replacing the artificial cardboard figures of the user and the author with a single figure, who I will call the situated user because that user is situated within his or her own culture.

We can then lay out a model of creativity organised around the situated user that has five essential parts:

- First – situated users engage with artistic and cultural works for multiple intertwined purposes, including consumption, communication, self-development, creative play. These activities shade into one another, and are impossible to disentangle, or understand, out of context. The ways in which situated users interact with creative works are so diverse as to defy easy characterisation. They use creative works to inform themselves and to fuel their own creative input and output, but also to imitate others, to perform cultural identities, and to build and sustain relationships. Some of these activities map to the economic user. They are just straightforwardly consumptive. Some activities map to the romantic user. They are bold exemplars of dissent. Many activities are mundane, and lie somewhere in between in that grey area that we haven't looked at hard enough.

- Second – the state of being a situated user entails cultural constraint. The everyday practice of users is constrained by the various social and cultural networks within which users find themselves. When those users become authors, their own creative output is subject to the cultural path dependencies that those networks create. Consider the following simple question: What should a painting of the female face look like? [Images shown from a YouTube video titled "Women in Western Art".] We are not going to watch the whole thing, but you get the point. This woman looks a particular way. Quite surprisingly, in every one of these paintings this woman does not look like the women in this room, or in this city, or in this country, or in this world. The images are much more uniform than they would be if creativity were simply an internal proposition rather than constrained by cultural demands. At the same time, though, the boundaries of the networks are fluid, so boundary crossings are frequent. Forms of expression can migrate from one network to another with astonishing speed. Consider first what happens when you cross traditional Malian music with the American blues. A result is the music of Ali Farka Toure. [Music played.] Then when you cross the music of Ali Farka Toure with that of Led Zeppelin, Jimi Hendrix, and other assorted American rock and roll influences, you get this: the rock music of Tinariwen. [Music played.] Boundary crossings between cultures happen because, of course, people within cultural networks are opportunistic. They see things that float in front of them and they grab them and mix them with what they already know. A different kind of cultural boundary crossing is illustrated by the obamicon.[3] The boundaries between mass culture, high art, and popular grass roots culture are very fluid. Things circulate, and recirculate, across those boundaries.

- Third – boundary crossings can create conflict because the artistic influences come into contact with the values of particular social groups. On your left is Tjangala's *Emu Dreaming*, which became the subject of litigation when it was put onto a carpet without the original Aboriginal people's permission, and in direct conflict with their religious practices. On your right is a nativity family that you could have bought from Target last year at Christmas time, showing you that Christianity does not take the same view of the commercialisation of its religious symbols. We have culture then as a kind of contest, in which different groups struggle about the forms of artistic expression, about what is permissible, and about what these expressions mean.

Sometimes the struggle is resolved one way, and sometimes another. I don't mean to be making an argument about how the carpet case should have been resolved. What I mean to be making is a more general point about what keeps the system of culture in motion. Situated users appropriate and use works of creative expression in many ways which are intertwined with and channelled by the forms of expression within those networks.

---

[3] A reference to the obamicon.me website. The site allows users to create stylised images generated by uploading personal photographs that are electronically integrated on a template of Shepard Fairey's "Hope" portrait of Barack Obama.

- Fourth, the creative practice of situated users is embodied and materially situated. Situated users use their bodies to communicate works to one another – for example, singing and dancing to popular songs, or repeating lines from favourite TV shows. Sometimes it is really obnoxious but this is what we do – dancing the Macarena, for instance. [Video played.] I looked for the video of Peter Costello being taught to do the Macarena on a talk show that you have here, but sadly it seems to have been taken down. [Video of teacher showing the Macarena moves.] This is very mundane stuff, not sexy remix culture, but this is a common denominator. This is what people do, and it is important, because this is how we process our culture. Sometimes the mundane way we process our culture is remixed into something more elevated. [Clip from the film *Muriel's Wedding* with characters lip-synching to Abba music.] Here this music is more than just a shallow pop song. It's embedded in a movie about ultimate female empowerment, although you would have to watch the whole movie to get there. Sometimes embodied cultural practice is strange. This is a prison in the Philippines where they do dance therapy. [YouTube video of prison inmates dancing to Michael Jackson's "Thriller".] That's fun to watch on video and it's probably on the list of 100 things you have seen on the internet unless you are a loser, or old or dead or whatever. The loftier point is that culture is an embodied conversation. The body is how people process their culture. This has implications not just for whether we can copy, but for the scope of the rights of public performance and communication to the public, whichever name they are called in the country you are in. That is why I prefer the term "cultural landscape" to "public domain". Creative practice by situated users involves working through what is ready to hand in the cultural landscape that is there around them. This means that often works of mass culture will be the raw material for a new creative effort. To experience, assimilate, appreciate, and have a conversation about works of mass culture requires behaviours like this. When we create our own works, we begin with real bodies and spaces.

- Finally –The creative practice of situated users relies on interplay between what is ready to hand and familiar in the cultural environment, on one hand, and serendipity or play on the other. People are opportunistic. They latch onto whatever they encounter. Always the familiar, but also the unpredicted and the unpredictable. For authors, creative practice is most fruitful when it includes these encounters with the unpredicted – and when it includes the freedom to exploit the serendipitous encounter without asking permission to do so first. This interaction between the familiar and the unexpected in the cultural landscape is exactly what we refer to when we talk about why art and intellectual culture are important on a personal level. We talk about art opening time and space for reflection. We talk about how the serendipitous encounter and its unexpected creative fruit contribute to a dynamic culture, a culture that moves and avoids becoming calcified and rigid. These things are what we mean when we talk about why art is important. They ought to be what copyright seeks to promote.

A LOGICALLY DISCONTINUOUS COPYRIGHT LAW

I want to close with some brief thoughts about how copyright ought to respond to the reality of creative practice. To begin, we need to acknowledge that copyright plays a relatively small role in stimulating many of the processes that I have just described and shown to you. That doesn't mean that copyright is unimportant. Copyright is extraordinarily important. It simply serves a different set of goals than the ones that we have become used to thinking that it serves.

Copyright serves roles that are primarily economic. It creates predictability in the organisation of cultural production, and this is important, particularly in capital intensive industries like film and television. It generates revenues, exports, jobs – all things that are good – and it enables the production of mass culture, which is so extraordinarily important. It's quite fashionable among free culture advocates to pooh pooh mass culture and talk about how bland and banal it is. I couldn't disagree more. Mass culture is a crucial ingredient in the process of circulation I described. We need the mass culture to enable everything else. At the same time, we need to acknowledge that the single-minded pursuit of economic predictability and fixity, and of the copyright primacy of mass culture, frustrates creative practice by situated users. We would be worse off if people couldn't do things like those we have just seen and heard.

A good copyright system needs to hold both of these goods, economic fixity and cultural mobility, in the balance. That means that the rules that establish rights in creative works need to ensure sufficient breathing room for creative practice as it actually occurs. The rules should ensure degrees of freedom, if you will, within which the serendipitous encounter can take place, and within which serendipitous appropriation and reuse can occur.

This requires narrower rights, with gaps and discontinuities between them. A logically discontinuous copyright law – a regime characterised by incomplete rights, by logical gaps that permit imitation and reworking, is exactly what is required.

This is easy to say but very hard to do for three reasons. We resist setting limits on rights, and this resistance is deeply embedded in the form of legal reasoning our culture prizes most highly. I will illustrate it with an anecdote. The other day I asked students in my upper level seminar to describe their law school exam taking strategy. I asked them to imagine that they were taking an exam in some non-copyright-related subject like torts or constitutional law, and they had been given a long complicated fact-pattern and asked whether the plaintiff would succeed with any number of theories of relief. I asked, do you think you would get a better grade by arguing that the plaintiff could succeed or fail? They unanimously agreed that they thought they would get better grades by attempting to show how the plaintiff could succeed even if it required an expansion of the grounds recognised by the law as the basis for recovery.

Now, to some extent, this response reflects successful internalisation of the common law method of flexible incrementalism that is so beloved of our Anglo-American legal system. To some extent, it reflects successful internalisation of the principle that you should seek to please your clients, by getting rights extended if necessary. But students also understood arguments for extension as demonstrating more skill at lawyering, and more true understanding of the subject matter. You really understand torts, or you really understand constitutional rights, or whatever, when you can explain why a particular rule really extends to cover situations to which it has never before been applied. That's what lawyers do, and skill at doing it is a key indicator of professional and intellectual excellence. Within that analytical frame, it makes sense that arbitrary barriers to copyright expansion, for example, should fall away before the relentless logic of good lawyering.

The second reason that we resist setting limits on copyright stems from a set of convictions that are essentially technocratic. We believe that if we try hard enough, we can define in an extraordinarily precise fashion the rules of a good copyright system. If we really use our language to the full extent of our ability, we can define rules that separate the economic exploiters from everyday users – the people who make the good technology from the people who make the bad technology, and so on. When those technocratic instincts are coupled with our expansionist inclinations, the result is a seemingly iron-clad case for broad open-ended rights with narrow precisely defined exceptions.

The third reason, the icing on the cake, is what I call a naïve restitutionary impulse, the idea that commercial gain to anyone other than the right holder constitutes an injury that demands compensation, so that the right holder can be made whole. If we need to expand copyrights to do this, then we ought to do it. Yet there is a deep irony here. When we commit ourselves to a legal methodology that treats limited, discontinuous rights as logically disreputable, no matter what the context, we detach means from ends. When you have competing, equally important goods on both sides of the equation, as we do in copyright, it becomes impossible to balance the competing and equally important interests that the copyright system must serve.

In order to have a good copyright law that is logically discontinuous in the way I just described, we need to invert some of those most fundamental assumptions. I think that this quite a tall order.

Thank you very much.

PART THREE

INNOVATION, ACCESS, TRANSPARENCY, FAIRNESS

PERSPECTIVES ON COPYRIGHT POLICY

12

INNOVATION POLICY

Dr Terry Cutler [1]

INTRODUCTION BY PROFESSOR BRIAN FITZGERALD

This session is about copyright and innovation policy. Now Dr Terry Cutler requires little introduction to those of you who have an interest in innovation policy and practice in Australia. He's been closely involved in this area for many years.

For the benefit of our international visitors, I would introduce Terry Cutler by explaining that he was the person who was entrusted by the Federal Minister for Innovation with the very important, I'd say crucial, job of running a review of our national innovation system which commenced in early 2008, just a few months after the Rudd Labor Government came to office in late 2007.

The need for such a review, and the real interest in kick starting innovation in Australia was clearly demonstrated by the fact that really, thousands of people turned up in person at the public hearings that the Innovation Review convened, right around Australia, and the fact that more than 700 written submissions were received, many of them very substantive, and it was really an unprecedented number of written submissions received to a Review Enquiry.

So from the perspective, as head of the Innovation Review which consulted widely around Australia, Terry really is in a unique position to comment on the relationship

---

[1] Dr Terry Cutler chaired the Australian Government's 2008 Review of the National Innovation System which culminated in the Report, *Venturous Australia*. He is deputy chairman CSIRO, chairman of the advisory board, Centre of Excellence for Creative Industries and Innovation and a member of the Innovation Economy Advisory Board, Victoria. He holds numerous other domestic and foreign appointments, and was chairman of the Australia Council 2001–2002. He is a Fellow of the Australian Institute of Management, a Fellow of the Australian Institute of Public Administration, a Member of the Institute of Company Directors, and the Australian Society of Authors. In 2002 he was awarded an honorary doctorate by Queensland University of Technology and in 2003 was awarded Australia's Centenary Medal.

between intellectual property, specifically copyright, and innovation. When we look at the relationship between copyright and innovation over the last twenty years, it's very much a story of how copyright applies, or is adapted to apply, to digital materials distributed through online networks.

These issues specifically are exactly the kind of thing that Terry has been writing and thinking about for a long time. My first introduction to Terry was through his written materials in this area through reports such as *Commerce and Content* in the early 1990s. So without more ado I'd like to bring Terry up to the stage.

DR TERRY CUTLER

Thank you, I'll start with an apology if I croak a lot, I've got a bad cold. My second apology is for not being a lawyer, so I feel quite intimidated to be in such company today.

One of the arguments I think I want to make is in fact the next conference you have Brian, should not be opened by an Attorney General, it should be opened by the Treasurer. One of the points I'd want to make today is that, to me, intellectual property issues, copyright and innovation is all about economic policy and needs to be thought of in the context of economic policy.

I also don't know why I thought the colour red was appropriate as a background today, but perhaps it was because of the incitement to think about freedom and cry freedom. I think one of the interesting issues when we talk about freedom is the wonderful phrase that Amartya Sen, the great development economist, coined when he talked about unfreedoms. The lack of access as a barrier to development at all levels. I think unfreedoms is a very useful way to think about some of the issues we're talking about today.

I want to make some really very simple observations today, but I think it's often good to go back to basics. The first point I want to make is that when you think about innovation and innovation policy, we often think in Pollyanna-like terms that innovation is good, but we need to remind ourselves that it is in fact not morally neutral at all. If you think about some of the messes we're in today, they were all caused by innovation. The global financial crisis was a dazzling example of how innovative financial instruments crippled an economic system. Think about 200 years of breakneck technology innovation that has produced the global warming problems we have today. So innovation is not a good or a bad thing in itself, it depends on the purposes to which we are directing it. So it's about purposeful change.

The second point is that innovation is all about the clash of vested interests. I think we spend too little time articulating the nature of these vested interests and what they involve. During the review last year, one of the interesting things we did was to say to people making submissions "You can only make your submission if you actually declare your interest in what you are submitting about". It was a modest attempt to put some of these issues on the table.

At the core of the problem here, when we talk about innovation and change, it is about the problems of incumbency of established interests, and the often weak voice of people trying to introduce something new, the insurgents if you like. So it is fundamentally about conflict and vested interest, and I think we need to be far more up front about what's involved here.

Now this is not only vested interest in the marketplace, we also have vested institutional interests. One of my disappointments, I suppose, with the Government's response to our Innovation Review, is the institutional push back we've seen from our proposals to create a new focus for innovation within central Government, and particularly our proposal for a National Innovation Council at the centre of Government.

We've put a lot of emphasis on innovation within the public sector itself, and here you're really talking about public sector reform. Also about rediscovering the centrality of public interest in the innovation debate. And here our focus today I think is about recognising that so many of the great challenges that our society faces are global challenges like climate change, ageing populations, peak oil, food security, can only be resolved through massive investment in innovation.

The third point I want to make is that when we talk about the innovation agenda, I think we're often in danger of ignoring half the picture. During the Innovation Review I was often asked what do we mean when we talk about a national innovation system. My simplest explanation of an innovation system is to say it's a bit like the money supply. You have stocks of currency, you have bank notes which you can have in a vault, but they actually have absolutely no value until they're in circulation. It is all about circulation that matters, the flows as well as the stocks. Often we focus all our attention on investment in the stock of innovation, whether its talent pools, human capital facilities, or even information and data. We pay too little attention to the issues of flows, the networks that we talked about before. Anything from social networks, information flows, trusted transactions, and crucially, access. So the core of innovation policy is this notion of the importance of information flows, and information networks.

The fourth point I wanted to make is that Australia has a particular innovation challenge. We often don't face up to the hard realities that everything is going against Australia as a country when you look at the map. I love this NASA earthlights map, because it really does put us in our place. We're right at the end of the line in the wrong hemisphere. In real estate terms of location, we fail. Also, though, we're a huge country with a very low population density. This means we have a huge disadvantage in terms of infrastructure overhead requirements that are much, much higher than in virtually any other country. And we're a long way from our major markets.

We're also a very small economy. On any major metric we represent about 2% global market share. What we often neglect to think about is, "Okay, if we produce 2% of the world's new knowledge and innovation in R&D, how do we best access the 98% that is being produced elsewhere in the world?" That is one of the greatest innovation and public policy challenges I think small country economies like Australia have, and one which is very seldom addressed.

This is not a level playing field, and it seems one of the great challenges we still have to come to grips with is how do we avoid being a chronic intellectual property price taker, where other people set the price and the terms of access to that 98% of knowledge not produced here. Not a level playing field so we need to think carefully about what are the David and Goliath strategies that we need as a small player. Again, I think we spend far too little time thinking about those. But what does that mean for copyright policy for intellectual property rights and policy in a small country economy like Australia? And are our intellectual property interests best served by those defined by the world's dominant intellectual property markets?

My fifth point is that innovation thrives in a free trade environment, and we need a free trade of knowledge. When we talk about systems we need to distinguish between open and closed systems. Closed systems do not produce innovation. In fact one of my favourite throw away lines comes from William Blake where he describes closed system as stagnant pools which breed reptiles of the mind. An open system by contrast is where you have active feedback loops, it is about open networks. Again that concept of network information and how we promote that with our intellectual property thinking is a crucial challenge I think for all of us.

I want to get back to the point I started with, that we need to think about intellectual property issues outside of narrow legal frameworks. Copyright information knowledge is at the core of a economic agenda and we need to think about it in the same way as we think about competition policy and issues around open access that we talk about in most other areas of competition policy, particularly with respect to utilities, whether it's telecommunications, water, electricity, or I would suggest, information and knowledge.

Now information flows, therefore, I see as being at the heart of any innovation system. That means that information access is a central issue underpinning freedoms to innovate. There are three areas that I think we need to look at here. First of all the issue about freedom to access prior art and knowledge. We all know that knowledge builds on knowledge, it's a cumulative process. Unless we can build and preserve and have access to that accumulated knowledge efficiently, including economically efficiently, we're shooting ourselves in the foot.

A secondary issue that is important about this freedom to access prior art and knowledge is around the role of publicly funded content, and access to public sector information. I think we've talked about that at conferences like this for many years now, and it's time we actually did something about it.

The second aspect of information flows and information access is around search and navigation. It is about finding relevant information for the problem solving that you're addressing. So issues around format, discoverability. If you like, global positioning systems for information and knowledge are absolutely crucial. I don't think we pay enough attention to the issues of search and navigation within our innovation frameworks.

Finally, innovation only delivers economic and social benefit when its diffused and put to use. So diffusion and the ability of end users to pick up, absorb, and adapt, and use knowledge and ideas is absolutely fundamental to any innovation policy framework. So the issues of usability and remix therefore become central issues for us to think about.

So I've suggested that innovation and IP law are not morally neutral. Innovation is about the conflict of vested interests and we need to identify and look at those interests. It is about change versus incumbency. We need to really put a focus on the importance of information flows, information networks and access as crucial issues in any innovation agenda. We need to rise to the 2% challenge that everyone in Australia faces, of how we access the 98% generated and held elsewhere. How do we avoid being an IP price taker? We need to recognise the importance of open systems and feedback loops.

So my bottom line is that when the circulation stops, when the circulation of information stops, innovation dies. So information policy therefore needs to be at the centre of any national innovation strategy, which is why in our review last year, we called for a far more active focus on a national information policy framework and strategies. It seems to me that one of the challenges here is that no-one in Government is really taking ownership or responsibility for the sort of issues I've been outlining. It's like an orphaned policy area. It's a challenge because it's an area where we do need a whole of Government framework and way of thinking about this. A national information policy is something that affects every aspect of Government, as does innovation itself.

It strikes me, as I was thinking about this, that it's ironic that in a digital economy, information policies should be a central policy priority. I think we've gone backwards over the last decade or so. I was recalling that in the mid 1990s, when we were confronting the emergence of the internet, and trying to think about the policy implications and what sort of policy frameworks we should develop around the internet, we had far more coherent responses and approaches than we do today. Perhaps it's because I've got a vested interest, but I remember the Government of the day set up an Information Policy Advisory Council, which I chaired, to address the frameworks for internet regulation, or to make sure in fact that we didn't inappropriately constrain the development of the online world with inappropriate regulation.

We established the national office for the information economy as a whole of Government executive agencies, to make sure that a coherent approach to information policy was developed and implemented. Now I think it's a great pity that we've let that policy focus lapse. I don't think we're going to have the right economic or development framework around information policy, the right context within which to think about copyright and intellectual property issues until we recapture that centrality of having a national information strategy.

Thank you.

QUESTIONS AND ANSWERS

QUESTION:

Dr Cutler I congratulate you on your presentation, and I always ask myself that very question. Why aren't more economists at these sorts of enquiries and meetings? That's really the question I have for you. This is a field which is rich for economists and research, and yet we have such paucity of empirical data on the very things that you were discussing today. The value of these information flows, not just in terms of copyright, but in terms of patent law. Can you explain to me why economists have essentially left this area well alone, and allowed lawyers, unfortunately, to dominate?

TERRY CUTLER

A very good, and provocative, and brave question in this environment. The short answer is I don't know the answer to your question, because it really puzzles me. I think it's partly a lack of public policy leadership generally. We can all assume some blame for not being more active in making this a more mainstream agenda.

On the other hand, I look back and think you can change over time. Remember a time when trade practise were seen to be a narrow preserve of Attorney General's and lawyers, rather than being seen as a central element of economic management, and the shift of the responsibility for the *Trade Practices Act* to Treasury. That's exactly the sort of shift I think we need to see today. If I had one wish it would be that we could shift copyright and patent law out of Attorney Generals and put it smack bang into Treasury. That would be the recommendation I'd love to see coming forward from this conference.

QUESTION:

Hi, thank you very much Terry. I don't think you quite meant to say take patent law out of Attorney General's because it doesn't reside there, but it gives me the segue, as the Americans say, to my question, which was why Treasury, rather than say the IP Australia, which is where patents, plant breeder's rights, designs and trademarks currently reside. I agree with you absolutely that I don't think Attorney General's Department has covered itself in glory over the last 100 years, and certainly the last 15, and 10, and 5 years on copyright policy, I don't think it has. But Treasury versus say an innovation department, why Treasury not the Department of Innovation?

TERRY CUTLER

I think because I really want these issues to be looked at in the context of competition policy, and because I think the core issues to me go to issues of access. I think the same principles we apply to access frameworks in other areas of competition policy could very usefully be applied to intellectual property issues.

QUESTION:

Terry, Oliver Freeman. I'd just like to add something here. I welcome the emphasis of what you've been saying of course, I'm just wondering whether you're going far enough. It seems to me we have a big issue with economists at the moment. They are rather on the nose in terms of what's happened in the last 12 months, and I'm not sure that I would like our future to be delivered from lawyers to economists.

TERRY CUTLER

There is a difference between economists and financial engineers.

QUESTION:

Okay, but I want to add two things. There seem to be two other planks that we're missing here. The first is all about a world in which some of us feel we've reached a stage of enoughism. That is a sense that we are depleting the resources of our planet in an unregulated and stupid kind of way, and that the whole issue around sustainability – and I'm not taking a narrow ecological view of sustainability – I'm talking about strategic alignment between the way we live our lives, and what the life we want to live has to offer us back. So there's a whole issue about sustainability.

The other issue, which of course is already implicit in the title of this conference, is to do with social equity. It seems to me I don't want to go into bat with the economists with our social equity and sustainability in the same frame, thank you.

TERRY CUTLER

Both really terrific points. When I think about open systems I think about open societies. So I think innovation is inherently around a democratic instinct, and that's very important. Your first point is also incredibly important, and I probably didn't emphasise it enough. You're quite right. The great challenge for our age is around sustainability. When you think about how we're going to resolve those challenges, we need massively different approaches to the way we do science, the way we collaborate, the way we share knowledge. I think that needs to become a mainstream part of the agenda at discussions like this. So I totally agree with you.

QUESTION:

Thanks very much, Tim Hollow, I'm an advisor to the Australian Greens and thank you for that wonderful presentation. One of the things that I picked up on what your point about the incredible need for public interest research and innovation. I guess I'd ask if you've got any policy prescriptions for how one rediscovers that. Obviously we have a situation, as you yourself have discovered in your career, you noted that even within the public sector you get these stagnant pools breeding reptiles of the mind, and you get Government directed research and innovation which actually constricts where we're going, which through public policy, directs innovation into areas where it might not be best placed. So do you have any prescriptions for how you might actually get around that?

TERRY CUTLER

In our report last year we spent quite a bit of space talking about promoting innovation in the public sector. Part of it is through the promotion of experimentation and freeing up scope for bottom up pilot activity and so forth. There's been a lot of work done, particularly in recent years in the UK, that I think gives us role models. One of the crucial things is actually to give people permission to innovate. One idea being pushed very much in the UK is the notion of having almost an Innovation Ombudsman who can unplug all the nay sayers and blockers, and have an override for innovative proposals. Essentially, it's a leadership issue at the end of the day, like all these things are.

13

RELATIONSHIP AND COMMUNALITY: AN INDIGENOUS PERSPECTIVE ON KNOWLEDGE AND EXPRESSION

Maroochy Barambah[1]

PROFESSOR ANNE FITZGERALD

We're going to talk about indigenous peoples and law, and this session is going to be chaired by Dr Terry Cutler. I don't think Terry needs any further introduction to you, and I'm sure this is going to be a fascinating session.

Maroochy Barambah and Ade Kukoyi have been known to me and Brian for many years. In fact I actually first met Maroochy in New York when she was studying opera singing there. The film in which she starred, *Black River*, had actually just won the Paris Opera Film of the Year Award. The commentator for this session will be Professor Susy Frankel from New Zealand, who's been very much involved with indigenous IP issues in New Zealand.

Terry, over to you.

DR TERRY CUTLER

Thank you Anne.

It gives me huge pleasure to chair this session. At the beginning of our conference we had a very moving welcome to country. Then we tend to proceed to marginalise, or make very unwelcome, any discussion that isn't within an Anglo-Saxon, or a Commonwealth Club framework. I think one of the great gaps in public policy discussion in Australia is our neglect of this whole area of traditional knowledge and the role of indigenous people in intellectual property discussions. This is even worse I

---

[1] Maroochy Barambah is an Australian Aboriginal mezzo-soprano singer and songwoman and law-woman of the Turrbal-Dippil people from the Brisbane region. She performed in the acclaimed Australian Metropolitan Opera production *Black River* in 1989.

155

think as we sit in a region where this is a very real issue. So this session is I think very important in putting a neglected area on the agenda.

Let me just briefly tell you a story about a discussion I had recently that really brought the importance of this home to me. It was with a fabulous Indian scientist who, a few years ago, saw that an American drug company was trying to patent some of the components of turmeric, a traditional herbal remedy in India. So he challenged the patent, and he did so on the basis of digging out all these old Sanskrit scripts that referred to traditional healing, and established through those scripts the prior art that had existed. Now of course when we get to areas of oral tradition, and when we get to areas like music, performance, that is so much harder.

I'm really delighted to welcome Maroochy and Ade who are going to talk about what they've been doing. So can you please welcome them.[2]

MAROOCHY BARAMBAH

Let me begin by paying my respects to the Ngunnawal people and the ancestral spirits of this land for letting us be here in their country. I thank Brian Fitzgerald and his colleagues for their tremendous effort in organising this conference, and inviting me to share some of my knowledge and experience in this jurisdiction with all of you.

I am the Songwoman and the Law-woman of the Turrbal people – the original people of Brisbane. I will share with you later about my role. For the benefit of our delegates I'll just tell you a bit about my country. I was going to show you where it is on a map, but we had some problems trying to locate one. Nonetheless, I'll talk about it now. Our ancestral homeland extends from Elimbah Creek/Beerburrum Creek in the north, to the Logan River in the south; from the Pullenvale catchment in the west, and Woogaroo Creek in the south-west; to the Moreton Bay in the east. Within the Turrbal tribe were smaller family groups which are often referred to as "clans". Today, rather than use the term "clans", Aboriginal Australians use "mobs". Some of you may have heard of this term.

Within the Turrbal country, for example, we had the *Daki Yakka* mob which occupied the Brisbane City to the Pine River in the north; the *Dalaipi* mob which occupied the North Pine/Caboolture areas; the *Mulrobin* mob which occupied the southside of the Brisbane River / Coorpooroo areas; the *Yerongpan* mob which occupied the Yerongpilly / south-west Brisbane area; the *Chepara* mob which occupied the area

---

[2] Maroochy Barumbah presented with Ade Kukoyi, founding president of the Australia-Nigeria Business Council, and native title lawyer assisting the Turrbal people. Ade answered questions after Maroochy's speech.

south to Logan; and the *Ningy Ningy* mob which occupied the Redcliffe/Deception Bay and the Toorbul Point areas. That is our ancestral homeland.

In approaching this topic, I felt I should begin by sharing with you some of the fundamental principles of the Turrbal system of traditional laws and customs. It is only within this context that our traditional knowledge, expression and what I refer to as "land-people relationship" can best be understood.

Our laws are unwritten – they are kept in songs, stories, dances, paintings … etc. and passed down from one generation to the next.

In my view, a great deal of misconception continues to exist in this area, the more so among contemporary writers such as anthropologists, and then there are the historians and others, who are merely curious about Australian Aborigines. Let me say up-front, and with all due respect to the delegates here today, that, unless you live for a considerable period of time in our community, you will not fully appreciate, as well as comprehend, the true workings of our traditional laws and customs. There is an incomparable gap between what I call "living it" and "merely observing or examining/ analysing it".

TURRBAL TRADITIONAL LAWS AND CUSTOMS

Certain elements constitute our system of traditional laws and customs, such as: *Bloodline Connection to Country; Invitation to Enter Country; Permission to Enter Country; Who can Speak for Country; Kinship system; Marriage; Totemic identity; Proprietary issues.* In essence what we have is a very complex layering of numerous elements, processes and inter-relationships that are kinship-based and totemic-related. What does this mean I hear you say?

In short, our system of customary law is underpinned by religious practices, beliefs and values which are pre-determined by one's totemic identity at birth. It is completely different from the Anglo-Australian legal system and pointless somewhat for anyone to try to make comparison. Obviously, I cannot possibly share all you need to know in my allotted time. My intention is to focus mainly on some key aspects. Before discussing our kinship system, let me turn my attention first to my role as a Songwoman.

SONGWOMAN'S ROLE

As a Songwoman and a Law-woman, it is my responsibility to educate, inform and enlighten other members of our community in customary law matters. I also have the responsibility to protect as well as enforce our laws and customs. Under Turrbal traditional laws and customs, our laws are kept in songs, stories and dances. Those songs, stories and dances have come down through generations – dreaming stories that we still hold, that have been handed down to us.

I was born on a reserve because the Queensland Government had an Act called *Aborigines Protection Act* 1897 ("APA"). Under the APA, the Queensland authorities went around the State rounding up people deemed to be of Aboriginal descent, and dumped them unceremoniously onto Reserves at the turn of the twentieth century. This policy continued up until the 1967 Referendum. There were three main Government reserves, namely: Palm Island, Woorabinda and Cherbourg. I was born on Cherbourg Reserve. In essence, several people were taken away from their country as far away as Cape York to Cherbourg.

However, some still managed to retain their stories. Ironically, the same 1897 APA that was meant to remove Aborigines from their ancestral homeland to Cherbourg and elsewhere was also instrumental and contributory to the Turrbal, Gubbi Gubbi and Wakka Wakka Peoples' continued physical connection to country. Unlike what happened with the Stolen Generation –where people of mixed race were taken away from their parents and ties severed completely from country, our cultural network and activities flourished on the Cherbourg Reserve.

In the case of the APA, it was mainly full bloods and half caste that were removed and taken to the reserves. If you had less than 50% Aboriginal blood in you, you didn't qualify for protection under the APA – this was the *Assimilation policy* of the day. So, today there are some people of Aboriginal descent who are going around now trying to reconnect with their Aboriginal ancestry, but they've lost that connection. Some I suppose will never make that connection, but there are others who will, or whose old people may reconnect with them spiritually and be able to point them in the right direction – this is very much a personal journey for such people in life. As a Songwoman, I have been privileged to assist some individuals over the years in their search to reconnect.

I myself was taken to Melbourne – some 2,000 miles away from Cherbourg. However, I maintained my contact and connection with my Elders and family.

It is not uncommon today to find Aboriginal people wanting to go back to that place where their old people came from – it's a spiritual calling. Yeah, that's something that I've experienced myself, and I've seen it with some other people. I also know that there are lots of other people still searching. That's just a little side story of land-people relationship. That old connection with Aboriginal laws and customs, with the songs and dances, people have to get permission to do this, you have to talk to certain elders. We have certain protocols within our society, even though we're a city-based, traditional owner group.

On the question of permission to enter country, just a couple of days ago, I was filling up petrol in my car at a petrol station. A gentleman came up to me, shook my hand

and asked me: "What are you doing now"? I replied: "I'm working with my mum on her native title claim because we are the original people from Brisbane". He then asked me "Oh, can I stay in your country"? "Can I stay here"? He was Aboriginal. Initially, it didn't dawn on me exactly what he meant by "can I stay in your country".

Upon clarification, I realised that he was seeking permission from me as a Turrbal Songwoman to live in my country. So things are gradually changing, I believe, for the better. We now receive this type of request from people in Brisbane all the time – "Can I stay in your country?" I don't think that would have happened that much pre-Mabo. These days, I perform many traditional Welcome to Country ceremonies in Brisbane to give permission to visitors entering our ancestral homeland in Brisbane.

I now turn my attention to other important aspects of our laws and customs.

KINSHIP SYSTEM

Our kinship system comprises the Turrbal and the Dippil people. The people who comprise the Dippil are commonly referred to today as the Gubbi Gubbi (Gabi Gabi or Kabi Kabi) and the Wakka Wakka. The Gubbi Gubbi People are from the Wide Bay area and the Sunshine Coast area of Queensland; whilst the Wakka Wakka People are from the Burnett River area. The Turrbal, Gubbi Gubbi and Wakka Wakka Peoples belong to the same kinship, and historically marriage was common among these three different tribes.

A strong cultural network also exists within this kinship – for example, during *Kurbingai*[3] ceremony at Redcliffe. Within these groups are smaller groups. "Hard yakka" got its name from our group. "Yakka" means to work, to work hard. I suppose the name came into English when Brisbane was a penal settlement, Moreton Bay, and as we say in Queensland, old Murri/Goori probably saw the convicts chipping away there, trying to break the stones to make the roads and things like that. So it was, that one of the very early words that the broader, non-Aboriginal people of Australia, got to know, from around the Brisbane area, was "yakka".

That was one of our words that had become very much a part of the Australian vernacular these days. It's also become a brand name of a successful clothing line. So, maybe we should be looking at something there in copyright terms. No, just joking.

Daki Yakka was the name of my great, great, great, great grandfather. His name gradually became anglicised to the "Duke of York", and if you look in history books of early Queensland in particular, and maps of Aboriginal tribes, you'll see the reference to the Duke of York tribe. Daki Yakka was the head man of the Brisbane tribe, and

---

[3] See C.C Petrie, *Tom Petrie's Reminiscences of Early Queensland*, UQP, 1904, pp. 37–38

back in the 1830s, 1840s, and 1850s he was called the Chief of the Brisbane tribe. I'm his direct descendant.

DREAMING TRACKS

Dreaming Tracks and *Dreaming Sites* are an integral part of our connection to country (the land-people relationship). Embedded within the Dreaming Tracks and Dreaming Places is our belief system which regulates what we ought to do and not do. Under our laws and customs for example, places such as Fisherman Island (Yangan), Mt Coot-tha (Kuta) and Spring Hill (Taggan) – remain culturally significant to us irrespective of any structure/s or development which may be erected upon them. At this point in time, I do not know if you are aware that the Port of Brisbane situated at Fisherman Island is on the list of assets earmarked for sale by the Bligh Government in Queensland. The Turrbal People are opposed to this proposed sale because Fisherman Island is a *healing site*[4]. Further, such an act contravenes our traditional laws and customs.

So, our Dreaming Tracks are very important; the kinship system is also very important. Our cultural network is most important. Historically, in southern Queensland, there's a place called the Bunya Mountains where most of the tribes travelled to for the triennial Bunya Festivals. During this time, message sticks were sent by the host tribe to other neighbouring tribes, and thus were allowed to cross their tribal boundaries in order to be able to travel to the Bunya Mountains.

TOTEMIC IDENTITY

Maroochy means the "red nose one" in Turrbal language. It refers to the black swan which is my totem. By this, I have the responsibility of taking care of sites along the Brisbane River dreaming track to Maroochy River on the Sunshine Coast. Consequently, I frequently visit Dowse Lagoon at Sandgate (north of Brisbane) where black swans abound aplenty. Under our traditional laws and customs, black swans are my spirit sisters and brothers.

Let me conclude my presentation by saying that I am hopeful that more non-Aboriginal Australians will get to learn about our laws and customs. In doing so, they get to understand it, and in the process get to show more respect for our beliefs and value system. We don't expect non-Aboriginals to fully comprehend every aspect of our traditional laws and customs. Personally, I am of the view that we are at a stage

---

[4] See C.C Petrie, *Tom Petrie's Reminiscences of Early Queensland*, UQP, 1904, pp. 65–66. Traditional knowledge possessed by the appropriate Turrbal People corroborates Petrie's accounts.

where the Anglo-Australian law and our traditional laws and customs are trying to co-exist. Whether the two systems meet in the middle or not remains to be seen. We are all trying to figure out where the pendulum should sit. Perhaps time will tell. That would go on, I think for some time yet.

Thank you all for listening.

14

CROWN COPYRIGHT

Anne Fitzgerald [1]

Copyright protects much of the creative, cultural, educational, scientific and informational material generated by federal, State/Territory and local governments and their constituent departments and agencies. Governments at all levels develop, manage and distribute a vast array of materials in the form of documents, reports, websites, datasets and databases on CD or DVD and files that can be downloaded from a website.

Under the *Copyright Act 1968* (Cth) , with few exceptions government copyright is treated the same as copyright owned by non-government parties insofar as the range of protected materials and the exclusive proprietary rights attaching to them are concerned. However, the rationale for recognizing copyright in public sector materials and vesting ownership of copyright in governments is fundamentally different to the main rationales underpinning copyright generally. The central justification for recognizing Crown copyright is to ensure that government documents and materials created for public administrative purposes are disseminated in an accurate and reliable form. Consequently, the exclusive rights held by governments as copyright owners must be exercised in a manner consistent with the rationale for conferring copyright ownership on them. Since Crown copyright exists primarily to ensure that documents and materials produced for use in the conduct of government are circulated in an accurate and reliable form, governments should exercise their exclusive rights to ensure that their copyright materials are made available for access and reuse, in accordance with any laws and policies relating to access to public sector materials.

---

[1] Anne Fitzgerald LLB (Hons) (Tas) LLM (London) LLM, JSD (Columbia University) is a Professor in Law Research at Queensland University Law School where she is involved in research on several projects including access to public sector information. Anne was a member of Australia's two principal federal government-appointed standing advisory committees on intellectual property: the Advisory Council on Intellectual Property which advised IP Australia from 1996 to 1999 and the Copyright Law Review Committee's Expert Advisory Group (1995 to 1998). She participated in the CLRC's major review ("the simplification reference") of the Copyright Act.

While copyright law vests copyright owners with extensive bundles of exclusive rights which can be exercised to prevent others making use of the copyright material, in the case of Crown copyright materials these rights should rarely be asserted by government to deviate from the general rule that Crown copyright materials will be available for "full and free reproduction" by the community at large.

GOVERNMENT COPYRIGHT OWNERSHIP

Ownership of copyright by government agencies is dealt with in Part VII of the *Copyright Act 1968* (Cth) (the "Crown copyright" provisions).[2] While the power to legislate in relation to copyright is a concurrent power under s 51 (xviii) of the Commonwealth Constitution, s 109 provides that "when a law of a State is inconsistent with a law of the Commonwealth, the latter shall prevail, and the former shall, to the extent of the inconsistency, be invalid". Since the Commonwealth has enacted a comprehensive legislative framework governing copyright, any State legislation dealing with subsistence, ownership or infringement of copyright or limits to its scope would be invalid by virtue of s 109 of the Constitution.

The principal provisions on which government copyright is based are ss 176 – 179 of the *Copyright Act 1968*. Sections 176 and 178 provide that the government owns copyright in literary, dramatic, musical and artistic works, sound recordings and films "made by, or under the direction or control of the Commonwealth or a State". Section 177 further provides that the government owns copyright in a literary, dramatic, musical or artistic work that is first published in Australia "by, or under the direction or control of, the Commonwealth or a State".[3] The operation of ss 176– 178 can be displaced by an agreement between the government and the person who created the copyright material that copyright is to belong to that person or some other party specified in the agreement.[4] The effect of these provisions is that governments own copyright in a vast range of materials in hard copy and digital form, including legislation, judgments, parliamentary materials, reports of government-commissioned

---

[2] See generally, A Fitzgerald, B Fitzgerald and N Hooper (2010) Enabling open access to public sector information with Creative Commons Licences: the Australian Experience, in *Access to Public Sector Information: Law, Technology & Policy*, Sydney University Press, eprints.qut.edu.au/29773/; A Fitzgerald and K Pappalardo, (2009) "Report to the Government 2.0 Taskforce: Project 4 – Copyright Law and Intellectual Property", eprints.qut.edu.au/29416/.

[3] Sections 176–178 are subject to any agreement between the Crown and the maker of the work or subject matter under which it is agreed that copyright is to belong to the author or maker or some other specified person (s 179).

[4] Copyright Act 1968, s 179.

review bodies, art works, computer programs, digital databases, photos and audiovisual works.[5]

These materials come into existence in different ways. A large amount of material is created within government, through the efforts of government employees and other persons who are not employed by government but produce copyright materials while working as volunteers (for example, interns, students on work experience placements and members of emergency services teams[6]). However, a significant part of the materials held by government is produced externally, by recipients of government funding (such as research institutes) and persons who make submissions to inquiries and online consultations. Governments commonly commission independent contractors to produce materials and enter into arrangements to fund work in universities and research institutes that results in output in the form of reports, academic publications and data. An important category of material is prepared by non-government parties and lodged with government pursuant to a statutory or regulatory direction to provide information or a report (for example, environmental impact assessments and information about water use, greenhouse gas emissions and results of mineral or petroleum exploration activities).[7]

RIGHTS OF GOVERNMENTS AS COPYRIGHT OWNERS

As the *Copyright Act* 1968 does not generally differentiate between the rights of government as copyright owner and the rights of private parties who own copyright, governments enjoy the same range of exclusive rights in their copyright materials as private sector copyright owners.[8] One of the few points of difference between the rights of government and private sector copyright owners is that the duration of

---

[5] For a listing of the various kinds of copyright materials produced by or for governments, see Copyright Law Review Committee, *Crown Copyright,* 2005 at pp 10-11.

[6] For example, emergency services volunteers typically vastly outnumber departmental employees (by as much as a factor of 10) and produce risk management plans, incident reports, news updates and other copyright materials.

[7] There are numerous examples of documents of this kind, including mining and petroleum exploration reports, flood studies, soil surveys, traffic analysis reports, noise studies, cultural heritage assessments, environmental impact statements, licence applications (eg for liquor licences, certified traders, etc).

[8] Section 182 specifically states that, apart from the provisions in Part VII of the *Copyright Act* 1968 (in ss 176-181) relating to the subsistence, duration and ownership of copyright, the provisions of Part III and Part IV of the Act apply.

copyright for materials within the scope of ss 176 – 178 is 50 years from the end of the calendar year in which the copyright item is first published or is made.[9]

The primary rights of copyright are the rights to:

- reproduce;
- publish;
- publicly perform;
- make an adaptation; and
- communicate the copyright work to the public in electronic form (eg on a website or as a digital file).[10]

Other rights of copyright owners are the rights to ensure that electronic rights management information (ERMI) is not removed or altered and to prevent the circumvention of technological protection measures (TPM) they apply to their copyright materials to control access to or copying of it. ERMI is electronic information (including numbers or codes representing such information) which is either attached to or embodied in the copyright material, or appears in connection with a communication or the making available of the copyright material.[11] It typically includes information identifying the copyright work, its author or copyright owner or indicating the terms and conditions on which the material can be used, or that the use of the material is subject to terms or conditions of use. It is an infringement of the copyright owner's rights to remove or alter ERMI relating to a copyright work or other subject matter without the permission of the copyright owner or exclusive licensee, if the person doing the act knows or ought reasonably to have known that the removal or alteration would induce, enable, facilitate or conceal an infringement of copyright.[12] In certain circumstances the removal or altering ERMI relating to a copyright work may be a criminal offence under the *Copyright Act*.[13] The anti-circumvention provisions enable copyright owners to protect their materials by applying technical measures that control access to or copying of the work. It is an infringement to knowingly deal in devices designed to circumvent TPMs[14] and, where the TPM

---

[9] *Copyright Act* 1968, ss 180, 181.

[10] *Copyright Act* 1968, ss 31, 85-88.

[11] The main provisions dealing with ERMI are set out in Division 2A, Subdivision B of the *Copyright Act* 1968. Section 116D sets out the legal remedies (including an injunction or damages) available for the removal of and interference with ERMI.

[12] *Copyright Act* 1968, ss 116B-116D.

[13] *Copyright Act* 1968, ss 132AQ-132AS.

[14] *Copyright Act* 1968, s 116AO(1).

controls access to a copyright work, it is an infringement to knowingly circumvent the TPM.[15]

As well as the rights described above, individual authors of copyright works can exercise moral rights, which are personal to the author and cannot be transferred. Although government does not, itself, have moral rights, it may own copyright in materials in respect of which individual authors can continue to exercise their moral rights. This situation may arise where government obtains an assignment of copyright in materials that have been produced by an individual author who has not agreed to waive the exercise of their moral rights. As moral rights cannot be assigned, if the author has not agreed to waive them, they will continue to be exercisable by the author. The moral rights that can be exercised by individual authors are the rights:

- of attribution, that is to be attributed (accredited) as the author of the work, where reasonable;

- to object to false attribution, that is to prevent someone else being wrongly identified as the author of the work; and

- of integrity, that is to prevent derogatory treatment of the work that would prejudice the author's reputation.[16]

RATIONALE FOR GOVERNMENT COPYRIGHT OWNERSHIP

Although the rights exercisable by governments as copyright owners under the provisions of the *Copyright Act 1968* (Cth) are for most purposes identical to those of private parties, there are fundamental differences between government and private copyright. The *Copyright Act 1968* (Cth) does not generally differentiate between public and private sector parties either with respect to the scope of materials in which copyright subsists or the exclusive rights that can be exercised in respect of them. However, it would be a mistake to assume that government copyright is exactly the same as copyright in non-government materials. Although statutory recognition of government copyright ownership was introduced into Australian copyright law in 1912 when the *Copyright Act* 1911 (UK) was adopted in Australia (No. 20 of 1912), the rationale for copyright in government materials is quite different from the reasons why copyright in recognized in materials produced by individual authors and private sector organizations.

An obvious point of difference is that, since many government materials (eg reports, legislation, handbooks) are created in the ordinary course of activities by parliament, the courts and government agencies, the traditional justification of copyright as

---

[15] *Copyright Act* 1968, s 116AN(1).

[16] *Copyright Act* 1968, Part IX, ss 189-195AZR.

providing an incentive to produce and disseminate new information is much less relevant than for works produced by publishers with the expectation of a commercial return.[17] In fact, discussion of government copyright is strikingly lacking in the usual rationales for recognition of copyright generally such as encouragement of innovation or enterprise for commercial benefit; reward of creative effort; maximizing commercial return through sale or licensing; and securing some advantage through the exercise of the exclusive rights.

As observed by the Copyright Law Review (CLRC) in its *Crown Copyright* report (2005), works such as legislation and judgments "will be produced regardless of financial incentives, and therefore the traditional justification for copyright ownership does not apply". Similarly the Prices Surveillance Authority in its report, *Inquiry into the Publications Pricing Policy of the Australian Government Publishing Service* (1992), observed that the traditional rationale behind copyright law does not apply to material produced by the government itself:

> There appears to be less justification for the existence of Crown copyright than copyright in general ... The information being copyrighted has been developed not by private individuals but by tax payer funded sources. Copyright monopoly rights are not necessary to ensure incentive for adequate developments of such information. It is information produced using public money to facilitate government. Such information should be freely available.[18]

Government copyright has its origins in the Crown prerogative.[19] The scope of the Crown prerogatives is uncertain, and they may change over time. It is generally accepted that the prerogatives are not lost by disuse but must be expressly removed by statute.[20] The Crown prerogative in the nature of copyright arose from the Crown's role in "ensur[ing] the integrity and authenticity of official government publications".[21] As Monotti explains, from the late 18th century:

---

[17] Copyright Law Review Committee (CLRC), *Crown Copyright,* 2005, para 4.23 at p38: www.clrc.gov.au/www/agd/agd.nsf/Page/RWPBB79ED8E4858F514CA25735100827559 .

[18] Prices Surveillance Authority, *Inquiry into the Publications Pricing Policy of the Australian Government Publishing Service,* Report No. 47, 19 December 1992, at p 91.

[19] For discussion of the Crown prerogative, see CLRC, *Crown Copyright,* 2005, Chapter 6. See also J Gilchrist, *Crown Copyright: An Analysis of rights vesting in the Crown under statute and common law and their interrelationship,* LLM thesis, Monash University, 1983; H V Evatt, *The Royal Prerogative,* Law Book Co, 1987 (publication of H V Evatt's doctoral thesis, *Certain aspects of the Royal Prerogative: a study in constitutional law,* 1924).

[20] See CLRC, *Crown Copyright,* Chapter 6, at pp 90–91.

[21] CLRC, *Crown Copyright,* 2005, para 4.66 at p 53.

a consistent theme emerged, namely that the sovereign has a duty, based on the grounds of public utility and necessity, to superintend and ensure authentic and accurate publication of matters of national and public concern relating to the government, state and the Church of England. That duty carries with it a corresponding prerogative which is not specifically defined in any of the cases, but clearly extends to publishing and printing that material.[22]

This understanding of the prerogative accords with the judgment of the Supreme Court of New South Wales in *Attorney-General (NSW) v Butterworth & Co (Australia) Ltd*[23], where Long Innes CJ stated that the Crown prerogative stems from the historic duty of the monarch "to superintend the publication of acts of the legislature and acts of state of that description, carrying with it a corresponding prerogative".[24] Over the years, the scope of the prerogative was cut back, such that, as explained in *Copyright Agency Limited v State of New South Wales:* [25]

> [b]y 1911 the Crown only claimed the exclusive right to publish the following works: the authorised version of the Bible (*The Universities of Oxford and Cambridge v Richardson* (1802) 6 Ves 689; (1802) 31 ER 1260); Acts of Parliament (*Basket v Cambridge University* (1758) 1 W Bl 105; (1758) 96 ER 59); proclamations (*Grierson v Jackson* (1794) Ridg. L. & S. 304); law books (*Roper v Streater* (1672) Skin 234; discussed in (1672) 90 ER 107); *Millar v Taylor* (1769) 4 Burr 2303; (1769) 98 ER 201); almanacs (*Gurney v Longman* (1806) 13 Ves 493; (1806) 33 ER 379); and what were compendiously described as government publications.

The Crown prerogative is preserved under s 8A of the *Copyright Act* 1968[26] and its operation is not otherwise affected by the Act.

These insights into the nature of the Crown prerogative with respect to official documents resonate with a theme that permeates the commentary on statutory Crown copyright in Australia and other jurisdictions: continued recognition of government copyright is justified by the "need to ensure the integrity and authenticity of official

---

[22] See A Monotti, *Nature and Basis of Crown Copyright in Official Publications* [1992] 9 EIPR 305, at pp 306-307. Note though that, in Australia, the Crown prerogative was never considered to apply to religious works, as there is no established state religion: CLRC, *Crown Copyright,* 2005 at para 6.07, p 88.

[23] (1937) 38 SR (NSW) 195.

[24] Ibid, p. 229.

[25] [2007] FCAFC 80 per Finkelstein J at para 179.

[26] Section 8A was inserted into the Act by the *Copyright Amendment Act* 1980. Previously, Crown prerogative was preserved by s 8(2) of the *Copyright Act* 1968.

government publications".[27] The need to ensure the reproduction and distribution of government materials in an accurate and reliable form is a constant concern in discussions about the existence and exercise of government copyright. Familiar phrases recur: the need to ensure the authentic and accurate publication of documents, to be able to rely on the veracity and accuracy of government materials and to indicate the status and authority of government materials.

Academic commentators[28] and many submissions to the CLRC's review of Crown copyright supported the view that the integrity and authenticity of government copyright materials can be ensured by distribution under copyright licensing conditions which enable infringement actions to be brought for misuse or misrepresentation of the material.[29] For example, the Victorian Government's submission stated that:

> [t]he State must ensure the continued integrity and authenticity of official government publications so that the public can be aware of the status of each publication. Continuing to maintain Crown copyright is essential to achieving [this] outcome.[30]

The justification for Crown copyright as providing a safeguard for the "integrity and authenticity" of official works has consistently been raised in the United Kingdom (even if no further rights existed in such works).[31] In 1996, Gordon Robbie (then) Head of Copyright in Her Majesty's Stationery Office (HMSO), explained:

> [C]opyright is … a means by which copyright holders can ensure that their material is used properly and responsibly by third parties. This is of particular importance where that material is authoritative, and where the general public, in one way or the other, are placing reliance on its veracity

---

[27] See Copyright Law Review Committee, *Crown Copyright,* 2005 para 4.66 at p 53, available at www.clrc.gov.au/www/agd/agd.nsf/Page/RWPBB79ED8E4858F514CA25735100827559 .

[28] See J Gilchrist, *The role of government as proprietor and disseminator of information,* (1996) vol. 7, no. 1, Australian Journal of Corporate Law pp 62-79, at p 79. On this point, see also J Bannister, *Open Access to Legal Sources in Australasia: Current Debate on Crown Copyright and the Case of the Anthropomorphic Postbox* (1996) 3 Journal of Information, Law and Technology (JILT), available at www2.warwick.ac.uk/fac/soc/law/elj/jilt/1996_3/bannister/. Bannister is commenting on *Baillieu and Poggioli (of and on behalf of the Liberal Party of Australia, Victorian Division) v Australian Electoral Commission and Commonwealth of Australia* [1996] FCA 1202.

[29] See CLRC, *Crown Copyright,* 2005, footnote 93, para 4.66 at p 53.

[30] See CLRC, *Crown Copyright,* 2005, para 4.68, at p 53, referring to Submission 64 at p 1.

[31] See S Picciotto,'*Towards Open Access to British Official Documents',* 1996 (2) Journal of Information Law and Technology (JILT), available at www2.warwick.ac.uk/fac/soc/law/elj/jilt/1996_2/picciotto/.

and accuracy. The Copyright Unit [of HMSO] does come across cases of abuse and is able to pursue and prevent them.[32]

The 1999 UK White Paper, *The future management of Crown copyright*, referred, without explanation, to the need to "preserve the integrity and official status of government material".[33] It noted that there was a general perception among the public that Crown copyright "operates as a brand or kitemark of quality indicating the status and authority of much of the material produced by government". [34] The justification of government copyright "as a means of retaining quality control over PSI and the way it is used" was raised more recently in the United Kingdom Office of Fair Trading's 2006 report, *The Commercial Use of Public Information* (CUPI), which found that improved availability of public sector information for commercial reuse was not incompatible with the continued recognition of Crown copyright.[35] The CUPI report made recommendations on improving the commercial use of PSI without abolishing Crown copyright and stated that:

> [i]n fact, the existence of Crown copyright is a key part of the control mechanisms which we want to build on to ensure that [public sector information holders] act in a fair and transparent manner.[36]

A similar approach to the justification for government copyright was taken in a study commissioned from KPMG by the Canadian Government in 2001. The report recommended that digital geospatial data should be licensed to users at no cost for use and redistribution, and that copyright and licensing should continue to be used to protect the quality of geospatial data originating from government agencies, rather than to prevent use.[37]

---

[32] G Robbie, Crown Copyright - Bête Noire or White Knight?, 1996 (2) *The Journal of Information Law and Technology (JILT)*, available at www2.warwick.ac.uk/fac/soc/law/elj/jilt/1996_2/special/robbie/.

[33] United Kingdom government, Minister for the Cabinet Office, *The future management of Crown copyright*, Cm 4300, HMSO, 1999 at para 5.1. See also C Tullo, *Crown copyright: the way forward – access to public sector information*, The Law Librarian, Vol. 29, No. 4, 1998, 200–3, at p200.

[34] Ibid, para 5.1.

[35] United Kingdom government, Office of Fair Trading, *The Commercial Use of Public Information*, December 2006, at para 4.74, available at www.oft.gov.uk/advice_and_resources/publications/reports/consumer-protection/oft861. November 2009) .

[36] Ibid, para 4.76.

[37] KPMG Consulting, Executive Summary: *Geospatial Data Policy Study - Project Report*, 2001, recommendation 5 at p 25, available at

EXERCISE OF EXCLUSIVE RIGHTS BY GOVERNMENTS

Although the same set of exclusive rights applies to the same materials, it was not intended that those rights would be exercised by governments in the same way as non-government copyright owners exercise their exclusive rights. Just as the rationale for government copyright ownership differs from that for private sector copyright, there is clear evidence that it was intended that government rights would be exercised primarily to ensure the distribution of government publications in a reliable form. Research by Ben Atkinson and John Gilchrist has uncovered historical documents in the Federal Government's archives, which strongly indicate that the concept of Crown copyright in United Kingdom and Australian law was, at least from the time it was first codified in statutory form, inextricably linked with what would now be termed "open content" licensing practices. At the time the first Crown copyright provisions were enacted in the United Kingdom and Australia, it was explained that the Crown's rights would be exercised to permit the "full and free reproduction" and widespread dissemination of the great bulk of government copyright materials. [38]

A United Kingdom Treasury Minute of 1912 [39] described the practice to be followed to give effect to s 18 of the United Kingdom *Copyright Act* 1911. [40] The 1911 *Copyright Act* (UK) was adopted in Australia in 1912 (No 20 of 1912) and s 18 of that Act (the precursor to the current Crown copyright provisions in ss 176–179 of the *Copyright Act*) provided that:

> Without prejudice to any rights or privileges of the Crown, where any work has, whether before or after the commencement of this Act, been <u>prepared or published by or under the direction or control of His Majesty or any Government department</u>, the copyright in the work shall, subject to any agreement with the author, belong to His Majesty, and in such case shall continue for a period of fifty years from the date of the first publication of the work. [emphasis added]

---

www.geoconnections.org/programsCommittees/proCom_policy/keyDocs/KPMG/KPMG_E.pdf . An earlier report produced for Industry Canada in 1995 by the Information Highway Advisory Council, *The challenge of the information highway* had recommended the retention of Crown copyright. See also A A Keyes and C Brunet, *Copyright in Canada: Proposals for a Revision of the Law*, Department of Consumer and Corporate Affairs, Ottawa, 1977, at p 225.

[38] See B Atkinson, *The True History of Copyright: The Australian Experience 1905–2005*, Sydney University Press, 2007 at p 277; B Fitzgerald, A Fitzgerald et al, *Internet and E-Commerce Law: Technology, Law, and Policy*, Lawbook Co/Thomson, Sydney, 2007 at pp 267-268.

[39] Dated 28 June 1912.

[40] 1 & 2 Geo 5, Ch 46.

An earlier Treasury Minute presented to the House of Commons on 31 August 1887[41] had identified seven classes of government publications in which the Crown claimed copyright: (1) reports of select committees of Parliament and of Royal Commissions; (2) papers required by statute to be laid before Parliament; (3) papers laid before Parliament by command; (4) Acts of Parliament; (5) official books; (6) literary and quasi-literary works; and (7) charts and ordnance maps. As noted by Finkelstein J in *Copyright Agency Limited v New South Wales* [2007] FCAFC 80 (at para 177):

> According to the Minute, Crown copyright would not be enforced in the first five classes but copyright in the last two would be strictly enforced. The Minute is reproduced in L.C.F. Oldfield, The Law of Copyright (1912) at 111–113.

Publications in the first five categories described in the Minute, such as reports of Select Committees or Royal Commissions and Acts of Parliament, were regarded as having been produced for the "use and information of the public and it [was] desirable that the knowledge of their contents should be diffused as widely as possible". A "general rule permitting full and free reproduction" of such works was to apply and, while the rights of the Crown would continue, no steps would ordinarily be taken to enforce the Crown's copyright. For works falling into the latter two categories – "often produced [by government] at considerable cost"[42] – the government objected to their reproduction, "by private enterprise for the benefit of individual publishers"[43] and made it clear that unauthorised reproduction would incur liability as if "the copyright had been in private hands".[44]

In December 1913, a copy of the 1912 UK Treasury Minute was brought to the notice of the Commonwealth Government by the Secretary of State for the Colonies, to provide information on UK practice regarding Crown copyright. In January 1914, Robert Garran, Secretary of the Commonwealth Attorney-General's Department, wrote to the Secretary of the Prime Minister's Department, attaching a Minute on Crown Copyright and requesting that the Prime Minister communicate with the respective State Premiers on the subject. Copies of the United Kingdom Treasury

---

[41] No 335 of 1887. This earlier Treasury Minute was referred to in the 1912 Treasury Minute.

[42] See G Robbie, *Crown Copyright - Bête Noire or White Knight?*, (1996) 2 Journal of Information Law and Technology (JILT) www2.warwick.ac.uk/fac/soc/law/elj/jilt/1996_2/special/robbie.

[43] Ibid.

[44] Ibid. Robbie quotes from a Treasury notice published in the London Gazette of 23 November 1886: "Printers and Publishers are reminded that anyone reprinting without due authority matter which has appeared in any Government publication renders himself liable to the same penalties as those he might under like circumstances have incurred had the copyright been in private hands."

Minute of 1912 were circulated by the Prime Minister to the States, attached to a letter dated 27 January 1914, informing them that the Commonwealth Government intended to follow the practice adopted in the United Kingdom.

From the historical background to the Crown copyright provisions – which survive to the current day in much the same form as in 1912 – it is clear that they were enacted with the expectation that they would rarely be exercised to restrain reproduction and copying of government materials. Although there is no clear statement of the circumstances in which governments may rely on their exclusive rights to restrain the unauthorised reproduction and distribution of their copyright materials, such instances would be limited.

However, appreciation of the fact that Crown copyright is intended to encourage rather than deter the distribution and reuse of government materials seems to have diminished with the passage of time. The UK's Power of Information Taskforce found that Crown copyright was often misunderstood by creators and reusers of data:

> When the public sector publishes information people should understand that it is intended for re-use ... Crown copyright, despite its historic name, is designed to encourage re-use in the majority of cases.[45]

Consequently, the *Power of Information Taskforce Report* (February 2009) recommended that steps should be taken to improve understanding of the permissive aspects of Crown copyright.[46]

CAL v NSW

The operation of the Crown copyright provisions in ss 176 – 179 of the *Copyright Act 1968* (Cth) was considered directly for the first time by the Full Federal Court in *Copyright Agency Ltd v New South Wales* (2007) 240 ALR 249; [2007] FCAFC 80, a case involving survey plans produced by surveyors and lodged with the Land and Property Information division of the State Department of Lands. Survey plans are protected under the *Copyright Act 1968* (Cth) as artistic works.[47] The New South Wales Government argued that it would not be liable to make payments to the Copyright Agency Ltd (CAL) (acting on behalf of surveyors) under the statutory licence in ss 183 and 183A of the Act if the survey plans were made or first published "by, or under the direction or control of" the State, as it would be the copyright owner

---

[45] Ibid, p25.

[46] R Allan, *Power of Information Taskforce Report*, February 2009, recommendation 12 at p 7, available at poit.cabinetoffice.gov.uk/poit/category/final-introduction/.

[47] *Copyright Act 1968*, s 10(1) defines "artistic work" as including "a painting, sculpture, drawing, engraving or photograph, whether the work is of artistic quality or not".

by virtue of ss 176 and 177 of the *Copyright Act*. The Full Court held that the survey plans could not be regarded as having been made or first published "by, or under the direction or control of the State" and the State did not therefore acquire copyright ownership through the operation of s 176 or 177 of the *Copyright Act*.

In delivering the principal judgment, Emmett J (with whom Lindgren and Finkelstein JJ agreed) considered (at [122]) that the reference to works made "by" the Crown was concerned with "those circumstances where a servant or agent of the Crown brings the work into existence for and on behalf of the Crown". The reference to works made under the "direction" or "control" of the Crown was concerned with situations "where the person making the work is subject to the direction or control of the Crown as to how the work is to be made" which, in the context of copyright law "may mean how the work is to be expressed in a material form". Taking into account standard dictionary definitions of "direction" and "control",[48] Emmett J stated that the reference in ss 176 and 177 to a work being made under the direction or control of the Crown (as opposed to being made by the Crown) "must involve the concept of the Crown bringing about the making of the work" but did not "extend to the Crown laying down how a work is to be made, if a citizen chooses to make a work, without having any obligation to do so". His Honour continued (at [126]):

> The question is whether the Crown is in a position to determine whether or not a work will be made, rather than simply determining that, if it is to be made at all, it will be made in a particular way or in accordance with particular specifications. The phrase "under the direction or control" does not include a factual situation where the Crown is able, de facto, to exercise direction or control because an approval or licence that is sought would not be forthcoming unless the Crown's requirements for such approval or licence are satisfied. The phrase may not extend much, if at all, beyond commission, employment and analogous situations. It may merely concentrate ownership in the Crown to avoid the need to identify particular authors, employees or contracting parties.

Finkelstein J also addressed the question of what works can be considered to be made under the direction or control of the Crown, stating (at [186]):

> There is probably a degree of overlap in the case of works made "under the direction of" or "under the control of" the Crown. Broadly speaking, however, where the Crown has power to require a work to come into existence, the work is made under the "direction" of the Crown. If the Crown has dominion over the execution of the work then it is made under

---

[48] *Copyright Agency Ltd v New South Wales* (2007) 240 ALR 249; [2007] FCAFC 80 at [123], [124] per Emmett J.

its "control". The assumption that underlies each concept (direction and control) is the existence of a relationship between the Crown and the author that authorises the Crown to give the direction or exercise the control as the case may be. That authority may be found in statute, including regulations made under a statute, contract or elsewhere. But, whatever its source may be, the authority must exist.

Since the survey plans were prepared on the initiative of the surveyor (or their client), rather than under the compulsion of the State, they could not be considered to be produced "by, or under the direction or control of" the State. This conclusion was reached notwithstanding that the State had issued very detailed instructions about the form the plans were required to take in order to be accepted for registration. The State had argued that it had directed and controlled the making of the survey plans within the meaning of s 176 by virtue of the fact that the plans were produced to satisfy the legal requirements for the creation of interests in land and the public record of rights and interests in land; it issued detailed requirements (in legislation, instructions and directions) about the information required to be included in survey plans and how it was to be expressed; and that survey plans could only be regarded as finished upon being acceptance for registration by the State, following examination and amendment where necessary. In rejecting these arguments, Emmett J explained (at [137], [138], [141]):

> There can be no doubt that, before a Survey Plan can be registered and so become a registered plan and effect the framework for the existence of a title to land in New South Wales, very stringent requirements and prerequisites laid down by the State and its instrumentalities must be met with respect to the Survey Plan. In a sense, the State, by the provisions to which reference has been made above, directs and controls the preparation of any Survey Plan that is to be registered under any of the provisions so described.

> However, there is nothing in the statutory and regulatory framework that compels any surveyor to prepare a Survey Plan that complies with the requirements of that framework. Of course, it is a condition precedent to the registration of a Survey Plan that it does comply precisely with those requirements. Nevertheless, a Survey Plan that is intended to become a registered plan is not prepared by reason of any compulsion from the State. A Survey Plan is prepared by a surveyor to satisfy the contractual obligation of the surveyor to his client.

> ...

> A person who prescribes the criteria for the registration of a Survey Plan does not direct or control the making of the plan. By laying down conditions for the grant of some privilege in respect of a work created by a

citizen, the State does not control or direct the making of that work. It is of no consequence to the State whether or not a plan that satisfies its requirements is lodged for registration. Section 176 is concerned with direction or control of the making of a work where the State has some reason or purpose for having the work made. A surveyor's practice is not controlled or directed by the State. Section 176 is directed to the activities and conduct of a person who is in some way answerable to the State.

Neither the surveyor nor their client (usually the owner of the land to which the survey plan relates) could have been compelled by the State to prepare, or to arrange the preparation of, a survey plan. Further, at any time before the registration of a survey plan, the owner of the land could have discontinued the application for subdivision or the surveyor could have declined to continue preparation of the survey plan. Finkelstein J agreed (at [191]) that s 176 does not apply to works "brought into existence by the voluntary act of the author", notwithstanding that the work takes "a form dictated by the Crown if the work is to be used for a particular purpose".

On the question of whether the State acquired copyright as the first publisher of the survey plans, the court held (at [148] per Emmett J) that the plans were in fact first published when the surveyor provided the completed plan to the land owner for signature. Although the State made survey plans available to public in hard copy and electronic form immediately following their registration – and these acts involved publication of the plans by the State – this was not the first instance of publication which would be required for the State to acquire ownership under s 177: at [145], [146].

The finding that copyright did not vest in the State through the operation of s 176 or 177 of the *Copyright Act* meant that copyright in survey plans was owned by another party, which would usually be the surveyor who produced the plan or the land owner who commissioned the production of the plan. In the appeal to the High Court, *Copyright Agency Limited v New South Wales* (2008) 233 CLR 279; [2008] HCA 35, the Full Federal Court's finding on copyright ownership was not challenged by New South Wales and this issue was not considered by the High Court.

Although the nature and operation of Crown copyright was not fully explored by either the Full Federal Court or the High Court in *CAL v NSW*, the case highlighted the fact that it must be considered in the context of the role, powers and functions of government. In considering the extent of the materials in which Crown copyright exists, the words "by", "direction" and "control" must be construed in light of the actions of governments – what they do, direct or control – that result in the creation of materials within the categories of protected works and other subject matter. Rather than limiting the meaning of "by", "direction" and "control" to their literal or dictionary meanings, the words must be read in a constitutional context so as to ascertain what materials can be considered to have been produced as a result of government actions falling under these headings.

COPYRIGHT LAW REVIEW CROWN COPYRIGHT INQUIRY – A MISSED OPPORTUNITY

In December 2003, the Attorney-General gave a reference to the CLRC to examine the law relating to government ownership of copyright material.[49] An "important impetus"[50] for the reference to the CLRC was the recommendation of the *Review of Intellectual Property Legislation* under the *Competition Principles Agreement* (the Ergas Committee) in its 2000 report that s 176 of the *Copyright Act 1968* be amended to ensure that the government is not given preferential treatment with respect to copyright, as compared with other parties.[51]

The CLRC's *Crown Copyright* report (2005)[52] recommended major changes to government copyright ownership. A key recommendation was that the special Crown copyright provisions in ss 176–179 of the *Copyright Act 1968* should be repealed[53] because they "are not clearly drafted and it is difficult to envisage situations where they would be relied upon today", "the ambit of the ownership provisions is uncertain" and it is unjustifiable "for government to have a privileged position compared with other copyright owners".[54] The CLRC also recommended that copyright be removed entirely from a wide range of materials produced by the judicial, legislative and executive arms of government, including Bills, statutes, regulations, judgments and court orders, official records of parliamentary debates, reports of Parliament, and reports of commissions of inquiry.[55]

Unfortunately, the main focus of the CLRC's inquiry and report was narrowed down to the issue of copyright ownership. Adopting a limited perspective meant that the CLRC avoided the core issue of the fundamental rationale for the introduction of statutory recognition of government copyright and how it was intended to operate. Rather than working from the premise that the best way to improve access to and

---

[49] For information on the Crown Copyright reference, see website, n 694. The CLRC released an Issues Paper in February 2004, a Discussion Paper in July 2004 and received almost 80 written submissions, many of which are available on the CLRC website.

[50] CLRC, n 694, p xix.

[51] Intellectual Property and Competition Review Committee, *Review of Intellectual Property Legislation under the Competition Principles Agreement* (September 2000) p 114: www.ipaustralia.gov.au/pdfs/ipcr/finalreport.pdf.

[52] CLRC, n 694.

[53] CLRC, n 694, Recommendation 1, p xxii and [9.09].

[54] CLRC, n 694, p xxi.

[55] CLRC, n 694, Recommendation 4, p xxvi and [9.38].

reuse of government materials would be to shift ownership of copyright from the government to the private sector,[56] or remove copyright from many materials altogether,[57] a preferable approach would have been to examine the rationale for government copyright and how it should be managed to achieve that outcome.[58]

CONCLUSION

In the absence of provisions in the *Copyright Act 1968* (Cth) that expressly limit or provide guidance on the exercise of copyright by government, it is necessary to have regard to the clear intention underlying the introduction of statutory recognition of Crown copyright. Government copyright exists primarily as a mechanism by which governments can ensure that documents and materials related to public and governmental functions are circulated in an accurate and reliable form. The fact that governments can, by relying on their exclusive rights as copyright owners, restrict access to, and copying and distribution of, copyright materials does not mean that they should do so without clear justification and authority.[59] Copyright is not, in itself, the driver of policy and practice in relation to copying, distribution and use of government materials and must be exercised in accordance with established government policies relating to the use of public sector materials.

Government ownership of copyright does not, in itself, justify entering into a commercial arrangement to obtain a financial return if doing so would restrict the

---

[56] For materials produced or first published under the direction or control of the government, and in the absence of a contract addressing the issue of ownership, this would be the result of implementation of the CLRC's recommendation that the provisions relating to subsistence and ownership of Crown copyright in ss 176–179 of the *Copyright Act 1968* should be repealed: see CLRC, n 694, Recommendation 1, p xxii and [9.09].

[57] For materials including Bills and Acts, judgments, records of parliamentary debates, and reports of inquiries, this would be the outcome of implementation of the CLRC's recommendation that copyright in such materials should be abolished and they should be in the public domain: see CLRC, n 649, Recommendation 4, p xxvi and [9.38].

[58] See further, B Fitzgerald, *Submission to CLRC on Crown Copyright* (Submission 17): www.clrc.gov.au/agd/WWW/clrHome.nsf/Page/Present_Inquiries_Crown_copyright_Submissio ns_2004_Sub_No_17_-_Professor_Brian_Fitzgerald; AEShareNet Ltd, *Submission to the Crown Copyright Law Review* (Submission 28): www.clrc.gov.au/agd/WWW/clrHome.nsf/Page/Present_Inquiries_Crown_copyright_Submissio ns_2004_Sub_No_28_-_AEshareNet_Limited.

[59] Note that in carrying out its inquiry into Crown copyright, the Copyright Law Review Committee's Terms of Reference required it to consider "the extent and appropriateness of reliance by government on copyright to control access to and/or use of, information": CLRC, *Crown Copyright*, 2005 at p xii.

"full and free reproduction" of public sector materials. While there are circumstances where copyright materials are developed at government expense and it is necessary to recover the costs of development in part or in full, any decision to impose charges for access or use should be in accordance with established policy or regulatory provisions.[60] Nor should copyright, as a standard practice, be relied upon by governments for secondary purposes not directly related to the rationale for Crown copyright (such restricting access to government documents containing confidential or otherwise sensitive information. Crown copyright should, as general rule, be exercised to foster the dissemination of government materials in an accurate and reliable form rather than be used as authority for the imposition of restrictions designed to limit their availability and use.

---

[60] For example, there may be circumstances where only the government possesses the expertise or resources required to produce a copyright work which is not required for purposes of public administration but is required by the general public. Unless the government is able to recoup the costs involved in producing the work it may not have the incentive or authority to expend public monies to do so.

15

THE PUBLIC DOMAIN

Professor Graham Greenleaf [1]

As only an occasional visitor to copyright law, I am rather awed by the company that Professor Fitzgerald has put me in today. He asked me to talk about how we should move ahead with the public's side in copyright. What I'm looking at is some aspects of what institutional arrangements we might need to protect, as Professor Fitzgerald put it, Australia's public domain in the future.

The question I will start with, is "What rights do the public have to use works or other forms of creativity". I think we have to identify four categories of rights.

First is the uses of works which are outside the exclusive rights of the copyright owner, including those that fall short of being a substantial part of the work, and other matters like that. Second is uses of works where there is no copyright owner. In Australia that primarily means works in which copyright has expired. This is because our Copyright Act doesn't exclude from copyright protection things that are often excluded in other laws like Government documents and legislation. Thirdly, and the part on which copyright practitioners concentrate, are the many different types of statutory rights that are given to members of the public to use works in different ways. These may be fair dealing exemptions or under Statutory Licences or other situations where there is a copyright owner but the uses that are allowed would otherwise be part of the exclusive rights of the copyright owner. Finally, we need to also recognise those *de facto* uses of the owner's exclusive rights which, as a matter of practice, go unchallenged. This is what I've described in other contexts as sometimes constituting

---

[1] Professor Graham Greenleaf, AM, is Professor of Law at the University of New South Wales's Faculty of Law, and International Scholar, Kyung-Hee Law School, South Korea. He is co-director, and co-founder of the *Australasian Legal Information Institute,* the internationally renowned legal information portal that makes publicly available in electronic form its comprehensive, and continually updated, holdings of Australian law. AustLII is, by far, the most utilised source of online legal information in Australia. Professor Greenleaf is one of most penetrating analysts in Australia of the policy of information regulation and a recognised expert in the law governing information technology.

"a commons by friendly appropriation" or some US scholars have referred to as "tolerated use".

Of course there has been a great deal of discussion about the theoretical aspects of all this, particularly from American academics such as Professors Boyle, Lessig, Cohen and Benkler to name but a few. They debate whether we should collectively refer to this bundle of rights that the public have as "the public domain" in a more extended usage, or perhaps simply use the expression "the commons" to describe all these things. I'm not going to do either, because I think those usages are ambiguous in their scope. I understand the motivation for wanting to use them: to try to appropriate some of the rhetorical value of the terms "public domain" or "commons" to describe this whole area. I do that myself, but I'll stick to the more prosaic expression, "public rights in copyright" to encompass all of one to four, that whole range of rights.

A slightly more technical definition is that that "public rights" are all those aspects of copyright law and practice that provide the ability of the public to use works without obtaining a licence on terms that are set and changeable (even if only at the end of the licence term) by the copyright owner. The corollary is that private or proprietary rights are the rights that owners of copyright in a work can effectively exercise to refuse to allow another person to use their work except on terms set or changeable by them. There's a lot of value in recognising the commonality in these four categories.

There is another distinction that we need to make before leaving any theoretical discussion and that is that the origins of the public rights that I am talking about are found in both global and national matters. I think it's reasonable to talk about global public rights, those elements of public rights that are common to most jurisdictions, for two main reasons. First, the formal elements of the global public domain are essentially the constraints that are placed on what public rights can exist because of the near universal adoption of the Berne Convention and TRIPs. We have heard the details from other speakers this morning. These constraints include the fact that no registration formalities can be required. In the USA when re-registration of copyrights was required 90% of works were not re-registered after the initial statutory term expired. Our public domain would be vast in comparison to what it is now if re-registration was allowed by Berne to be required (even though initial registration was still not required). Berne's minimum term for copyrights is another reason: would we seriously think that the term of copyright for software would have been set at the life of the author plus 50 years if nations around the world had been given a free hand? Of course there are other constraints like the "three step test", too complex to address here.

Berne is by and large on the negative side. On the far more positive side of the global equation are the informal elements, arising mainly from the global effects of some aspects of the Internet. Of particular importance is viral licensing and the way in which it has created certain content specific commons such as open source software and the commons of text (found most notably in Wikipedia). Also, search engines have created a commons for searching text which would otherwise involve infringements of exclusive rights in many jurisdictions in the world. These are matters that Australian policy alone can't change much, as Adrian Sterling was noting earlier in relation to the formal constraints.

We then have a long list of national influences which affect, in our particular case, Australia's public rights in copyright. I won't go through all of those there, but as you can see (from the list below) there are many aspects which have a significant effect on what public rights we have. None of them are unique to this country. Some of them are unusual, like our long history of legal deposit requirements. In combination, Australian law is relatively inhospitable to the creation of public rights.

NATIONAL ELEMENTS AFFECTING AUSTRALIA'S COPYRIGHT PUBLIC RIGHTS

- Lack of any constitutional limits on copyright (probably!)
- The long history of legal deposit requirements
- Crown copyright in legal/administrative documents
- No significant other limits on the scope of copyright subject-matter
- Protection of compilations perhaps even beyond the EU
- Narrow, specific, fair dealing exceptions: inflexibility
- Limited implied licences, broad authorisation doctrines
- More extensive compulsory licences than many other countries
- Highest international level of copyright duration, but no retrospectivity
- Moral rights, but only co-extensive with economic rights
- The need to accommodate indigenous rights

What do we need to do to try to more effectively protect this whole range of public rights? First, those who are interested in some of these aspects of copyright law need to recognise that they have a common interest in all these aspects of public rights. If there is a common thread, perhaps it's the recognition that all forms of creativity must draw on and rely upon previous creations, 'standing on the shoulders of giants', as it's often referred to. Once we recognise that common interest other things follow.

Second, we need to better articulate a set of principles on which the protection of public rights in copyright are based. Copyright laws clearly articulate many of the interests of authors and other creators simply by listing the exclusive rights of the different types of copyright owners in convenient sections in the Copyright Act, and then having various other things flow on from that, like enforcement provisions. Public rights are rarely so clearly and neatly articulated.

They are usually implied. They're the things that Professor Larry Lessig talked about earlier today such as the fact that you don't have to have any exceptions in order to read a book or to lend a book to someone else. You can't find that public right clearly stated in the Copyright Act but it's essential to understanding what we're talking about. Alternatively, if they are written down, they're scattered all over the place, often in immensely complex legislative provisions. Those of us who are interested in this side of the fence need to try to articulate in an understandable fashion the set of rights that we are interested in defending.

In the interests of provoking discussion, I have made an initial attempt to set out 10 Principles for public rights in copyright (titles below, and detailed in the Appendix). After listening to both Professor Lessig and Adrian Sterling I suspect that I'm probably too conservative. The principles need to be general and kept separate from any short term strategic goals.

10 PRINCIPLES FOR PUBLIC RIGHTS IN AUSTRALIAN COPYRIGHT

1. Balance
2. Limits on exclusive rights
3. Minimum term
4. Preservation of Australian publications
5. Fair & flexible exceptions
6. Fair compulsory licences
7. Support for voluntary licensing
8. Protection from technology & contracts
9. Proportionality in enforcement
10. Free/open access to publicly-funded content

First we need to articulate the types of balance in copyright law that we need. Copyright law should be protecting our national interests and not the interests of other countries (unlike the Australia-US Free Trade Agreement). There's a place marker in the first principle for the interests of Indigenous people, but I don't know how to expand that and I'm interested in hearing the rest of the Conference on that question. Picking up from the Adelphi Charter, there's a principle that the proponents of any expansion of the scope of copyright protection should have the onus of proving the need for expansion.

In relation to national interest, I've missed something which Terry Cutler has prompted me to think should be added. In our role as the 2% copyright exporter 98% importer, we need to expressly recognise that Australia should contribute its share to the global pool of information that's available to be exercised with public rights by anyone in the world. This is our part of the global bargain from which we will benefit as an importing country.

Some of the other principles are fairly obvious: the need for limits on exclusive rights; the attempt to minimise as far as possible the duration of copyright and not to extend it any further; and the need to preserve works so that they can be later re-used in other creative works. This is to say, we need to preserve the content of Australian publications so that at the end of their copyright term others can use them. A strategic goal that follows is to ensure that that the current review of legal deposit extends it to digital and audio visual works.[2]

We need to obtain fair and flexible exceptions to copyright law that can adjust with changes in technology. In contrast, our existing law with its specified fair dealings does not allow such flexibility at present.

We need to ensure that compulsory licences and collecting societies operate in ways which give appropriate protection against potential anti-competitive conduct. Specific goals may include ensuring that collecting societies do not impede their members' use of voluntary licences and do not collect fees in relation to content on the Internet which is supposed to be available for free. But that, in a sense, is the negative side. We shouldn't forget the positive side of compulsory licensing.

As Professor Lessig points out, most notably in *Free Culture*, much of the entertainment industries of the 20th Century in the USA have been based around the conversion from what once was called "piracy" into something that's become a statutory licence and has produced revenue and benefits for both producers and consumers. Compulsory licences constitute a lot of the most important content of our public rights. As people interested in that side of the copyright picture, we should be actively trying to make those compulsory licences work better to give a better result to everyone, both the copyright owners and the users of the collectively licensed materials.

Another principle is that we should actively provide support for voluntary licensing. Creative Commons licences, open source licences and the other licences of the last 10 years or more, have given us enormous benefits and expanded the scope of public rights. We should be looking at what our copyright law needs to do to actively support those voluntary licences. One example in Australia may be that we need an amendment to the Copyright Act to clarify the means by which public domain

---

[2] Commonwealth *Review of Legal Deposit* 2008.

dedications can be made, because that's not at all clear under our law. And, while there are no obvious impediments to the enforceability in Australia of say, Creative Commons licences or the GPL,[3] we should be looking at whether we need to strengthen our copyright law proactively to make sure we don't get a nasty surprise 15 years down the track.

I will skip over other obvious things like proportionality in enforcement and the "no brainer" of getting around Crown Copyright in Australia and opening content up in relation to both public sector information and the outputs of academic research in this country.

The last thing I wish to say is that public rights need a peak body in Australia. There are a lot of reasons why the public rights side is disorganised in comparison with copyright owners and authors who are very well organised. We need to establish a public rights peak body that represents all of the new types of interests and organisations who have an interest in the various types of public rights that I'd sketched out. One question that we in Australia need to ask is whether we already have the nucleus of such a public body in the Australian Digital Alliance. ADA does exceptionally good work, has a set of principles that are narrower than what I've sketched although containing many of the elements, and has a membership that is far narrower than the group of organisations that are relevant to all the issues I have canvassed in my "10 Principles". There needs to be a conversation within and without ADA as to whether it should become a more general public rights body for Australia.

The conclusion of my Centre's submission to the Cutler Inquiry was that the third thing we needed was a thorough-going law reform review of the Copyright Act with its principal focus being the public rights side of copyright. A public rights focus is needed, rather than the little scattered bits of public rights reform always being an afterthought to some other law reform inquiry, usually one conducted by the Attorney General's Department. My suggestion is that the Australian Law Reform Commission would be the best body to do a research-based analysis on what we need with public rights in the Copyright Act, not one that's merely driven by submissions from the most well organised organisations in this field.

Finally, public rights need a good public image and perhaps a mascot. So I suggest, for the benefit of all the Australians in the room, that the best candidate is Norman Lindsay's Magic Pudding, an icon of Australian literature, created in 1918. Lindsay didn't die until 1969. Philip Pullman says, "It's the funniest children's book ever written" and it's on Wikipedia so it must be true. The hero for those of you who don't know, is Albert, the "Cut and Come Again Puddin'".

---

[3] GNU General Public Licence, a free software licence written by Richard Stallman for the GNU Project, identified with the free software movement.

We've heard a lot about cakes today, and now I'm offering a puddin' as our mascot – the little guy on the right. Lindsay says, "There's nothing this puddin' enjoys more than offering slices of himself to strangers, the more you eats the more you gets, Cut and Come Again is his name and Cut and Come Again is his nature". He's the inexhaustible self replenishing resource, by analogy, similar to our public domain, on which further creativity can be built. He's non-rivalrous and inexhaustible. So I commend to you Albert as our potential mascot for public rights.

He also represents the difficulties faced by the public domain because although he's a national icon who's now approaching his Centenary, being born in 1918, his literary form will not be in the public domain until the year 2039 when young Albert is the grand old age of 120. So we should ask, "Is that the sort of public domain we want, or can we do better?"

16

ADAM SMITH 2.0: EMERGENT PUBLIC GOODS, INTELLECTUAL PROPERTY AND THE RHETORIC OF REMIX

Nicholas Gruen[1]

I

In a landmark article proposing a "politics of intellectual property", James Boyle mentions two contrasting principles of intellectual property (IP). With IP being a public good, property rights can help bring IP into existence by reducing free riding on others' efforts.[2] Yet Boyle points to another legal tradition (1997, p. 97). Privatising knowledge restricts free speech. As Boyle points out:

> [C]ourts are traditionally much less sensitive to First Amendment, free speech and other "free flow of information arguments" when the context is viewed as private rather than public, or property rather than censorship. Thus, for example, the Supreme Court will refuse to allow the state to ban flag burning, but it is quite happy to create a property right in a general word such as "Olympic", and allow the word to be appropriated by a private party which then selectively refuses public use of the word. Backed by this state-sponsored "homestead law for the English language," the United States Olympic Committee (USOC) has decreed that the handicapped may have their "Special Olympics," but that gay activists may not hold a "Gay Olympics." The Court saw the USOC's decision not as state censorship, but

---

[1] Dr Nicholas Gruen is CEO of Lateral Economics, expert economics commentator. He advised the federal government on economic reform policy, was economic policy adviser to two federal government ministers, a former Associate Commissioner to the Productivity Commission and Chair of the Government 2.0 Taskforce. He is a recognised expert in tariff reform, competition policy, innovation policy, and intellectual property regulation policy. He is a regular contributor to leading newspapers, and has published in national and international academic journals.

[2] With others simply watching and waiting for IP to be created so that they can free ride on his efforts, the IP might never come into existence.

as a mere exercise of its private property rights. (Emboldened, Chief Justice Rehnquist applied the same argument to the American flag.)

Boyle proposes a new politics of IP. Admiring the way in which environmentalism imputed to environmental causes far greater ethical urgency than is conveyed in a cost benefit analysis, he seeks a similar politics of IP, one which engages us more deeply than mere accounting or economics.

In this paper I suggest that paradoxically enough, economics can offer some help in this quest, or at least economics as its founder hoped it might become. Like Darwin, Adam Smith was a plodder and a perfectionist, pondering things for many years, seeking ways to minimise any offence they might cause, before setting out his views in print. Smith's first major book was *The Theory of Moral Sentiments* published exactly 250 years ago. It contained Smith's most fundamental thoughts about human beings and the society which they create, and which of course creates them.

In this paper I argue that way back at the beginning of economics, Smith pioneered an approach to the creation of public goods which has gone largely ignored. This is very relevant to the philosophy of IP. Even more, Smith saw human development whether it was cultural or economic, as at bottom an expression of human sociality. And as Web 2.0 burgeons before us, Smith's thinking helps us see it in it's most promising, it's most glorious light: As a scaling up of human sociality itself.

Against a backdrop in which certain Christian teachings had demonised self-interest, Smith sought to revive aspects of ancient traditions in which the pursuit of true enlightened self-interest is bound up with the quest for virtue.

Along with other Enlightenment figures, Smith was in awe of the power and economy of Newton's system of celestial mechanics involving as it did, "an immense chain of the most important and sublime truths ... connected together by one capital fact, of the reality of which we have daily experience".[3] Emulating Newton, Smith's economics was built from a single principle – in this case human beings' tendency to "truck barter and exchange". And his meta theory of society in *The Theory of Moral Sentiments* was built upon the single principle of sympathy. Today the word "sympathy" typically

---

[3] Smith, A, 1795, 'The principles which lead and direct philosophical enquiries; illustrated by the history of astronomy', in *Essays on Philosophical Subjects*, Oxford: Oxford University Press, 1980. See also Smith's observation in his lectures on rhetoric that the Newtonian system was "vastly more ingenious and for that reason more engaging than the other. It gives us a pleasure to see the phaenomena which we reckoned the most unaccountable all deduced from some principle (commonly a well-known one) and all united in one chain, far superior to what we feel from the unconnected method..." (Lectures on Rhetoric and Belle's Lettres, Oxford: Oxford University Press, 1980; in lecture 24). (Cf. TMS, VII. ii. 2. 14).

denotes some sentimental well-wishing towards another. Smith's use of the word sometimes suggests this. But more fundamentally Smith argues that sympathy is our engine of social epistemology. As the second paragraph of *The Theory of Moral Sentiments* explains:

> [Having] no immediate experience of what other men feel, we can form no idea of the manner in which they are affected, but by conceiving what we ourselves should feel in the like situation. Though our brother is upon the rack, as long as we ourselves are at our ease, our senses will never inform us of what he suffers. They never did, and never can, carry us beyond our own person, and it is by the imagination only that we can form any conception of what are his sensations.

Imaginative sympathy gives us the tools to understand what others are thinking. Just as Shakespeare observed that all the world was a stage, Smith introduced a similar idea to social science (or moral philosophy, as he called it). Reflecting on our own observation of others, we realise that others observe us, and form opinions about us, just as we do about them. And from the cradle to the grave, we are hard wired to care deeply what others think of us.

II

Homo economicus – the pure, calculating egoist optimising his profit or 'utility' without regard for others' views or conduct (except where they're useful to his ends) is nowhere to be seen in Smith. With one possible exception. A newborn baby is a kind of inchoate *homo economicus,* a blob of infantile egoism – *infans economicus* if you like. But beyond this, the process that we now call socialisation progressively deepens and transforms us.

As Smith makes clear, socialisation begins from infancy. Indeed, even if it were "possible that a human creature could grow up to manhood in some solitary place" there is no exposure to society without socialisation.

> he could no more think of his own character ... than of the beauty or deformity of his own face ... Bring him into society, and he is immediately provided with the mirror which he wanted before ... all his own passions will immediately become the causes of new passions. He will observe that mankind approve of some of them, and are disgusted by others. He will be elevated in the one case, and cast down in the other. His desires and aversions, his joys and sorrows, will now often become the causes of new desires and new aversions, new joys and new sorrows: they will now, therefore, interest him deeply, and often call upon his most attentive consideration.

So much for *homo economicus*.

Our craving of approval, our dread of disapproval, and our ability to understand others by imagining ourselves in their shoes, draws us into a lifelong dialectical social drama in which we're all actors and spectators, not just of others' actions, but ultimately of our own. We keep an eye on our own conduct contemplating what others might think of us. As we mature (and Smith knew that some mature more than others!) this internal questioning takes on its own moral force. We ultimately crave the love and approbation of those we most respect. And conscience emerges for Smith as a fictive impartial spectator which becomes the yardstick of our actions, and leads us towards virtue. For Smith, the whole of human society – its psychology, its sociology its economics, it's social customs and mores and perhaps even its religion – is built on these simple foundations.

Despite the enthusiasm with which it was met in Smith's time, *The Theory of Moral Sentiments* gradually slid into relative obscurity. Smith's foundational moral philosophy of society generated no school of followers, let alone a discipline as *The Wealth of Nations* did. Yet, ironically, remarkably, as the division of intellectual labour is splintering the study of man more and more, modern neuroscience is confirming Smith's theory. Just as modern genetics provided the missing biological underpinnings for Charles Darwin's theory of evolution, so modern neurology is discovering that animals with brains like ours – monkeys and primates – are hard-wired for sympathy.

In the 1990s, Italian neurophysiologists placed electrodes in monkeys' brains to study how they co-ordinated their hands and mouths to eat. Having located the small region that fired when an animal lifted food to its mouth, they found that the same region fired – only less strongly – when one monkey simply watched another lift food to its mouth. An extensive network of so-called "mirror neurons" was discovered, which fire and enable monkeys to recreate within their own brains what's going on in the brains of their fellows. Critically, mirror neurons don't respond in a mechanical way to given physical movements but only when the observer interprets such movements as having been made with a given intention – for instance, eating.

Just as Smith's *Theory of Moral Sentiments* had argued that we all share vicariously in the gamut of each others' emotions, from elation, through to horror and disgust, so recent experiments show that brain regions which activate when we experience pain, disgust, happiness and other emotions, also activate when we observe *others* having similar experiences.

III

Before proceeding, we pause to note the intensely rhetorical nature of Smith's theory. For we can misunderstand its emphases if we ignore its pervasive normative tone.

Smith's first lectureship was in rhetoric, and his scientific contributions are subsumed within the contemporary eighteenth century rhetorical tradition encompassing the threefold task of delighting, instructing and persuading the reader to identify with virtue.[4] The *Theory of Moral Sentiments'* theory of virtue is itself delivered in a rhetorical package which engages in that quintessentially rhetorical practice of praising virtue and blaming vice.

Almost invariably in the Moral Sentiments, whenever Smith praises virtue or points to our desire for approval, he mentions its shadow side – vice and our abhorrence of being thought unworthy by our fellows. Indeed a modern reader of Smith is likely to find him quite long winded and indeed – in the modern (pejorative) sense, rhetorical. Smith's books were like this because although they are also other things, Smith wrote them largely, perhaps principally, as invitations to his readers to virtue.

It's not appreciated how much even *The Wealth of Nations*, likewise conforms to this rhetorical tradition. To recap, let's note the rhetorical resonances in what might be the most passionate passage in all of Smith's writing. It is about the African slave trade.

> Every savage undergoes a sort of Spartan discipline, and by the necessity of his situation is inured to every sort of hardship ... Fortune never exerted more cruelly her empire over mankind, than when she subjected those nations of heroes to the refuse of the jails of Europe, to wretches who possess the virtues neither of the countries which they come from, nor of those which they go to, and whose levity, brutality, and baseness, so justly expose them to the contempt of the vanquished.

IV

Although Smith can be rightly seen as an apostle of self-interest, one might also portray his contribution as delineating those *public goods* which are preconditions for self-interest to be socially constructive. Here, in a famous passage, Smith explains how the self-seeking individual in a market turns the exchange of private goods towards the common good.

> He generally, indeed, neither intends to promote the publick interest, nor knows how much he is promoting it. . . . . [H]e intends only his own security; and by directing [his] industry [and capital] in such a manner as its produce may be of the greatest value, he intends only his own gain, and he is in this, as in many other cases, led by an invisible hand to promote an end

---

[4] Which is part of the reason for my arguing that "Adam Smith is to Markets as Jane Austen is to Marriage" (Gruen, 2006).

which was no part of his intention. He generally, indeed, neither intends to promote the publick interest, nor knows how much he is promoting it.

So far Smith's has illustrated nothing more than the optimisation of the production and exchange of *private goods*, not the emergence of a public good. Though it was not clearly defined in Smith's time, in modern economics public goods are characterised by non-rivalry and non-excludability. A wireless broadcast is non-rival because, unlike toasters or cars or fridges, if one house enjoys the broadcast it does nothing to prevent others from enjoying it. At least unencrypted, the broadcast is also non-excludable. Anyone can tune in. If someone must fund the broadcast, we may have a problem, because the potential for free riding undermines the ability to charge for the broadcast as we do for fridges and toasters.[5]

But look a little closer and there are public goods that are both the precondition and consequence of the invisible hand of the market. The precedent, as Smith explains at length, and with great force, in *The Theory of Moral Sentiments*, is a peaceful law-abiding citizenry, and the rule of law, or what Smith called commutative justice – respect for property.

Looking around we see other public goods in Smith. The emergence of currency is an emergent property of markets as they evolve, although, as in the case of public mores, the state may lend its authority to reinforce community norms. And the thing which most fundamentally distinguishes us from the animals is an emergent public good. Adam Smith wrote a treatise on the emergence of language in which he spelled out precisely this quality of language as an emergent product of individuals seeking only their own private ends. A rule of grammar would "establish itself insensibly, and by slow degrees" as a consequence of the human "love of analogy and similarity of sound" as people "would endeavour to make their mutual wants intelligible to each other".[6]

---

[5] There are a range of combinations of rivalry and non-excludability such that the quadrant defined by those two terms produces the four categories of public goods, private goods, common pools and club goods as follows.

	Excludable	Non-excludable
Rivalrous	Private good	Common pool good
Non-rivalrous	Club good Toll good	Public good

[6] Smith, Adam, 1762. *Lectures on Rhetoric and Belles Lettres*, oll.libertyfund.org/index.php?option=com_staticxt&staticfile=show.php%3Ftitle=202&layout=html accessed on 24th May 2009.

Thus, as Otteson has spelled out, Smith's "market model" in which public goods are the emergent and unintended product of private endeavours to meet private needs, applies not just to the way markets serve the common good and produce public goods, but also to the way language, currency and social mores emerge – all of which are foundations of a market order. We might summarise by saying that the public goods of language and widely shared social mores, and a currency, are the preconditions for the emergence of a sophisticated market order, which itself is the precondition for the emergence of the public good of market prices and liquidity.

V

And here's the thing. Since Smith, economics has always taken the central problem of public goods to be the difficulty of funding them, given the presence of free-riders. But by virtue of their very nature as emergent properties of self-seeking humans, within society no-one has had to pass round the hat to bring emergent public goods into existence. They're no more or less than the accretions of life itself!

Smith's Newtonian schema allows Smith to explain how social mores which underpin the ascent to increasing opulence in the economy and virtue amongst the people all emerge from a single source – human sympathy between free people. Neither the crown nor its government intrudes in any way although at some stage in the tradition of British Common Law (Smith also lectured in Jurisprudence) the state may publicly legitimate and re-enforce what are already private conceptions of justice.

And now Web 2.0 brings us a panoply of new emergent public goods: the epiphenomena of those seeking private benefits for themselves. Though it predates the coining of the expression Web 2.0, open source software is paradigmatic. Although sometimes driven by loftier motives, the motive for a great deal of open source software coding is the private interest of a user in solving their own problems by fixing bugs or adding features. Once coded the producer has an interest in having their code incorporated into the project and so donates it. One can tell similar stories about the other 'Public Goods 2.0' like blogging, Flickr and Wikipedia – though of course there are richer motives in play as well. It is to those we now turn.

VI

Smith's intensely, inextricably social, picture of the way we are constituted finds its way into his economics. Despite his desire to construct his economics around the single principle of our innate tendency to "truck barter and exchange", in lectures delivered before *The Wealth of Nations,* Smith permitted himself the thought that there was something even more fundamental, human sociality and (note Smith the rhetorician!) the desire to persuade. Here is Smith's 'oratorical' theory of a bargain.

> If we should enquire into the principle in the human mind on which this disposition of trucking is founded, it is clearly the naturall inclination every one has to persuade. The offering of a shilling, which to us appears to have so plain and simple a meaning, is in reality offering an argument to persuade one to do so and so as it is for his interest.

Of all economists, Smith would have understood the foundational proposition of what might be taken as an early Web 2.0 credo, "the cluetrain manifesto" – "Markets are conversations". And, although no doubt Smith would have been amazed at some of the more amazing things about Web 2.0 – like Wikipedia for instance – he might have been one of the least amazed. For so much of the engine behind Web 2.0 is the same as the engine Smith saw behind society – the dialectic of human sociality.

In this regard note Odlyzko's (2001) documentation of the how much larger a share of the economy is driven by our desire for interaction between two specific parties, compared with broadcasting or publishing from one source to many. Speaking of the US economy Odlyzko observes:

> What is striking is how highly valued [two way] communications is. . . . Our postal system alone collects almost as much money as our entire movie industry, even though the latter benefits from large foreign sales. For all the publicity it attracts, entertainment is simply not all that large, because people are not willing to pay very much for it. . . . [C]ommunications is huge, and represents the collective decisions of millions of people about what they want. It is also growing relative to the rest of the economy in a process that goes back centuries. As a fraction of the US economy, it has grown more than 15-fold over the last 150 years. The key point . . . is that most of this spending is on connectivity, the standard point-to-point communications, and not for broadcast media that distribute "content."

Odlyzko documents how pundits and market players have repeatedly overestimated our preparedness to pay for content, while underestimating our desire for inter-connectedness, from the underestimation of the value of Bell's telephone for social communication, to the ARPANET's engineers' surprise at the popularity of e-mail to the under-appreciation of the value of mobile phones, and scepticism that SMSs were anything more than a toy gimmick.

Smith doesn't write about the power of propaganda or anything much emitted from a single source, however powerful. He writes about human beings creating their own world through their communication, their interest in what each other are thinking – in his terminology their sympathy – and their interaction. And he writes about the strength of their social desires, from the desire to communicate to their desire to fit in and be well regarded by each other. Those forces are now the dominant force behind the burgeoning of social networks, and many other phenomena of Web 2.0, right now.

VII

Smith also gives us a more compelling portrait of the psychology of motivation and achievement. For *homo economicus* the attraction of power, fame or wealth is simple greed for more. Smith is a better psychologist. "[T]o what purpose is all the toil and bustle of this world?" Smith asks about the human drive towards avarice and ambition? Smith concludes "It is the vanity, not the ease, or the pleasure, which interests us."

> Is it to supply the necessities of nature? The wages of the meanest labourer can supply them.... To be observed, to be attended to, to be taken notice of with sympathy, complacency, and approbation, are all the advantages which we can propose to derive from it.

This rings true for me, and perhaps more importantly for Warren Buffett recently quoted in uncannily Smithian terms (Lewis, 2009):

> Basically, when you get to my age you'll really measure your success in life by how many of the people you want to have love you actually do love you. I know people who have a lot of money, and they get testimonial dinners and they get hospital wings named after them. But the truth is that nobody in the world loves them.

This striving for fame, glory, the respect of peers is an important, though not necessarily primary motive behind much coding of open source software and it surely lies behind a great deal of the voluntary work that is done on blogs, and any number of other Web 2.0 phenomena. Smith comments at some length on the intensity of our desire to discover something of ourselves in others, and our desire to reciprocate both the favours we are done, and the slights.[7]

> What most of all charms us in our benefactor, is the concord between his sentiments and our own, with regard to what interests us so nearly as the worth of our own character, and the esteem that is due to us. We are delighted to find a person who values us as we value ourselves, and distinguishes us from the rest of mankind, with an attention not unlike that with which we distinguish ourselves. To maintain in him these agreeable and flattering sentiments, is one of the chief ends proposed by the returns we are disposed to make to him.[8]

And Smith understood that there are all sorts of quirky, all-too-human motivations arising from our social instincts. They're powering Web 2.0 also. As Nicholson Baker

---

[7] *Theory of Moral Sentiments*, Part III, Chapter VI.

[8] *Theory of Moral Sentiments*, Part II, Section III, Chapter I.

wrote recently (2008), the initial sources, such as the 1911 Encyclopaedia Britannica, and other public domain publications, which provided a "seed" for many entries, and altruism, don't fully explain Wikipedia's success.

> The real reason it grew so fast was noticed by co-founder Jimmy "Jimbo" Wales in its first year of life. "The main thing about Wikipedia is that it is fun and addictive," Wales wrote. Addictive, yes. All big Internet successes – e-mail, chat, Facebook, Gawker, Second Life, YouTube, Daily Kos, World of Warcraft –have a more or less addictive component – they hook you because they are solitary ways to be social: you keep checking in, peeking in, as you would to some noisy party going on downstairs in a house while you're trying to sleep.

In a treatise on the history of astronomy remarkably prescient of Thomas Kuhn's *Structure of Scientific Revolutions*, Smith explained the motivation behind scientific progress as driven by the mental discomfort of things not quite "adding up". The mind seeks to relieve the "chaos of jarring and discordant appearances, to allay this tumult of the imagination, and to restore it, when it surveys the great revolutions of the universe, to that tone of tranquillity and composure, which is both most agreeable in itself, and most suitable to its nature." And indeed it's the stub, the niggling error, outrageous claim, the irritating infelicity that keeps some up at night

VIII

So where does this leave us in considering copyright in the world of Web 2.0 and remix. In fact Smith accepted copyright, at least for the fourteen years protection it spanned in his day, "as an encouragement to the labours of learned men".

> And this is perhaps as well adapted to the real value of the work as any other, for if the book be a valuable one the demand for it in that time will probably be a considerable addition to his fortune. But if it is of no value the advantage he can reap from it will be very small. These two privileges therefore, as they can do no harm and may do some good, are not to be altogether condemned. But there are few so harmless".[9]

Given Smith's scepticism about publicly sanctioned monopolies, one can't imagine him looking on the IP expansionism of our own time with either pleasure or surprise. My guess is that Smith would have continued to approve of copyright where it underpins production that would not otherwise take place, but not beyond that point.

---

[9] Lectures On Jurisprudence, oll.libertyfund.org/index.php?option=com_staticxt&staticfile=show.php%3Ftitle=202&layout=html, accessed on 24th May 2009.

My one practical suggestion combines my admiration for Smith and one of my own country's policy successes. We reined in the monster of protectionism that Smith warned against by insisting that any change to protection be preceded by an independent study analysing its net economic effects. Given the way in which IP protection has been ramped up in circumstances that make it highly dubious that it will lead to more production [10] I have for some time argued that we should agitate to enshrine the principle in international negotiations that no increase in IP be negotiated ahead of an independent study demonstrating its net global economic benefits.

Further the more I see of the politics of IP, the more I see international agreements operating simply as constraints on what national governments can do. They can indeed be constraints, and to some extent that is their point. But it's remarkable how often it seems to be forgotten that *we negotiate international agreements*. Given this, every time I hear someone tell me that sensible reform isn't possible under this or that international agreement, whether it be multilateral like TRIPS, or bilateral like the Australia US Free Trade Agreement, I'd like to hear them add words to the effect that we should bring up the problem at the very next international meeting where these agreements are discussed.

But I began this paper suggesting that Smith might help us meet James Boyle's challenge of going *beyond* contemporary economic concerns in conceptualising the issues at stake in intellectual property. To recap, Boyle wants something broader, more "human" than the simple totting up of costs and benefits typical of contemporary economics. Remarkably enough, Smith offers several promising leads.

- He shows us something that is usually impossible to find in most economics textbooks. There is a substantial class of pure public goods which are 'emergent'. Thrown off spontaneously by social and intellectual interaction they require no funding or outside intervention.

- Web 2.0 is now scaling up this miracle, generating a kaleidoscopic array of new global public goods funded from nothing more than the restless sociality of our species not least our desire for the esteem of our fellows. As Smith put it, our striving for wealth, or fame or glory isn't for the thing itself but for what it brought – an "easy empire over the affections of mankind". For the most part, a collaborative web can be funded without any monopoly in the content produced.

If this underscores the economic reason for avoiding excessive IP protection, it also hints at that "human" aspect that James Boyle is after. For as we extend IP we are

---

[10] This is most obviously the case where IP terms have been increased retrospectively where they can quite obviously have no effect in bringing forward additional production.

discovering areas in which our human instincts recoil. It may or may not entail more economic benefits than costs to allow the patenting of human genes – though somehow I doubt it. But it had better be economically worthwhile, because economic considerations aside, it seems kind of creepy. If I ask whether should I be free to use Tim O'Reilly's term "Web 2.0" as I like – and as I have, without payment and indeed, until now even without acknowledgement – economics says "yes". That's because the only case for providing monopolistic protection is to bring forth IP. And yet we have the expression delivered to the world, safe and sound without it.

But there's another, more "human" answer. Commonsense – if I might be permitted to invoke such an abused term – says "yes" too. We humans like communicating and interacting amongst each other. Our communication today is built on our own, and others', past communications. And it's easy to see harm coming from outside interference in that process and from commercialising it. At least as applied to the intimacies of daily life, it's kind of creepy. Smith surely reinforces that commonsense. Certainly for his time, but even today, a remarkable characteristic of Smith is his faith in human culture's capacity to build itself in a healthy way *from the ground up*, from the smallest interactions between the most ordinary people and his concomitant scepticism of what could be gained from any heavy handed interventions in that process.

In this regard, we should heed the lesson from the last thing Smith ever wrote for publication. The revolutionaries of France and America had warmed to Smith's confidence that people could be the authors of their own culture, and his faith in the way the small details of human life and human culture, when left to their own devices, within the rule of law ultimately build better lives. But like his friend Edmund Burke, Smith looked on the events of 1789 in France with great anxiety. As a result, the next year, the year of his death, he added a section to the final edition of his *Theory of Moral Sentiments,* which thus became both the first and last book he published.

Anxious like Burke about the way in which those in power could overreach themselves he penned a section against "the man of system".

> The man of system. . . is often so enamoured with the supposed beauty of his own ideal plan of government, that he cannot suffer the smallest deviation from any part of it. . . . He seems to imagine that he can arrange the different members of a great society with as much ease as the hand arranges the different pieces upon a chess–board. He does not consider that the pieces upon the chess–board have no other principle of motion besides that which the hand impresses upon them; but that, in the great chess–board of human society, every single piece has a principle of motion of its own, altogether different from that which the legislature might chuse to impress upon it. If those two principles coincide and act in the same

direction, the game of human society will go on easily and harmoniously, and is very likely to be happy and successful. If they are opposite or different, the game will go on miserably, and the society must be at all times in the highest degree of disorder.[11]

Finally, I can't finish without observing that Smith might have wanted to add one more thing. Amid the unruly mix of motives that have always powered the emergent phenomena of social life, and now power the emergent public goods of Web 2.0, we catch glimpses of our better selves. And we come to see ourselves as others see us – and encounter others doing the same. Something tells the blogger, the Wikipedian, the coder of the next distribution of Wordpress or Linux, that their quest for that "easy empire over the affections of mankind", is just a foretaste of our destiny, which can only be found on our halting journey towards that more distant and difficult ultimate destination – virtue itself.

Editorial note: quotations from Adam Smith and Edmund Burke are unexpurgated and contain anomalous 18th century spellings.

---

[11] TMS, Part IV, Chapter 2, Section ii.

17

CURRENT ISSUES: NATIONAL, REGIONAL AND INTERNATIONAL PERSPECTIVES

Professor Adrian Sterling [1]

PART I: GENERAL

A   Introductory

This year 2009 marks the 55th anniversary of my commencement of work in the field of international copyright law, for it was in 1954 that I first took part as a delegate at an international copyright meeting, namely the Berne Union Permanent Committee meeting in Lugano in June/July of that year, at which I was fortunate to meet the great copyright experts of that era: Marcel Plaisant, *Rapporteur* of the 1948 Berne Convention Revision Conference, Valerio de Sanctis, Eugen Ulmer, François Hepp, architect of the Universal Copyright Convention, Alphonse Tournier, co-founder of BIEM,[2] Georges Straschnov, Jacques Secretan, the then Director of the Berne Bureau, and his successors, George Bodenhausen and Arpad Bogsch.

How gracious these great men were to me, an unknown lawyer making his first appearance among them, and how important that is, encouragement to the young. Since then I have had the years representing a copyright interest (till 1974), of practice at the Bar and (since 1992) of teaching copyright at postgraduate level. You will be relieved to hear that I do not propose to regale you with anecdotes of the past, but rather to consider, as regards copyright, where I think we are going or should be going.

---

[1] LL.B. (Sydney, 1948); Bar of New South Wales (1949); Bar of England and Wales (1953). Professorial Fellow, Queen Mary Intellectual Property Research Institute, Queen Mary, University of London, Visiting Professor, King's College, University of London. This paper is based on an address given to the British Literary and Artistic Copyright Association, London, on 12 March 2009, and to the Copyright Society of Australia on 3 June 2009. © Text and Appendixes J.A.L. Sterling 2009.

[2] Bureau International des Societes Gerants Les Droits D'Enregistrement et de Reproduction Mecanique.

As you will see from the list of headings of this address, I am somewhat like the dramatist trying to contain a mighty battle within confining walls, but may I suggest that you let the challenges "on your imaginary forces work".[3]

During the 55 years which I have mentioned, there have been extraordinary developments on the technological level, which have brought into debate the whole question of how, and whether, traditional copyright concepts can cope with the new environment, in particular as regards digital recording and transmission processes, satellite communication and the internet. Looking at the present situation, we see national, international and regional attempts to deal with these developments, but these attempts have not succeeded as regards all the legal aspects involved (for instance in the application of the internet making-available right introduced by the WIPO Treaties 1996), or with the challenges to the exclusive right system posed by the opening of the floodgates of communication through the massive and increasing amounts of protected material available throughout the world on the internet. So what I seek to do here is to summarise the challenges as I see them, and suggest some approaches to be adopted to meet them. I do emphasise that my suggestions are for discussion and by no means submitted as the final, or only, answers.

I use the term "old era" to describe not so much a chronological stage, but what might be called the analogue age, and "new era" to describe the digital age, suggesting 1996 as marking the point when international law made its first attempt to deal with the internet challenges, in the WIPO Treaties.

B   Old era approaches

1   DISCRIMINATORY PROTECTION

(a)   At the international level[4]

The Berne Convention in its present version (1971) in general makes copyright protection depend on nationality of the author or place of publication (Article 3(1)), with certain additional territorial-based rules as regards cinematographic and architectural works (Article 4).[5] Thus, as far as the Convention is concerned, an

---

[3] Shakespeare, *Henry V*, Prologue.

[4] References herein to international instruments are to Berne Convention for the Protection of Literary and Artistic works 1886–1971; Universal Copyright Convention; Rome Convention for Protection of Performers, Producers of Phonograms and Broadcasting Organisations, 1961; WTO Agreement on Trade Related Aspects of Intellectual Property, 1994 (TRIPS); World Intellectual Property Organisation (WIPO) Copyright Treaty 1996 ("WCT"), WIPO Performances and Phonograms Treaty, 1996 ("WPPT"). Australia is a Contracting Party to all these instruments.

[5] See also the nationality and territorial criteria of the Universal Copyright Convention 1972 (Art. II), the Rome Convention 1961 (Arts 2 – 6) and the Phonograms Convention 1971 (Art.2). Note also the

author's work which does not fulfil the Convention criteria is unprotected. It was said in justification of this discrimination that these rules would encourage membership of the Convention, but this argument no longer has any validity, if it ever had any:

(i)   there are now over 160 countries bound to comply with the substantive provisions of the Berne Convention, and only 11 not so bound (not being Berne, TRIPS or WIPO Copyright Treaty members).[6]

(ii)   Article 27(2) of the Universal Declaration of Human Rights provides that "everyone has the right to the protection of the moral and material interests resulting from any scientific, literary or artistic production of which he is the author". Discriminating against authors on grounds of nationality or other grounds breaches this principle, and, it may be suggested, conflicts with natural justice, for why should a human being who is a national of one country be protected, but not a human being who is a national of another country?

(iii)   From the practical point of view, discriminatory protection adds to costs of recognition and administration of rights, to the detriment of owners of rights in protected material, and to the financial liability of users.

(b)   At the national level

With few exceptions, national copyright laws are on a discriminatory basis. Two reasons may be ascribed for this: firstly, the principle that a national law in general only deals with the actions of its subjects, or actions taking place in its territory, and secondly, because discriminatory protection is imposed by international or regional instruments. It is submitted that neither of these grounds provides sufficient justification for discrimination against authors or owners of related rights.

(c)   At the regional level[7]

---

national treatment provisions of TRIPS (Art.2), the NAFTA Agreement (Art. 1703), and the Cartagena Agreement (Art.2).

[6] Afghanistan, Eritrea, Ethiopia, Iran, Iraq, Laos, San Marino, São Tomé e Principe, Seychelles, Somalia, Turkmenistan.

[7] References herein to regional instruments are to the North America Free Trade Association Agreement (Canada, Mexico, USA), USA Free Trade Agreements (including US-Australia Free Trade Agreement, 2004), Cartagena Agreement (Bolivia, Colombia, Ecuador, Peru, (Venezuela)) and European Union legislation (including seven European Community "Copyright Directives"). Following the entry into force of the Lisbon Treaty (after the Canberra Conference), the European Community is subsumed into the European Union.

The EC Copyright Directives contain discriminatory provisions (i.e. on bases related to European Community membership), e.g. the Database Directive, 1996 (Art.11) and the Artist's Resale Right Directive, 2001 (Art.7).

2 BORDERED REGULATION

National laws and rules concerning assessment of infringement, and national practices as regards licensing are based in general on territorial considerations. In general, infringement is assessed according to the law of the country where the alleged infringing act takes place, and licensing for use of protected material is generally on a territorial basis. By means of reciprocal agreements, collecting societies may grant licences for use in several territories, but, as far as I am aware, no single collecting society at present grants licences permitting internet communication and downloading of all the material in its repertoire anywhere in the world (see II D 3 below).

3 EARTH BOUND DISCIPLINE

No international or regional instrument at present deals specifically with the question of infringement of copyright in Space (or, for that matter, in extraterritorial areas on Earth). See C.3 below.

C   *New era approaches*

1 NON-DISCRIMINATORY PROTECTION

It is submitted that all authors, performers, phonogram producers and broadcasters should be granted protection by copyright or related rights and that the present discriminatory rules in this respect should be abolished. The necessary amendments should be made to the abovementioned international instruments, and to national laws and the EC Copyright Directives and other regional legislation.

2 BORDERED AND BORDERLESS REGULATION

It is submitted that present practices as to bordered regulation should in general be retained, but that new procedures for use of protected material in the borderless environment created by the internet should be adopted, where effective procedures are not at present available. The precedent for this approach has been foreshadowed by the internet making-available right granted by Article 10 of the WIPO Copyright and Treaty, and Articles 10 and 14 of the WIPO Performances and Phonograms Treaty (replicated and expanded as to beneficiaries in Article 3 of the EC Information Society Directive). These instruments refer to the authors' right of communication to the public (as established in the Berne Convention) but add the vital specification, "including the making available to the public of their works in such a way that members of the public may access these works from a place and at a time individually chosen by them", in other words, on the internet. Using this approach, rules for the internet should:

(i)   clarify that the persons who make available online are the persons responsible for the websites carrying accessible material and those involved in effecting the relevant transmissions, with authorising or contributory acts of uploaders and link providers (see Part II.B. 2(a) below);

(ii)   clarify that making available online takes place at the location of the initial transmission of the accessed signal, and at all points of reception of such signal (see II B. 2(b) below);

(iii)   clarify the reach of limitations and exceptions and rules regarding private copying, peer-to-peer communication and upload to social networking sites; and

(iv)   distinguish between the transmission signal and the transmission content manifested by the signal, and indicating what rights there should respectively be in the signal and the manifestation.

The application of these rules should lead to recognition of borderless rights with bordered and borderless application, exercise and enforcement of rights.

3   LICENSING

In conjunction with the rules mentioned under (i)-(iv) above, systems or procedures allowing global licensing of material on the internet should be available, while preserving present practices as to licensing on a territorial basis. See II.F. Solution 6 below.

4   ENFORCEMENT

Particular rules as to enforcement of the internet making available right should be developed, permitting internationally enforceable orders in relation to unauthorised use of protected material.

5   COSMIC DISCIPLINE

The new era requires the formulation of rules concerning the creation of and regulation of the use of protected material in extraterritorial areas, including Space.[8]

---

[8] For proposals in this area see J.A.L. Sterling "Space Copyright Law: the new dimension" 54 Jour. Copr. Soc'y 348 (2007), on line at www.qmipri.org/research.html.

D   *The debate on principles*

1   THE JUSTIFICATION FOR COPYRIGHT

Among the arguments justifying copyright may be mentioned:

- Encouragement of creativity
- Recognition of human and moral rights
- Economic benefits
- Protection of investment
- Public interest in creation and dissemination of knowledge and the arts.[9]

In my submission, the main justification for copyright is that it protects and promotes the creative products of the human mind, and is based on the principles of respect and reward for the creator; such justification implies the necessity to ensure public access to protected material on fair and practical terms.

In the 300 years of copyright history to date, there has been much discussion on the justification for copyright, but in recent years arguments for abolition or restriction of the right have been advanced with increasing vigour. What has caused this? At present we can only surmise, but two factors seem to be prominent in the debate, namely the technical advances that have made protected material widely accessible in easily copyable forms, and the expectation of users to have such material at their disposal anywhere, anytime.

These two factors have led on the one hand to new means of creativity and on the other to massive use of protected material in ways not authorised by the rightowner, in particular unauthorised file sharing and other forms of unauthorised copying. Thus the lines of the pro- and anti- copyright battle are drawn, and it is, I suggest, appropriate to examine the arguments advanced, not by polemic exaggeration, but by logical and objective analysis of the facts before us.

2   THE RIGHTOWNER AND THE DISSEMINATOR

(a)   The author and the content provider

A tendency has grown up in recent years to delete the individual author from overall assessments in the field of copyright law. Authorship is regarded by some as a romantic idea, with the authors disappearing in a general mêlée of "content providers" in a sort of supermarket of entertainment and information. The fact that the individual author is the originator, the *fons et origo* of literary, dramatic, musical and artistic works should never be forgotten, nor should John Milton's great statement in

---

[9] For fuller listing of justifications for copyright see J.A.L. Sterling *World Copyright Law* (Sweet & Maxwell, 3rd ed, 2008) ("WCL") paras 2.27–2.42: for contrary arguments see para.2.43.

Aereopagitica: "a good book is the precious life-blood of a master spirit". We should, at all costs, recognise, preserve and protect that spirit.

(b)   Rightowner/disseminator partnership

Works, performances and productions lie hidden from humanity unless they are disseminated. Conversely, without such material, disseminators (publishers, producers, broadcasters, website operators) would have nothing to disseminate. At the same time, disseminators are usually rightowners, e.g. performers in their performances, producers in their sound recordings and films, broadcasters in their broadcasts and publishers in their publications. The rights and interests of rightowners and disseminators are thus inextricably entwined. Consequently, I submit that the future of copyright depends for its success on the effective collaboration and mutual recognition of the respective interests of these parties.

3   COMBINING REGULATION AND FREEDOM

In the new era, there is a call for greater freedom for the use of disseminated material, so that new creativity based on pre-existing material will flourish. This fact must be recognised, but such recognition must be linked to the preservation of the rights of those who produce protected material.

E   *Current issues*

1   GENERAL

In Annex I some of the current issues in the field of copyright are listed under three separate headings, to which reference should be made.

As to Section 1, the issues listed may be divided into those relating to legal issues (points (1)-(4)) (diversities in systems and private international law), while the issues under points (5)-(7) (balancing interests of rightowners and the public, discriminatory protection, developing countries) may be regarded as political issues. The use of protected material in Space (point 8) could be regarded as involving both legal and political issues.

2   PARTICULAR, OTHER THAN TECHNOLOGICAL AND   INTERNET

As to Section 2, the issues listed under points (1) and (2) concern definitions with important practical implications: the definition of joint authorship (at present often different in different countries) having repercussions both on exercise of rights and term of protection, and the definition of place of broadcast (place of transmission, place of reception, or both) affecting questions of licensing and infringement. Issues under points (3) and (4) concern diversities in the definition of authorship of cinematographic works: is an author of a cinematographic work under the law of one country entitled to claim protection in another country with difference authorship criteria, and is an employee who is initial owner in one country, entitled to claim protection in a country where, according to the general provisions of the local law, the employer is the initial owner?

Point (5) concerns scope and content of moral rights, a subject on which there are fundamentally different approaches in national laws (e.g. those of the United States and France). Points (6)-(9) relate to questions of protection of databases, audiovisual performances and broadcasts, all the subject of study in WIPO with a view to formulating new international instruments. Protection of traditional works (point 7) is an ongoing issue likely to become of increasing importance as the commercial value of such works increases. Terms of protection for performers and record producers (point 10) are the subject of widespread discussion and the introduction of EU proposals for extension of terms.

The issue as to whether there should be a right to make transformative use of pre-existing material lies at the heart of the debate on the function and purpose of copyright, and is particularly relevant in the context of material made available online (see II below).

Issues in rights management and licensing, including those relating to orphan works and other orphan material (points (12) (13)) raise problems in the fields of definition and of administration, and come to the forefront in relation to online libraries (see 3 below). Decoder cards (point 14) are mentioned as an issue raising, as regards trans-border use, questions of licensing and competition law.[10] On the horizon, we have the problems which will undoubtedly arise in relation to cloud computing.

3   TECHNOLOGICAL AND INTERNET

The issues listed in Section 3 deal in points (1)-(4) with general challenges resulting from the borderless nature of the modern communication environment, issues which arise in general because copyright has traditionally been formulated as a system of territorially based rights, whereas online communication is in principle borderless, but with possibility of territorial limitation.

Specific issues in the online field are listed in points (5)-(10), including the widely discussed issues of the licensing of the use of protected material in library digitisations for online availability[11], and of liability of internet service providers in point (10).

---

[10] In relation to the European Union, see the UK case *Murphy v Media Production Services Ltd.* [2007] EWHC 391 (Admin.).

[11] See Part II E.1 below. As at 1 January 2010, the Google Book Settlement awaits final approval by the New York District Court (18 February 2010) and if so approved will, undoubtedly mark a milestone in the history of copyright.

Format shifting (point (11)) raises fundamental points as to whether purchasers may, for private purposes, do what they wish with purchased copies. Another fundamental issue arises under point (12), namely whether private copying exemptions allow or should allow circumvention of technological protection measures.

4   PRIORITIES

It is submitted that the issues concerning developing countries, transformative use, rights management and licensing, orphan works and other orphan material, peer-to-peer file sharing, user-generated content and liability of internet service providers should be regarded as of top priority for the finding of rapid and practical solutions if copyright is to be effectively recognised in the new era.

F   *Current aims*

1   UNIVERSAL AVAILABILITY OF ALL KNOWLEDGE

Proposals for the creation of online digital libraries as part of projects to place all material in the field of knowledge and the arts at the disposal of the public raise questions of the practical means of licensing of protected material for such uses (see E. 1. above).

2   *Regulated use of all material available online*

Hand in hand with the aim of the universal online availability of the contents of libraries, and similar projects, go the desire and requirement of the public to have access to such facilities online by unfettered means. Should such access be free, or subject to payment?

PART II: ONLINE AVAILABILITY OF PROTECTED MATERIAL

A   *General*

Making protected material available online involves the exclusive rights of reproduction and communication to the public, and possibly other rights. It may be said that everyone using the internet makes copies and communicates. The alternatives for the administration of the exclusive rights are:

1   TOLERANCE OF INFRINGEMENT

A right that is not exercised becomes outmoded and liable to repeal – so tolerance of infringement threatens the continuance of copyright as a comprehensive means of protecting creativity and its associated activities and investment.

2   REGULATION OF USE

Regulation of use of protected material online represents an area of copyright and related rights in which many challenges remain to be confronted and resolved, as outlined in B. – E. below.

B   *Relevant rights*

1   INTERNATIONAL, NATIONAL AND REGIONAL LEGISLATION

Clarity in the scope and content of the reproduction, public communication and distribution rights is essential for ordered regulation of copyright and related rights. National, international and regional legislation contains provisions in this regard but leaves many gaps, of which the following problems are examples.

2   SOME PROBLEMS

(a)   Who makes available online?

There should be clarity in defining the liability (whether primary, or on the basis of authorisation or contributory infringement) of those involved in making protected material available online, including program providers, file uploaders, hosts, file storers, central index providers, link providers, telecommunicators and accessors (clarifications not provided by the WIPO Treaties).[12]

(b)   Where does making available online take place?

The WIPO Treaties 1996 do not make clear where it is that the making available online takes place. It is suggested that it should be accepted that the points where making available online takes place include the point of initial transmission and all points of reception of the transmitted material.[13]

(c)   Meaning of "publication"

It is submitted that making available online could be held to constitute publication in terms of Article 3(3) of the Berne Convention (1971 version). This may depend on whether it is accepted that making available online constitutes distribution of copies, see below.

(d)   Is distribution of copies involved?

---

[12] For detailed listing of potential infringements by those involved in unauthorised making available online, see WCL para 13A.01.

[13] For discussion on points (a) and (b), and related issues, with reference to relevant cases in Canada, Germany, USA and other countries see WCL paras 9.29–9.44.

The question has arisen in a number of cases in the United States as to whether making available online constitutes distribution of copies.[14] One of the points of contention is whether the mere placing of material on site for online accessibility constitutes distribution of copies. It is, however, accepted in some decisions that where there is downloading, there is a distribution of copies.

The implications of the decision as to whether, and if so in what circumstances, online distribution of copies constitutes publication of the material involved will affect the administration of rights, both as to ascertaining subsistence of protection (if a distribution constitutes first publication) and as to exercise of the exclusive right to distribute copies, as distinct from the right to communicate to the public: furthermore, definition of the place of distribution (e.g. place of site, place of download or both) will need clarification.

C   Limitations and exceptions

Legislation in the United States and the European Union provides certain "safe harbours" for internet service providers ("ISPs"), e.g., release from liability for infringement caused by, or possibly through, specific acts of hosting, or caching, or mere conduit, where certain conditions are fulfilled.[15] There seems to be a general misconception that in some way these provisions provide a general release from liability, but it must be emphasised that release is only obtainable on fulfilment of the respective conditions, and in the case of the requirement of takedown notices, there can be infringing acts unless and until the valid notice is given and acted upon.

The difficulties in international regulation by specific limitations or exceptions are manifold. The factors militating against obligatory international rules in this area are:

    (i)   the need to adopt provisions which conform to the three step test.[16]

    (ii)   the need to revise the relevant international instruments (Berne Convention? WIPO Treaties?).

    (iii)   The Great Divide between the United States "fair use" exception on the one hand and on the other hand the more limited "fair dealing"

---

[14] See WCL para.9.05.

[15] For details, see WCL paras 13.42–13.47.

[16] Berne Convention, Art.9(2); TRIPS Agreement, Art.13; WIPO Copyright Treaty, Art.10(2); WIPO Performances and Phonograms Treaty, Art.16. For the complexities involved in the interpretation and application of the three step test, see the French *Mulholland* case quoted in F. Solution 2 below, *ProLitteris v AargauerZeitung AG et al*, Swiss Supreme Court, 27 June 2007, (2008) 39 IIC 990, and C. Geiger "Rethinking copyright limitations in the Information Society – the Swiss Supreme Court leads the way" (2008) 39 IIC 942.

approach of the UK and other more restrictive approaches of the civil law system, as in France.

In this connection, the area of transformative use is of particular importance. In addition to traditional means of modifying protected material, online manifestations of such material can be digitally altered in ways not previously available, e.g. by addition to, or deletion from, digital images, and "remix" and "mashups", in particular of audio and visual recordings.

Internet users, young and old, carry out these transforming processes, and the question arises as to whether such activities require the permission of the relevant rightowner, or whether they fall under some exception or limitation such as private copying or parody. The difficulties in answering this question in any particular case are manifold – firstly, because the rules on private copying and permitted transformation differ from jurisdiction to jurisdiction, (see (iii) above), and secondly, because judgment in determining whether a permitted limit is exceeded is by its nature subjective, since there are no specific measuring rules for calculating infringement.

These aspects have in particular received the attention of Professor Lawrence Lessig, who is concerned with "criminalising" of children (and others) as a result of sanctions imposed under the criminal provisions of copyright law concerning infringement; furthermore, Lessig considers that what he calls "amateur creativity" can be stifled by the exercise of exclusive rights concerning copying and transformative use.

Lessig is by no means an abolitionist; he does not "support people using technology to violate other people's rights", and believes that it is appropriate "to create mechanisms to make it simple for copyright owners to collect revenues for work made available", and that "we ought to be enabling an amateur and regulating the commercial"[17], and considers that "Congress needs to decriminalise file sharing, either by authorising at least non-commercial file-sharing, with taxes to cover a reasonable royalty to the artists whose work is shared, or by authorising a simple blanket licensing procedure, whereby users could, for a low fee, buy the right to freely file share".[18]

Certainly one can argue that art is built on transformative use, and that to stifle such use is to stifle art. But that does not mean that such use should be unfettered or uncontrolled, or allowed to bring harm to the creator's economic or moral interests.

Here, then, in the context of the internet, is the crux of the problem. On the one hand we can envisage laws and court decisions being sympathetic to children, and others, who, in the privacy of their homes remix and mashup the works of others. But what of

---

[17] As reported in an interview published in *Managing Intellectual Property* March 2009, 26–30. I am grateful to Malcolm Langley for reference to this interview.

[18] Lawrence Lessig "*Remix: making art and commerce thrive in the hybrid economy* (Penguin 2008) at 271

the communication of such transformations to other persons? Let us consider, first of all, the situation in the analogue world, and assume that Leonardo da Vinci is still alive, and that without authorisation someone publishes in a book a transformation of the painting of Mona Lisa, showing the addition of a long red beard to the lady's face.

In most countries, the rightowners in the painting will have remedies where the publication is commercial, but even here the "fair use" defence in the United States may run in that country, but not in other countries. Then what about non-commercial use – supposing the user simply makes copies of the transformation and distributes them to all his/her friends, or to all the world? Even if "non-commercial" transformative use is to be permitted, what is "commercial use"?[19] And even if the use is non-commercial, what about the author's moral rights? If you insult me, you cannot escape liability merely by saying that you did not make money out of your insult.

In the internet context, the same problem arises. One can envisage a blanket licensing system in which (by, or on the analogy of, a Creative Commons licence) the author permits transformative use of the protected material for non-commercial purposes. Even leaving aside the definition of commercial, what is to be done when the transformative use damages the integrity of the work? Surely the author (and the performer) must be able to reserve exercise of the moral rights.[20]

In sum, it is suggested that there is a clear distinction to be made between:

(1)   copying and transformation of protected material by a private individual for that individual's private purposes: such copying should, it is submitted, be permissible without specific authorisation by the rightowners, provided that the material copied or transformed has come into the possession or control of the copier legitimately;

(2)   communication of protected material to persons outside the private and domestic circle of the communicator, whether, in the internet context, this is by way of file-sharing, or upload to a social networking site, or otherwise: here it is suggested that, in the global context, licensing is necessary for legitimation. Such licensing can validate communication of the untransformed material, or of the transformed material, but in either case, the licence should, it is submitted, be subject to the exercise of the moral rights concerned. The global licence is necessary because limitations and exceptions applying under specific national laws do not have international application and validity. Preliminary consent case by case does not seem to be a practical

---

[19] On the difficulty on drawing the line between "commercial" and "non-commercial" see Paul Sugden "How long is a piece of string? The meaning of "commercial scale" in copyright piracy" [2009] EIPR 202

[20] Such reservation may be covered in the proposed global licensing system: see F. Solution 6 below.

option. For a proposal which would enable such licensing to take place on a global scale, see F Solution 6 below, and Annex II.

D   Cross-border licensing

1   THE NEED TO CO-ORDINATE CONTROL, LICENSING   AND ENFORCEMENT

Control of use of protected material should embrace the ability to prohibit or license particular uses. Cross-border licensing should embrace a system which will effectively authorise the use of the protected item concerned for making available online for access anywhere in the world. Enforcement should embrace the ability to pursue and obtain remedies for infringement wherever it occurs. Rights cannot be effectively exercised unless each of these elements is available to the rightowner, or the rightowner's representative, permitting co-ordinated recognition of rights.

2   THE BLESSING OF OBTAINABILITY AND THE   NEGATIVE EFFECT OF UNOBTAINABILITY

In today's world, uploading and downloading of protected and unprotected material are activities as easily undertaken as breathing in and out. Since such actions may include the associated actions of transforming material which is accessed, as abovementioned, users will expect facilities allowing instantaneous licensing of the intended use, subject to conditions which are accepted as maintainable in the interests of rightowners and the public. If the desired licences are obtainable on equitable terms, the exercise of copyright will be accepted by the public. If such licences are unobtainable, public opinion or influential sections of public opinion may rise against the recognition of copyright itself.

3   MANDATED RIGHTS

(a)   Split rights, split ownership, split territorial reach

One of the factors militating against the effective recognition of copyright and related rights in the internet context is that the initial rights comprised in copyright (for instance the reproduction and public communication rights) can be split as to exercise, one person or body administering one right, another person or body another right. Ownership of rights may also be split between different territories.

(b)   Split collecting society mandates

Collecting societies historically administer rights for their respective territories and conclude reciprocal licences for the exploitation of their repertoires in other territories. The terms of such reciprocal agreements give problems,[21] but even when these are overcome, there remains the point that there are rights which are not mandated to a collecting society or societies for all territories.

(c)   Compulsory collective exercise?

Article 9(1) of the EC Satellite and Cable Retransmission Directive (93/83/EEC) provides that Member States shall ensure that the right of copyright owners, and holders of related rights, to grant or refuse authorisation to a cable operator for a cable transmission, may be exercised only through a collecting society. The question arises whether a compendious solution to the problem of internet licensing could be achieved by a similar provision that the internet licensing right could only be exercised through a collecting society. However, internationally agreed legislation would be necessary for the effective institution of such a provision, and it is difficult to envisage the achievement of such legislation within the foreseeable future.

4   UNMANDATED RIGHTS

(a)   Identifiable non-member material

Non-member material may be defined as material in respect of which the relevant rights are not administered by the collecting society concerned.

A collecting society can (in default of special legislation) only legitimately authorise use of material covered by its mandates or those of societies with which it has the necessary reciprocal agreements. Non-member material can be licensed by the rightowner concerned, but legitimate licensing of such material by a collecting society needs legislation, see (b) below.

(b)   Extended collective licensing

Undoubtedly the ability of collecting societies to license the use of material in which the relevant rights are owned by non-members (the "extended collective licensing system", as applied in Scandinavia) would facilitate the administration of the right of making available online.[22] Such a system may (as in Scandinavia) be used to license the use of orphan material (see (c) below).

---

[21] For description of some of these problems, and cases before the European Commission in this connection, see WCL para.26.21.

[22] For description of the extended collective licensing system, with references to commentaries thereon (including the Scandinavian systems), see WCL para.12.24, and Annex III (3).

(c)   Orphan material

The problem of licensing material where the rightowner is unidentifiable or untraceable has been the subject of extensive studies.[23] But no regional or international solution of this problem has yet been reached.

I make so bold as to present at this Conference a legislative proposal concerning the licensing of orphan works and other orphan material under provisions of amendments to the Australian Copyright Act 1968: see Annex III.

5   IDENTIFICATION: THE SINE QUA NON

What is being copied and communicated must be identified, otherwise the use of protected material cannot be properly regulated. How will protected material be identified? I submit that for effective global exercise of the internet right there must be some form of notification of all items of protected material, to an administering body or administering bodies, with linked databases permitting access for rights administration purposes.

All material protected by copyright or related rights can be recorded digitally. So I submit that if I want to protect my creation, performance, recording, broadcast or database in the digital world effectively, I must notify its details to the relevant administering body. Ideally, the notification will include a copy of the item concerned. With computerised facilities, I can make the notification by a touch on a key or a pad.

Collecting societies already have extensive and sophisticated databases covering their respective repertoires. It is understood that YouTube also has in its Content Identification and Management System an extensive means of searching and recording data concerning protected material, as provided by rightowners.[24] The availability of a global database of interlinked information concerning all notified protected material is not beyond the bounds of possibility; indeed, it is a development we could see within a relatively short period.

Notification must be distinguished from compulsory registration as a condition of copyright subsistence, such formality being forbidden by Article 3(2) of the Berne Convention.

---

[23] See WCL paras 12.32–12.37 for general description of the problems involved in orphan material and my proposal for a solution in UK law, online at www.qmipri.org/research.htm. As to the USA, see the US Copyright Office Report on Orphan Works, January 2006, and Bills presented to Congress, S2913, HR 5889. In the UK, the Digital Economy Bill 2009 contained a provision empowering the Secretary of State to authorise extended collective licensing schemes concerning use of orphan works (cl.43) (cf Annex III), but this provision was the subject of debate and was dropped from the Digital Economy Act 2010.

[24] See www.youtube.com/t/contentid.

6   EXERCISE OF RIGHT

(a)   Prohibition: With respect to prohibition of use of protected material, we have to take into account the concerns expressed by Professor Lessig; and other writers. Lessig accepts the value of copyright in encouraging and sustaining creativity, but as abovementioned his concerns include:

(i)   the challenge of the effective exercise of the exclusive rights of copyright in the modern communication environment, and

(ii)   the criminalising of those (particularly children) who copy or communicate without authorisation.[25]

I believe these concerns must be taken into account in the exercise of copyright in the new era.

Consequently, we need first to establish those conditions in which the exercise of the prohibition right will be justified in the digital (copying) and online (communication) environment.

Here the three step test, now law throughout countries bound by the TRIPS Agreement, including the USA and all countries of the European Union, must be taken into account.

(b)   Legitimated use

(i)   Potential infringements: where material is hosted online, unauthorised use of such material involves infringement (or authorising of or contributing to infringement) by the uploader, the host, the link provider and the accessor (and by the storer, where the material is stored for use by the host), and possibly, where knowledge of infringement subsists, by the program provider. A multiplicity of separate rights will be infringed by unauthorised use, e.g. in the case of sound recordings, those of the author, the performers and the sound recording producer, and in the case of films, depending on the applicable national law, of the director, performers, producer and others.[26]

Accordingly, permissions covering a multitude of rights and, at present, from a multitude of rightowners must be obtained to ensure global legitimacy of use.

---

[25]See C above.

[26] For a detailed description of the potential infringements involved in unauthorised file sharing and file hosting, see WCL para. 13A.01.

(ii) Particular areas: in the context of the internet, two areas need particular consideration in formulating rules for legitimated use:

    (i) peer-to-peer file sharing of films and sound recordings;

    (ii) upload of protected material to social networking sites such as YouTube, and public communication following such upload.

The questions involved include:

    (a) Legitimation of the initial act of sharing, or uploading to site.

    (b) Legitimation of hosting, onward transmission and storage facilities.

    (c) Legitimation of accessor downloading and subsequent use (e.g. further use of material on a social networking site such as Facebook).

(iii) Individual and collective licensing: two forms of licensing are available:

    (a) individual licensing: that is, licensing by the rightowner (or rightowner's representative) without the intervention of a collecting society as where, for instance, a rightowner:

        (i) provides sites with the facility of legitimated download (as in the case of iTunes): whether such facilities will eradicate unauthorised peer-to-peer file sharing remains to be seen, but such an outcome at present seems unlikely;

        (ii) licenses the social networking site directly, e.g. where the rightowner has a contract with the site operator permitting online use of specific material on specific conditions: such contracts will only cover the particular networking site concerned;

    (b) licensing by collecting societies: here one of the problems will be the territorial scope of the licence.

(c) Peer-to-peer file sharing

I believe that it will be generally accepted that an overall exception for peer-to-peer file sharing will not conform to the three step test – it is not a special case, it affects the normal exploitation of the material and it is prejudicial to the rights of the author, since it deprives him or her of the right to determine the conditions of copying and communicating the work.

So how will peer-to-peer file sharing be regulated? I submit that this can be comprehensively achieved by a system of permission rather than prohibition, see F. Solution 6. below.

(d) YouTube and similar facilities

YouTube and similar social networking sites allow upload of material for making available online. Without the necessary authorisations, such activities involve, where protected material is concerned, infringement of copyright or related rights by the uploader, the host, and the accessor, and possibly other persons (see above).

The status of all material which it is proposed to use on the internet must be identified before such use, if infringement of rights or other unlawful acts are to be avoided.

The preliminary establishment of status of the material concerned in this context, in a rapid and comprehensive manner, is thus essential for the effective control of the use of protected material on the internet.

Systems are already in use for the identification of the subsistence and scope of rights, but there can be gaps in these systems, for instance as regards geographical extent and orphan material, see below. However, we may proceed by considering material of which the protection status is established.

Protected material uploaded to social networking sites may be described as "user-generated" and may consist of various categories of material, including

(i) "User solo material": the production of the uploader alone: in this case the uploader may, if the production consists of such material alone, and subject to legislative limitations or exceptions, and any conditions imposed by the website operator, determine the conditions of copying and communication, for instance by a Creative Commons or similar licence, or by notification to an administering body;

(ii) "Identified third party non-transformed material": protected material not created, performed, produced etc. by the uploader. To forbid all such uploading without providing legitimation, or offering of the possibility of such legitimation, in my view adopts an attitude which does not take into account the realities of the present situation.

(iii) "Identified third party transformed material": While third parties may authorise in advance the uploading of non-transformed material in which they own rights, the licensing of upload of transformed material presents particular problems in two areas, namely the exercise of limitations and exceptions, and the application of moral rights. A limitation or exception which is applicable in one country may not free an upload from infringement in another country: for instance, an uploading of substantial extracts of a protected work may be permissible in the US within the "fair use" provisions of the US Copyright Act, but not under French law, so that download in France would infringe.

As regards moral rights, it is unlikely that authors would wish to give preliminary permission for transformations which infringe the integrity right, and, indeed, in some countries such permissions would be invalid because of the unwaivability of moral rights. It seems, therefore, that to achieve legitimation in this area the choices are

(a)   a system of preliminary reference to the author or performer of all transforming uploads of the work or performance concerned, for decision as to whether moral rights are infringed, and, if so, the necessary takedown (a system which hardly seems practical) [27], or

(b)   an internationally accepted exception covering transformative use on social networking sites (a provision which is unlikely to obtain universal acceptance), or

(c)   a system of licensing under which (i) the rightowner permits transformative use, subject to the exercise of moral rights in the material concerned, and (ii) the site owner permits upload subject to possible claims for infringement of rights, the uploader to be responsible in this respect.

(iv)   "Non-identified third-party material": For the site operator legitimately to license the uploading of orphan material, some form of universally applicable extended collective licensing would need to be available. National systems for dealing with orphan material may be different. Possibly a solution would be for the site operator to allow upload on the basis of indemnity by the uploader against subsequent claims, and other conditions.

---

[27] Note that, in addition to the moral rights granted to the author by Art.6*bis* of the Berne Convention, Art.5 of the WIPO Performances and Phonograms Treaty grants the performer certain moral rights of attribution and integrity regarding live aural performances and performances fixed in phonograms.

(v)   "Incidentally included material": It seems possible to envisage a situation where incidental use of protected material in uploads could be covered in the licensing provisions.

Legitimated use may be achieved by direct licensing by the rightowner or rightowner's representative concerned, or through agreements concluded between collecting societies and the networking site concerned. However, as indicated above, such agreements will not at present necessarily give global cover for access to the online material throughout the world.

E   Present studies and procedures

1   EUROPEAN COMMISSION

Among the extensive series of legislative reports, proposals and studies issued by the European Commission are those concerning management of copyright and related rights, and digital libraries.[28]

Here, I would only mention that, in my view, proposals for the establishment of European Union-wide licences for the online use of protected material do not meet the practical requirements of rightowners, disseminators and users, namely licences which cover global accessibility on the internet. It is of limited use to the prospective licensee seeking geographically unrestricted licences to be offered an EU-wide licence which does not cover access in any country outside the EU.

2   UNITED KINGDOM

Extensive studies and reviews of copyright law, including aspects of such law in the context of online use of protected material have been carried out in the UK: these include the Gowers Review on Intellectual Property, issued by the Intellectual Property Office, 2006, the Department for Business Enterprise and Regulatory Reform (BERR) Consultation on legislative options to address illicit peer-to-peer file sharing, July 2008, the Intellectual Property Office "Rights Agency and P2P", 2008, the BERR Interim Report "Digital Britain", January 2009 and "Copyright in the digital world: what role for a Digital Rights Agency?", March 2009. The proposals in and issues raised by these documents are under continuing study and here I would only mention

---

[28] For studies concerning the copyright problems involved, see European Commission Recommendation on collective cross-border management of copyright and related rights for legitimate online music services, 18 October 2005 and summary "Monitoring of the 2005 Music Online Recommendation", 7 February 2008; "i2010: Digital Libraries High Level Expert Group-Copyright Sub-Group Final Report on Digital Preservation, Orphan Works, and Out-of-Print Works" 4 July 2008, and related documents. For listing covering material issued 2004–2008, see WCL para.26.07.

the following passages with which, with respect, I entirely concur, and which are in line with the proposals which I make in this address:

> … In the new digital world, the ability to share content legally becomes ever more important and necessary. Traditional mechanisms to identify rights-holders and acquire legal consent to share often need radical updating to meet the near-instant demands of this new world. There is a clear and unambiguous distinction between the legal and illegal sharing of content which we must urgently address. But we need to do so in a way that recognises that when there is very widespread behaviour and social acceptability of such behaviour that is at odds with the rules, then the rules, the business models that the rules have underpinned and the behaviour itself may all need to change … Our aim, in the rapidly changing digital world is a framework that is effective and enforceable, both nationally and across borders. But it must be one which also allows for innovation in platforms, devices and applications that make use of content and that respond to consumers' desire to access content in the time and manner they want, allowing them to use it how they want, and at a price they are willing to pay." (BERR Interim Report "Digital Britain", January 2009, published by The Stationery Office, para.3.2)

The proposal for a UK Digital Rights Agency is not in conflict with the global licensing agency proposal made in F. Solution 6 below: rather it could complement the operation of the global entity. See also the proposals in the Digital Economy Bill (first reading in the House of Lords, 19 November 2009, *cf.* C4.(c) above.

3   ACAP

Automated Content Access Protocol (ACAP) is "a non-proprietary protocol, developed by publishers, which is designed to ensure that anyone who publishes content on the web, and who wants to ensure that web crawlers used by search engines, and other online aggregators, can read and understand the terms and conditions of access and re-use [is able to do so]".[29] Undoubtedly this and similar systems may contribute to means of control of the use of protected material on the internet, within the context of a global licensing system as proposed hereunder: see F. Solution 6.

---

[29] Quotation from ACAP website at www.the-acap.org, where details of the ACAP system and procedures are available.

F   Possible solutions

By way of example I take peer-to-peer file sharing and social networking sites and consider six possible solutions (there may be others):

Solution 1: *Continue as at present*

(a)   Regarding peer-to-peer file sharing: two streams of activities by rightowners as regards unauthorised peer-to-peer file sharing are at present discernable: (i) licensing of download of specific items from specific sites (e.g. iTunes), and (ii) bringing of legal actions against unauthorised file-sharers, hosts and downloaders.

As to licensed sites it is understood that at present these sites only offer download of protected material on a territorial basis. Since present solutions do not legitimate global download, the internet's fundamental feature of global access is therefore not satisfied, such satisfaction being, it is submitted, essential for a solution that will be in the interests both of rightholders and the public.

As to the bringing of actions for unauthorised file sharing activities, this is in the global sense ineffective, as witness the fact that, with new technology such as BitTorrent, the problem grows, and does not decrease. Furthermore, legal actions against non-commercial users can create a bad press for copyright, one that prejudices the continuance of copyright as we know it. In this connection, it must be doubted whether the "graduated response" system of enforcement in the French HADOPI legislation (2009), also being considered in the UK, will effectively eradicate unauthorised file sharing. Cf., in the UK, a somewhat similar procedure instituted by the Digital Economy Act 2010.

(b)   Regarding social networking sites: As above indicated, it appears that the present systems of individual and collective licensing do not give comprehensive global cover, either because, in the case of individual licensing they relate to limited repertoires, or, in the case of collective licensing because they are territorially limited, or limited as to the rights covered by the licence.

Solution 2: *Introduce limitations and exceptions*. Limitations and exceptions are the minefield of copyright. Try to extend limitations regarding private copying, and the French will rise in arms and cry "There is no right of private copying", as the *Cour de Cassation* has declared.[30] Try to cut down limitations and exceptions, by arguing, for

---

[30] *Perquin et al v Films Alain Sarde* ("*Mulholland Drive*" case) TGI Paris, 3 Ch. April 30, 2004, (2004) 202 R.I.D.A. 323; CA Paris, 4 Ch B. April 22, 2005, (2006) 207 R.I.D.A. 374, (2006) 37 I.I.C. 112; Cass civ. February 28, (2006) 209 R.I.D.A. 323, (2006) 37 I.I.C. 760; CA Paris, April 4, 2007, (2007) 213 R.I.D.A. 379 (sub nom. *Association UFC Que Choisir v Société Universal Pictures Video France*).

instance, that the US fair use system contravenes the three step test[31], and the United States will storm out of the room. Far better to leave the international rules basically as they are, and work within them.

Solution 3: *Require sites which host protected material to monitor and filter out infringing material.* Even if it were possible to introduce effective monitoring and filtering (which is contested), such actions will not, by themselves, regulate unauthorised file sharing, since in the now prevalent BitTorrent system there is no hosting website, no central list of copyable files – but everyone shares by individual exchange of constituent parts brought together through a myriad of transmissions of file segments to the accessor at the end of the process. By all means, as seems to be the present accent in legislative proposals, introduce provisions legitimating ISP activity, safe harbours and so forth – but without the other side of the medal, namely licensing, the eradication of unauthorised material from the internet gives only half the requisite.

Solution 4: *Abolish the right to control making available on the internet.* To achieve abolition of the right, the WIPO Treaties would have to be amended to delete basic provisions of the instruments (in WCT Article 8, in WPPT Articles 10, 14), national laws granting the right would have to be repealed as would the relevant provisions of the EC Information Society Directive (Article 3). Solution 4 is not a serious contestant, unless rightowners fail to provide practical licensing systems: in the case of such failure, the maintenance of the right itself would indeed be under threat.

Solution 5: *Introduce a levy system.* It may be that a levy system can provide part, but possibly not the whole of the solution. First and foremost we have to consider its international acceptability, and the modalities of its application.

Solution 6: *Provide global licensing of protected material.* I believe that it is axiomatic that the solution to the internet challenges, including unauthorised file sharing and the making available online of user-generated content on social networking sites, requires a global solution, not one based on territorial division of rights. The advent of the internet requires changes in copyright licensing procedures to reflect the borderless nature of internet transmission, which permits instantaneous access to online material throughout the world.

The right to make available online needs to be regarded as universal in character, with corresponding licensing facilities covering both reproduction and communication to the public.[32]

---

[31] *Cf.* Berne Convention, Art.9(2); TRIPS Agreement, Art.13; WIPO Copyright Treaty, Art.10(1); WIPO Performances and Phonograms Treaty, Art.16(2).

[32] *Cf.* the French Case *Perathoner and others v Paumier and others,* TGI Paris, 3 Ch, May 23, 2001: (2002) 191 R.I.D.A. 308; [2003] E.C.D.R. 76 (unauthorised digital communication on the internet infringes both reproduction and public communication rights).

This why I have proposed the GILA System for global internet licensing under which rightowners or their representatives will entrust (either directly or through a collecting society) a central body with the global administration of their rights in the context of internet use (existing practices regarding broadcasts, hard copy publication etc being maintained).[33]

In brief, the GILA licence covering global use of protected material on the internet would, with "tailor made" conditions, be available to file-sharers, hosts, storers, social networking site operators and uploaders, broadcasters, the press, and others wishing to upload to or use protected material on the internet.

The advantages of this system are:

1   No need for legislation introducing limitations or exceptions.

2   Legitimated use of protected material, meeting the concerns expressed by Professor Lessig and others concerning "criminalisation" resulting from unauthorised file sharing, and avoidance of disputes concerning infringing uploads on social networking sites.[34]

In my submission, global and territorial licensing of protected material should be on the basis of freedom of choice for rightholders. Thus a rightholder, or group of rightholders, may wish to license the material themselves, directly to hosts, networking sites etc. However, I believe there can be disadvantages for rightholders in so proceeding, since separate contracts need to be made with a multiplicity of uploaders, hosts or accessors, and users can be reluctant to seek licences from many sources. To an extent, the same applies where collecting societies can only give licences covering certain territories.

It would of course be open to individual rightowners or collecting societies to remain outside GILA. However, it is thought that it will be attractive for the licence seeker, and thus of advantage to the rightowner, to have a central point to which to refer for the necessary licence.

So, it may be asked, if the rights to make protected material available online are, at any rate to a certain extent, to be put in the hands of a central licensing agency, *quis custodi et ipsos custodes*? Who will control the controllers? Such control is in my view essential so that all concerned can be assured of fair and practical licence terms and that rights are not abused. Possibly one could consider that in case of dispute between the global licensing body and the applicant for a licence, the matter could be settled by the WIPO Arbitration and Mediation Centre, which already has extensive experience in the

---

[33] See Annex II for summary of the system, and for a fuller description see J.A.L. Sterling, "The GILA System for Global internet Licensing" online at www.qmipri.org/research.html.

[34] See C. above.

internet area through its domain names Dispute Resolution Service, and in any event, I believe that WIPO must be involved in seeking solutions of the issues to which I have referred in the course of this address.

Collecting societies should, in my respectful view, establish a global licensing system on the lines described, or find some other practical and comprehensive method of dealing with the global use of protected material on the internet. Failure to do so will threaten the preservation of copyright in the new era, and success should guarantee the maintenance of copyright in the ever-increasing domain of borderless communication.

We must not be like the Venetian Professors who met every Saturday evening to discuss how to prevent the flooding of Venice by the rising waters, and one evening looked down and saw that the waters had reached their knees.

My plea is that all those who are concerned with copyright as rightowners, disseminators or users should agree on the best way forward.

III THE WAY FORWARD AND CONCLUSION

A   *The way forward*

1   COMBINED APPROACH: RIGHTOWNERS, DISSEMINATORS, USERS

My view of the future of copyright is not confined to the challenges of the internet, but embraces the whole area of the issues in this field. A solution to the problems posed in the analogue and digital areas requires, in my view, collaboration of rightowners and their representatives, disseminators and users. I propose the formation of a universal copyright research alliance to achieve this. The alliance should bring together rightowners, and rightowners' representatives, disseminators (including broadcasters, internet service providers and search engine service administrators) and representatives of users of protected material.

The object of the alliance would be to undertake research in copyright and related rights issues, to seek consensus on such issues, wherever possible, and to make representations and reports to Governments and relevant national, regional and international organisations, academic and professional institutions, and others, concerning solutions to issues which have been the subject of research by the alliance, including but not limited to those raised by national and transborder communication of protected material. Participation in the alliance would be open to the relevant representatives of the respective sections, and their statements and views on the issues under study would be available for public comment. A convenor would be necessary to initiate the project, and the alliance would operate through internet communication.

2   FIXING THE GOALS

The goals to be achieved should in my submission provide solutions for the issues which I have described and, in regard to the specific problems raised by the internet, should include

(a)   acceptance by rightowners of the principle that the internet making-available right should as far as possible be treated as territorially indivisible and should be mandated accordingly;

(b)   establishment of a central licensing agency empowered to license on a global scale the use on the internet of all material protected by copyright and related rights;

(c)   within the ambit of global licensing of protected material for use on the internet, provision of conditions permitting copying and transformative use by individuals within the strictly private sphere, with necessity for the relevant licence for file sharing or any further transmission of any protected material whether transformed or untransformed.

In general, a major goal should be the education of the public (including students at the primary, secondary and tertiary levels) concerning the principles of, and practical information concerning the operation of, copyright and related rights.

3   PLANNING

Those interested in the maintenance and effective recognition of copyright should in my view now as a matter of urgency set about planning the achievements of the goals mentioned above. Whether this is done through the abovementioned alliance or otherwise is for those concerned to decide.

B   *Conclusion*

Summing up, I would say that the issues facing copyright generally are, on the one hand, those which might be put in the "traditional" field – issues like the definition of joint authorship, protection of audiovisual performers and broadcasters etc. Of these issues, I believe one of the most difficult is that of orphan works, since the solution will require internationally agreed definitions and procedures to be fully effective. However, the demand of satisfying the needs of the information society will, I am confident, lead to solutions.

On the other hand, the technological issues present a much greater challenge: the challenge is not so much, I believe, as regards enforcement – the collaboration of ISPs and technological tracing measures should ensure that. The negative aspect of enforcement is that it achieves no benefits for rightowners, or for the economy, if it is not matched with effective licensing procedures.

This is why I believe that, in a sense, the future capacity of copyright, as an effective legal discipline, to ensure recognition of copyright and related rights, lies not so much in the hands of the legislators, but, as abovementioned, in collaboration between rightowners and their representatives, disseminators and users. The creation of a global system of internet licensing should, where operating in conjunction with other licensing procedures, ensure the continuance of copyright and related rights and the benefits they bring to rightowners and the public alike.

Thus we may say that the ball is in the court of the collecting societies and disseminators to participate in the collaboration I have suggested. I plead with them to get together, and save copyright from being strangled in the tentacles of technology, or submerged in uncontrolled piracy, to their detriment, and the detriment of the public. Nature (and law) abhors a vacuum, and a present vacuum in copyright is the absence of global internet licensing. I hope that rightowners and collecting societies, in collaboration with disseminators, will fill that vacuum.

In the old era, the approach was "Give the author exclusive rights and let the legislator set the exceptions". In the new era the approach should, I submit, be "Give the author exclusive rights and offer the rightowner the possibility of effective exercise of those rights by accepting fair and practical terms applicable to the use of protected material in the modern communication environment". The alternative of uncompromising demand of the exercise of the exclusive right in the internet context will, in my view, result in the continuance and increase of unauthorised use, and, in the final scenario, threaten abolition of the right itself.

At the outset of the address I promised not to lapse into anecdotes. I do want to mention, however, that at the conclusion of the WIPO Diplomatic Conference in 1996, at which the WIPO Treaties on copyright and related rights were adopted, Dr. Arpad Bogsch (Director of WIPO) and I greeted each other, for the last time, had we but known it. "Sterling", he said "these Treaties are only a step in the history of copyright. You and I will disappear, but copyright will continue." Well, Dr Bogsch was always right, so that gives us confidence.

Finally: in Tennyson's great poem *Ulysses*, the old warrior looks back on his life and adventures, and he does not wish to remain in the past, but, in seeking the new, "to strive, to seek, to find and not to yield": these words may, I suggest, provide the fitting motto for the copyright lawyer in the 21st Century.

ANNEX I

Current issues in international, regional and national copyright

(The listing does not purport to be comprehensive.)

SECTION 1: GENERAL ISSUES

(1)   Diversities in national systems

(2)   Diversities in international systems

(3)   Diversities in regional systems

(4)   Private international law

(5)   Balancing the interests of rightowners and the public

(6)   Discriminatory protection

(7)   Developing countries

(8)   Use of protected material in Space

SECTION 2: PARTICULAR ISSUES (OTHER THAN THOSE CONCERNING DIGITIAL TECHNOLOGY AND THE INTERNET)

(1)   Definition and term of protection of works of joint authorship

(2)   Definition of place of broadcast

(3)   Authorship of cinematographic works

(4)   Ownership of rights in employees' works

(5)   Scope and content of moral rights

(6)   Protection of databases

(7)   Protection of audiovisual performances

(8)   Protection of broadcasts

(9)   Protection of traditional works

(10)   Performers' and record producers' terms of protection

(11)   Transformative use

(12)   Rights management and licensing

(13)   Orphan works and other orphan material

(14)   Decoder cards

SECTION 3: ISSUES CONCERNING DIGITAL TECHNOLOGY AND THE INTERNET

(1)   Challenges to traditional concepts

(2)   Challenges to definition and application of rights

(3)   Challenges to exercise of rights

(4)   Challenges to enforcement of rights

(5)   Peer-to-peer file sharing

(6)   User-generated content

(7)   Content aggregation

(8)   Virtual worlds

(9)   Online libraries

(10)   Liability of internet service providers

(11)   Format shifting

(12)   Technological protection measures

(13)   Cloud computing

ANNEX II

Global internet Licensing: legitimating file sharing and social networking: proposal for a global system

Part I: General

1   Introductory

Administration of licences for the reproduction, communication to the public, and distribution, of copies of protected material (including authors' works, performances, sound and film recordings and broadcasts) is, in general, conducted on a national basis, with reciprocal agreements between administering societies. However, online communication is basically global, and a general licensing system should be available which enables website operators, and others, to obtain globally effective licensing for the online communication of protected material.

2   Key issue

The challenge is to establish a general licensing system which enables prospective users to obtain permissions covering the online availability of protected material throughout the world, such system to be structured so as to afford, on the one hand, a practical and effective means of recognising rights in protected material, and on the other hand giving the public an effective means of prompt obtaining of the necessary licences on reasonable terms. The key issue is how to achieve this in a way that will provide legitimation for all forms of use of protected material on the internet, including file-sharing and social networking.

3.   Resolution

A central licensing agency should be established to provide global licensing of online use of protected material.

4   Proposal

It is proposed that collecting societies establish a central licensing agency (GILA) empowered to issue global internet licences for the uploading and transmission of protected material throughout the world. For description of the proposed system see Part II below.

Part II: The GILA System for Global internet Licensing: summary

A   Main features of the system

1   Establishment of a central internet licensing agency by existing collecting societies, the agency to administer the licensing of use of protected material

on demand on the internet ("the internet right"), without territorial restriction.

2   The structure of the system: the rightowner or rightowner's representative globally mandates a collecting society (which then accordingly mandates GILA) or GILA directly with the administration of the internet right for the material concerned.

3   Material mandated to GILA forms part of the GILA repertoire. Every item in the GILA repertoire has a GILA Identification Number (GIN), permitting administration of rights in, and tracing of online use of, protected material.

4   The GILA home site contains details of all items of the GILA repertoire, and of the various categories of available licence.

5   The prospective user (including file sharers and user-generated content uploaders) applies online for the required licence. If a global licence is required, this is issued by GILA. If a territorial licence is required, the applicant is referred to the relevant rightowner or rightowner's representative or collecting society, where this information is available to GILA.

6   Royalties paid to GILA are distributed to the rightowner, rightowner's representative, or collecting society concerned.

7   Structure, administrative procedures and licence conditions conform to competition rules.

B   The licence system in practice

Licences regarding hosting, file storage, file sharing, and social networking involving sound recordings or films, are taken as examples.

1   Website operator, storer, social networking site operator (e.g. YouTube) and internet connection suppliers (ISPs) apply to GILA for a GILA internet Licence and are issued with the appropriate licence, with conditions, including payment terms where applicable.

2   An internet user wishing to share files or upload items to a social networking site applies for a GILA File Sharer or File Uploader Licence to cover specific recordings. The licence is issued with conditions, including payment terms where applicable. The File Uploader Licence may be issued through the social networking site operator.

ANNEX III

Australian Copyright Act 1968: Orphan works and other orphan material: a legislative proposal

Part I: General

1 Introductory

The modern era demands effective and practical means for obtaining licences for the use of all legitimately available protected material (including authors' works, performances, sound and film recordings and broadcasts). However, the owners of the rights in protected material may be unknown or untraceable (such material constituting "orphan material").

In the Copyright Act 1968, there are a number of provisions on limitations and exceptions to copyright law, but these provisions do not cover all possible cases where use is intended to be made of orphan material.

2 Key issue

The key issue is how to achieve the establishment of the conditions of legitimate use of all categories of orphan material from the inception of such use.

3 Resolution of the key issue

Legitimation of online and offline use of orphan material should, it is submitted, be effected by legislative provisions giving the necessary coverage for intended use. It is submitted that eight essential conditions need to be fulfilled in order to provide effective and comprehensive licensing of use of orphan material, namely:

Condition 1: Legislative solution

Condition 2: Conformity to existing legislative structure

Condition 3: Conformity to international and regional instruments

Condition 4: Recognition of economic and moral rights

Condition 5: Provision of remuneration

Condition 6: Comprehensive coverage of rights

Condition 7: Operational practicability

Condition 8: Control of licence terms

In practical terms, two cases need to be distinguished: (1) cases where there is a collecting society which administers the right in respect of which permission is needed for the use of orphan material, and (2) cases where there is no collecting society administering the right concerned.

Existing national systems regarding licensing of use of orphan material include (1) the Scandinavian Extended Collective Licensing (ECL) system, under which national legislation permits accredited collecting societies to license use of non-members' works on approved terms, (2) the Canadian Tribunal application system (Canadian Copyright Act, section 77), and (3) the compulsory licence system (covering published works) under article 67 of the Japanese Copyright Law.[1] The proposal here made provides comprehensive coverage of both cases outlined above and combines the features of the Scandinavian and Canadian systems to provide as rapid and comprehensive means as possible for the licensing of the use of orphan material.[2]

4   Proposal

The national copyright law should provide that a collecting society managing the relevant right may license, under defined terms, the use of orphan material where the relevant owner is (following reasonable enquiry) unknown or untraceable. If no collecting society administers the right involved, the prospective user should be able to obtain the necessary licence through application to the respective judicial entity (e.g. Copyright Tribunal).

---

[1] For general summary of the problems involved in licensing of orphan material and of the Scandinavian and Canadian systems, see J.A.L. Sterling *World Copyright Law* (3rd ed., Sweet & Maxwell, 2008 paras 12.24, 12.32–12.37. For detailed description of the systems of Scandinavia, Canada and Japan, and of proposals considered in Australia and elsewhere, with comprehensive analysis of the issues involved, see Ian MacDonald "Some thoughts on orphan works", 24/3 *Copyright Reporter* 152 (October 2006), also available online. See also M. Rimmer "Finders keepers: copyright law and orphan works" (online at
www.digital.org.au/alcc/slides/OrphanworksMRimmer.ppt). For details of US proposals see the US Copyright Office Register's Report on Orphan Works, January 2006, at www.copyright.gov/orphan. The US proposals submitted to Congress (lapsed Bills S2913, HR5889) under which claims of persons suing for unauthorised use of orphan material would be subject to limited damages, did not, it is submitted, provide solutions comprehensively recognising the interests of the rightowners and users, since remedies under these proposals were limited by statute in advance, and on initial use the user would be an infringer. No statutory system for dealing with the licensing of orphan material has yet been adopted in the UK: see British Copyright Council proposal at
www.britishcopyright.org/pdfs/policy/2009_001.pdf, and note also the lapsed proposal in clause 43 of the Digital Economy Bill, see main text, II D 4 above.

[2] For a parallel proposal in the context of UK law, with detailed description of the operation of the system, see J.A.L. Sterling "Orphan works and other orphan material: proposed amendments to UK Copyright, Designs and Patents Act 1988: the "legitimated use" system" online at
www.qmipri.org/research.html.

The amendments to the Copyright Act 1968 as proposed in Part II below concern a system for the legitimation of the use of orphan material, based on (a) administration through a collecting society, or (b) where no relevant collecting society exists, consent obtained through application to the Copyright Tribunal. It is submitted that this proposal conforms to the eight essential conditions described under **3** above, and as regards Condition 2, the Copyright Act 1968 provides the legislative structure for administration of orphan material by collecting societies (in defined cases and under approved rules). It is emphasised that the proposals are for a basis of discussion, and there may be other forms of amendment to achieve application of these two principles.

Part II: Proposed amendments concerning orphan works and other orphan material

Insert new provisions in the Copyright Act 1968 as follows:

("Protected material" means any subject matter or performance in which copyright or performer's right of action exists by virtue of the Act, "declared collecting society" means a body declared to be a collecting society in accordance with the provisions of the Act, and "Copyright Tribunal" means the Copyright Tribunal of Australia.)

Provision 1	Provision that where an owner of a right granted by the Act has not transferred management of such right to a declared collecting society and where the identity or whereabouts of such owner cannot be ascertained by reasonable enquiry, a declared collecting society which manages rights of the same category shall be deemed to be mandated to manage such right in accordance with a licence scheme approved by the Copyright Tribunal, and a use covered by a licence validly issued by such society under such scheme as so mandated shall be treated as licensed by such owner.
Provision 2	Provision (a) that the Copyright Tribunal may, on the application of a person wishing to use an item of protected material, give consent to such use in a case where the identity or whereabouts of the person entitled to exercise the right to authorise such use cannot be ascertained by reasonable enquiry, and where no declared collecting society is mandated in accordance with Provision 1, in respect of management of rights of the category concerned, and (b) that such consent has effect as consent of the person entitled to exercise the right to authorise the use concerned.

Provision 3	Provision that no civil or criminal liability under the Act will result from issuing of, or acting in accordance with, a licence granted under Provision 1, or acting in accordance with consent given under Provision 2.
Provision 4	Provision that a rightowner to whom Provisions 1 or 2 apply, has the same rights and obligations, resulting from any relevant agreement between the licensee and the licensing body, as have rightowners who have transferred management of their rights to that licensing body.
Additional Provisions	Provisions concerning relevant functions and powers of the Copyright Tribunal, conditions to apply to licence schemes, claims by revenant rightowners and period within which such claims must be made etc.

ANNEX IV

Asian Pacific Copyright Association (APCA)
Proposal for formation
Part I: Introductory

The Pacific Region as a whole may be seen as composed of the regions to the west and east respectively of the International Date Line (IDL). The region to the west of the IDL may be called the Asian Pacific Region, including Russia, China, Korean peninsula, Taiwan, Vietnam, Cambodia, Thailand, Malaysia, Singapore, Indonesia, Brunei, East Timor, Japan, Philippines, Australia, New Zealand, Papua New Guinea and Pacific island States, e.g. Fiji. The region to the east of the IDL may be called the Eastern Pacific Region, including Canada, United States, Mexico, Panama, Colombia, Ecuador, Peru, Chile, the Hawaiian and Marshall Islands, Samoa etc.

All countries in the Pacific Region have copyright laws, and it is thus possible to envisage an overall association of countries of the Asian Pacific Region on the one hand and of the Eastern Pacific Region and the other, both coming together in a Pacific Region Copyright Association. That, however, is a long term prospect and irrespective of whether it is eventually achieved it is submitted that, as far as the Asian Pacific Region is concerned, the formation of the Asian Pacific Copyright Association (APCA), to provide a forum for the discussion and seeking of consensus on copyright issues in the region, will be of immediate value to the peoples of the whole area, who at present speak on copyright with different voices, often unaware of the views and needs of other countries in the region.

From the international point of view, it is notable that the European Union consists of 27 countries with facilities to formulate common copyright policies throughout the Union. With EU membership including countries such as the UK, France and Germany, which have influence in the copyright area, this gives the European Union a notable strength of negotiation in putting its views on copyright at the international level. There are also the provisions regarding copyright in the North American Free Trade Agreement (NAFTA) embracing Canada, Mexico and the USA, and in South America in the Cartagena Agreement.

In the Asian Pacific Region, there is at present no regional copyright association, yet the Region includes a large percentage of the world's population, and its countries are bound by economic and other ties: they also have important cultural traditions and authors, artists and musicians of world renown. The copyright laws of the region are also of interest, representing or reflecting, as they do, the three main traditions of copyright legislation: the common law system (e.g. in Australia, Malaysia, New Zealand, Singapore), the civil law system (e.g. in Cambodia, Russia, Vietnam), and systems combining features of the common law and civil law systems, and additional features (e.g. China, Japan).

Copyright law, or laws related to copyright, protect and foster the maintenance and protection of the rights of authors and of those engaged in the performance, production and dissemination of creative works, including performers, film and record producers and broadcasters.

Because of modern means of communication, including satellite broadcasting and the internet, national copyright laws need to be assessed in the light of international and regional considerations, as well as national. In addition, the advent of the internet and the facilities it offers renders it essential to ensure that material protected by copyright is accessible by the public on fair and reasonable terms, and in accordance with systems that guarantee, on the one hand, the preservation of the interests of rightowners, and on the other, the recognition of the public interest in ready access to all available material.

It is suggested that the nations of the Asian Pacific Region should, through their respective governments, academic and professional institutions, organisations representing authors, performers, film and sound recording producers and broadcasters should, in conjunction with those representing other disseminators of protected material (including internet service providers), and with representatives of the public interest and individuals interested in the maintenance of copyright, form the Asian Pacific Copyright Association (APCA) with the objective of promoting the maintenance and development of copyright and related rights in the Region.

The Association should seek recognition by the World Intellectual Property Organisation, the World Trade Organisation, UNESCO, and other international bodies so that it can put forward the views of APCA and ensure that the needs and concerns of the people of the Asian Pacific Area in the field of copyright and related rights are taken into consideration by the international community in all discussions and international treaty negotiations concerning such rights.

It is suggested that a Planning Committee be set up to forward the implementation of this proposal, with a view to holding a foundation meeting. As a start, prospective National Groups can be formed before the foundation of the Association, and two or more such Groups could effect such foundation.

Part II: Suggested structure and procedure

The following is suggested as a basis for discussion in planning the structure and procedure of APCA.

A	General
1	Constitution and objective
2	Membership

A   General

1   Constitution and objective

An association with the objective of promoting, through legislation, dialogue and education, the maintenance and development of copyright and related rights in the Asian and Pacific Region (i.e., that region embracing the countries and territories located in or bordering on the Pacific Ocean west of the International Date Line, including Russia, China, Korean peninsula, Taiwan, Vietnam, Cambodia, Thailand, Malaysia, Singapore, Indonesia, Brunei, East Timor, Japan, Philippines, Australia, New Zealand, Papua New Guinea and Pacific island States, e.g., Fiji).

2   Membership

Membership of the Association to be open to any person or organisation located in the Asian Pacific Region, and interested in the objective of APCA. Associate membership to be open to interested persons or organisations located outside the area (e.g., in Canada, India, U.S.A.)

3   Organs and Officers

     a   General Assembly of members of the Association.

     b   Officers: President, Vice Presidents, Secretary General: elected by General Assembly.

     c   National Groups consisting of members of the Association located in the respective countries.

	d	Regional Council consisting of the Officers and of delegates of the National Groups, one delegate per country.
	e	Executive Committee consisting of the Officers and of persons appointed by the Regional Council.
	f	Secretariat of the Association, headed by the Secretary General.

4   *Meetings*

Meetings of the General Assembly, the Regional Council, the Executive Committee and National Groups to take place in accordance with the respective rules of those bodies.

5   *Finance*

The funds of the Association to be constituted by membership fees, donations and subventions, and administered by the Secretariat.

6   *Areas of activity*

The areas of activity of the Association to include the following items, as determined and developed by the organs of the Association:

	a	APCA website to include Association documents and material on current issues, national, regional and international developments, etc.
	b	Establishment of common positions of countries of the Asian Pacific Region regarding representations on specific issues in regional and international conferences and initiatives on copyright and related rights.
	c	Research in copyright and related rights laws of the Asian Pacific Region including preparation of "Asian Pacific Copyright Guide" and other material on copyright and related rights.
	d	Participation in international discussions and negotiations concerning copyright and related rights.

B   Planning Committee

A Planning Committee to be established to initiate the steps necessary for carrying forward the proposal for formation of the Association, and the ways and means to accomplish this.

C   Foundation and Constitution

Two or more prospective National Groups to found and adopt the Constitution of the Association.

18

DINNER ADDRESS

Senator Kate Lundy[1]

I'd like to begin tonight by illustrating the beauty of open access to intellectual property. I am going to borrow a thought from Lawrence Lessig, who in turn is borrowing from someone else. I think it contextualises my comments.

Lawrence wrote this of the US Republican Party a couple of years ago:

> Increasingly, the party – as conservative columnist Bruce Bartlett says of George Bush in his book, Impostor – is "incapable of telling the difference between being pro-business and being for the free market. It favors specific competitors rather than favoring competition. What's good for the US is more and more often translated into what's good for powerful friends. Or so policy in America could be summarized today. Such pro-business and anti-efficiency policies will continue to prevail until someone in our political system begins to articulate principles on the other side. And given the way money talks in capitals around the country, this is a stance only those out of power can afford to take.

Now, me being me.

All political parties have difficulty lifting their thinking above the interests of entrenched incumbents within markets. More so now than probably at any time since the Great Depression.

The rise of organised corporate interest groups has created a tremendous imbalance in the volume of the voices in debates around public policy. That is not a mischief on the

---

[1] Senator Kate Lundy has been the Labor Party member for the Australian Capital Territory in the Commonwealth Parliament since 1996 and in 2009 was a Labor Party backbencher. In 2010, she became Parliamentary Secretary to the Prime Minister and Parliamentary Secretary for Immigration and Citizenship. She has a special interest in communications and intellectual property issues and is a long-term member of the Senate Environment, Communications and the Arts Committee. This speech and further information is at www.katelundy.com.au/2009/05/28/copyright-future-dinner-address/. She gave this speech on the evening of 27 May 2009.

part of the voices that are organised. They are just doing their job. But it does create a problem for policy makers.

When there is a considerable imbalance in power and influence, never underestimate how self-fulfilling it can become.

This is a potentially controversial thing to say, but this has been no more evident than in the debate about around intellectual property, and especially copyright. I don't want to give the impression that the problem is a party-political one. But it is a simple fact that those representing the case for the expansive and expanding use of copyright to protect their interests have all but drowned out alternative voices representing the broad public interest.

For example, routinely, pejorative terms like "pirate" have entered the vernacular to describe the people breaching what copyright owners claim to be their rights, even if no crime has been committed. This is despite the detailed and ongoing legal challenges from both sides about personal use. This is a reflection of the power and influence of these incumbent interests.

The observation I make is that the debate is decidedly one-sided. Perhaps more so here in Australia that the US, where there at least appears to be a more sophisticated debate around the purpose and merit of IP and copyright law in relation to rights protection in the digital age.

This concerns me greatly and if I can make a difference, I want it to be ensuring that the public debate is balanced and well-informed. I want to see that both sides in the copyright and IP debates have a voice, are heard in Parliament and their respective positions are equally understood and considered when decisions are made.

The first step to rectifying the imbalance in the public debate is to ensure that policy decision making is open: open to scrutiny and open to participation. It requires, in fact, a new openness in our democracy. The Labor Government is acting to restore confidence in democratic processes by opening up the operation of government and public sector information and removing the frustrating 'unknowns' of political and bureaucratic decision making that lead to cynicism and apathy.

It is a chance – maybe the last this generation will have — to give form and substance to the concept of, and I quote another famous American: *"Government of the people, by the people, for the people..., (shall not perish from the earth)"*. (Abraham Lincoln)

A quick read of a my colleague Senator Faulkner's Speech at the launch of "Information Awareness Month" will inspire you, as a dramatic change has occurred in the attitude of the Australian federal Government since the last election when Labor came to office.

The program for building the national broadband network provides the time frame and platform to reset the operating system of government. It will close the digital divide. Never has there been a greater genuine opportunity for positive and progressive change for active participation in our democratic processes.

The NBN combine with a raft of cross-portfolio initiatives to usher in a new era of greater freedom of information, earlier access to archived records, open government initiatives, more interactive citizen and business services online and the next steps in the digital deluge project, Australia is well and truly on the cusp of transformational change in how we function as a society. It's a chance to raise accountability through openness and transparency.

HOWEVER, working against a new way of making policy are the same old militating factors that in the past have inhibited participation by the broadest cross section of interests.

I have personal experience in just how pervasive the influence of sectional interest groups operating in a closed decision-making environment can be.

No-one, not even legislators are safe! While the Australian democratic system is free of some of the blatant corporate donation culture that is rife the US, power and influence is still very real and operates in a range of ways.

Not least of these is in the negotiation of trade agreements, where deals can be negotiated in virtual secrecy, and usually only legislated with the openness afforded by institutional parliamentary debate once signed.

I want to share with you some observations in relation to the Australia-US Free trade agreement.

In the lead up to the 2004 election, the Howard Government was in the throes of the final negotiations of the AUSFTA. The Labor Opposition was under the pump to declare a position on the proposed agreement. To help inform its view, Labor instigated a Senate Inquiry into the proposed agreement.

The Senate Select Committee embarked upon a detailed exploration of the issues, including the ramifications on IP law in Australia, including patent law and copyright.

It was clear from what the US was asking for that they were using FTA's to propagate the recent changes in IP law, such as the so-called "Mickey Mouse" amendments, to extend copyright protection and the provisions of the DMCA to digital content, to other nations: particularly those where the content owners had a large and specific interest in the market.

While I was not a sitting member on that particular Senate Committee, I took a deep interest in my capacity as shadow minister for information Technology and the Arts. It was, after all, the IP, copyright and local content provisions that directly impacted on these sectors in Australia, and their ability to innovate and grow into the future.

It seemed these provisions were unchallenged by the then Howard Government and they ended up being the subject of fierce contention at the Senate Inquiry. The voices of both sides of the debate were heard thanks to the Senate committee process.

It is a credit to many in this room that the implications of co-opting US-style IP and copyright law received a comprehensive airing. The difference between the interests of the market, in this case a thriving innovative Australian ICT sector, and business, being the incumbent corporate interests, WERE clearly articulated.

The 20-or so specific recommendations arising out of Chapter 3, which was devoted to intellectual property in the Senate Report, were prefaced by the following comment:

A major concern of Labor Senators is that Australia entered into the IP obligations of the Agreement in a manner that cut across established processes for copyright law reform and which did not appear to be part of a strategic vision of intellectual property.

Labor Senators were also concerned that it was difficult to get a comprehensive explanation from Government officials on many of the implications of the FTA on Australia's IP regime

Note that this second point starkly illustrates the lack of openness!

The big questions were these: were the reservations and concerns about the IP implications enough to have the ALP opposition either oppose or force modifications of the Proposed FTA? And, if so, would the Senate support the approach adopted by the ALP?

For my part, I spoke out about the innovation-inhibiting effects signing up to the AUSFTA would have on local content production, the local ICT industry, open source and other software development, scientific endeavour and related innovation and ICT procurement.

These comments received widespread coverage and a furore erupted in the media that gave a voice to the many citizens who had harboured concerns, but had not found a way to express them: and there was renewed interest in groups who had articulated concerns. Airing their views meant a spotlight fell on the intellectual property aspects of AUSFTA.

I can tell you now that the media interest in my comments did not endear me to the Leader. The AUSFTA had powerful support, on top of his concerns about being perceived as anti-American. But once the door was open to other voices, the balance of the debate shifted and the concerns with the agreement were seen as legitimate.

After lots of political machinations, the end result was that federal Labor successfully moved a series of amendments that modified at least some of the worst aspects of the Agreement.

I tell this story because it's an issue I know you are familiar with, but also as an example of the challenges in accessing the information necessary to make informed policy decision as well as showing our democracy in action.

In my view it was the combination of the institutional scrutiny provided by the Senate Committee process, AND the unleashing of community opinion through the media once facts were at hand that led to the changes in the Agreement.

It is a great example of how greater openness and improved participation becomes mutually supportive of alternative views. In this case, they were expressed first inside a small, informed community, then in the Parliament, and then in the broader community.

Ladies and Gentlemen: we need each other. And that is how the system of democracy is supposed to work.

In my opening comments I reflected on the opportunity the NBN creates to close the digital divide and become the enabling network on which to reset our democracy in firm principles of open government and freedom of information.

It is with these aspirations in mind that we need to work together to make sure the public debate that informs this transformation is balanced, inclusive and informed. This is the approach espoused by the Rudd Labor Government before, during and after the 2007 election.

The value of openness, sharing ideas, collaboration and collective innovation need to be re-inserted into the debates about IP. There is an opportunity for the Government to lead the way with public sector information and the signs are good. We all have a role to play to ensure this direction is supported and encouraged through widespread discussion and debate.

The tension between open information and copyrighted material will once again be heightened as the public debate proceeds about the merits of openness for public sector information.

What needs to change is the voices on the alternative side of the copyright debate need to be loud enough, co-ordinated enough, supported enough and endorsed enough to balance the currently one-sided domination of the debate.

I commend those initiating and involved in the idea of bringing together a group concerned about these issues. I understand the aims and objectives to include:

"Raising the standard of awareness of the full range of copyright issues affecting the various stakeholder and constituent groups, such that robust discussions on relative priorities and aims could be held across a wide range of organisations."

This development is essential and I look forward to supporting your application: well-organised and well-resourced representation of the public interest is long overdue.

It is also essential because the transformational effect of open and accessible public sector information will inform the benefits of open access and creative commons information across the private sector as well. We can lead by example.

Let's make the most of the opportunity it represents!

Thank you for listening.

19

COPYRIGHT FREEDOM: CONCLUDING REMARKS

Professor Brian Fitzgerald

In organising this conference it was my aim to put focus on the way in which copyright law might be used to incentivize both creativity and dissemination. In itself that is not such a revolutionary ideal. Creativity and dissemination have been the key components of copyright law since the Statute of Anne was first enacted in 1710.[1]

Yet copyright law and the freedom to disseminate have become enemies, if not in the last one hundred years certainly in the last ten years. The notion of copyright ownership as a sovereign right to control dissemination has become a core part of copyright law subject to limitations, exceptions and statutory licences. But in a world where the networked environment is throwing up endless dissemination possibilities many of which are beyond the reach and comprehension of the copyright owner the sovereign right to control seems out of place and potentially damaging at a social and economic level.

One starts to wonder whether we can decouple creation/production from dissemination/use and imagine a digital utopia in which anyone can lawfully (re)distribute anything on the proviso that adequate revenues flow back to the appropriate parties. The Google Book Settlement for all its flaws is leading us in this direction.[2] Google in setting up the project challenged the control of the copyright owners in the name of more widespread dissemination and ultimately the settlement provides for a flow of revenue, a fair share of which did not exist before.

While the Google Book Settlement is evidence that new possibilities are not too far off, the pace at which the established industries have embraced the new technologies is slow and unacceptable. In this regard it is worth noting a recent file-sharing case in the US in

---

[1] The Statute of Anne (1710) was stated to be an "Act for the encouragement of learning ..." See also *Harper & Row, Publishers, Incorporated, et al. v. Nation Enterprises, et al.* 471 US 539 (1985).

[2] See generally: "Google Book Search Settlement Agreement" in *Wikipedia* en.wikipedia.org/wiki/Google_Book_Search_Settlement_Agreement.

which Harvard law professor Charles Nesson somewhat controversially sought to argue the fair use defence.

While rejecting the notion that peer to peer file sharing was covered by fair use, Judge Nancy Gertener, presiding in the case, explained that, *"a defendant who used the new file-sharing networks in the technological interregnum before digital media could be purchased legally, but who later shifted to paid outlets, might ... be able to rely on the defense."*[3] This reasoning raises some interesting questions.

To what extent are the copyright owners obligated to engage with new technologies (to exploit the affordances of Web 2.0) in going about their business? Is it fair for copyright owners to dumb down dissemination to the point of inefficiency for their own private (yet at times sub-optimal) gain? Followers of the sovereign right to control ethos will argue that the copyright owner can do what they wish – they are the ruler of their manor.

Yet, as Boyle, and others, have highlighted through analogies with environmental law,[4] our legal system no longer accepts the unfettered exercise of real property rights in the face of negative externalities. Merely owning a factory no longer suggests a sovereign right to pollute the air or the waterway. To what extent can copyright owners limit or stifle the freedom to disseminate via digital networks by refusing to engage with it?

One hope is that the next ten years will see a period of uninhibited collaboration between the key stakeholders. How can we get the publishing, recording and film industries to join with the whiz kids of the Internet era to provide an environment where creativity can be disseminated to the broadest possible audience in the most efficient and effective manner? And what role for copyright?

It is hoped that market forces will draw these key actors together, but more could be needed. International stakeholder forums (convened by WIPO or the WTO) should be considered. Another approach would be to reconsider the role copyright law can play in incentivizing dissemination. Should copyright owners be obligated to engage more with new technology and if so how could copyright law accommodate such a concept?

Nesson saw it as fitting in with the notion of an exception or a defence while others might see it as being raised in a discussion about the scope of the "exclusivity" of the

---

[3] Memo of Justice Nancy Gertner in the case: *Sony BMG Music Entertainment v Tenenbaum* (2009) U.S. Dist Lexis 112845 (7 December 2009). pacer.mad.uscourts.gov/dc/cgi-bin/recentops.pl?filename=gertner/pdf/tenenbaumfairusedec7th09finalng.pdf at [8].

[4] J. Boyle, "A Politics of Intellectual Property: Environmentalism For the Net?" (1997) 47 *Duke Law Journal* 87, www.law.duke.edu/boylesite/Intprop.htm *Cf.* M Geist, "Brazil's Approach on Anti-Circumvention: Penalties For Hindering Fair Dealing" 9 July 2010 www.michaelgeist.ca/content/view/5180/125/.

owner's right.[5] On the other hand should intermediaries be obligated to work with owners to find solutions? If necessary this could entail restructuring secondary liability rules.

In an era where information flow is seen as a key ingredient to social and economic life[6] we need to shape a copyright law that accommodates social practices and builds prosperity on the back of dissemination. Taken slightly out context the words of Brett Cottle Head of the Australian Performing Rights Authority (APRA) are apt to describe the sentiment: "It's not an issue of control or permission, it's an issue of fair payment for use."[7]

---

[5] Competition or antitrust law also has the potential to play a role here: B. Fitzgerald, *"Digital Property: The Ultimate Boundary?"*(2001) *7 Roger Williams University Law Journal* 47 eprints.qut.edu.au/7406/1/DigitalPropertyRWUJOurnalFinalFeb2002.pdf , as might taxation law.

[6] See generally K. Dopfer and J Potts, *The General Theory of Economic Evolution* (2008) Routledge UK.

[7] ABC Radio National, *Background Briefing: Internet Piracy* www.abc.net.au/rn/backgroundbriefing/stories/2009/2726710.htm .

A second order issue will be what "use" is and should be remunerable? *Cf. Review of the Intellectual Property Legislation under the Competition Principles Agreement,* AGPS, 2000 (Ergas Report) at 5: 'Balancing between incentives to invest in innovation on one hand, and for efficient diffusion of innovation on the other, is a central, and perhaps the crucial, element in the design of intellectual property laws.'; L Ray Patterson, 'Free Speech, Copyright, and Fair Use', *Vanderbilt Law Review,* Jan 1987, Vol 40 No 1.

AFTERWORD

The Hon Greg James, QC[1]

The conference at which the papers which comprise this book were delivered was convened to mark the 40th anniversary of the commencement of Australia's *Copyright Act* in 1968. As can be seen from the papers, it sought to place the issues in copyright law in both their historical and their contemporary contexts. Those issues have increasingly attracted national and international scrutiny, as was pointed out to the attendees by Senator Lundy in her speech at the conference dinner.

In his foreword, the Hon Michael Kirby surveys the current debates on copyright law and intellectual property from an international and human rights law perspective. Those debates informed not only the conference papers, but also the robust discussions. The varied papers produced for the conference reflected those debates, as well as governmental and legislative views, and also the history of the legislation in Australia and internationally. The technological revolution has allowed the global public to access information through the internet, which, particularly recently, has dramatically changed the climate in relation to copyright and intellectual property law.

Since the conference, the release by Wikileaks of documentation of a broad-ranging kind relating to the affairs of various governments has fuelled the existing global debate as to what material might be retained confidentially, for what purposes, and what material should be disseminated or published or generated, so as to serve a public interest in being informed, and in rewarding creativity and providing access to knowledge. Those considerations have to be weighed in intensely political "democracy/free-speech" dialectic.

In that context, it is not surprising that the proceedings of the conference were vigorous. The papers covered a broad diversity of topics. The attendees plainly enjoyed, indeed even immersed themselves in, the more arcane history of copyright

---

[1] The Hon Greg James, QC, was one of the youngest Queens Counsel appointed in NSW history, and a leading advocate in Australian and international courts. He was a judge of the NSW Supreme Court and a South Australian Royal Commissioner. He is President of the NSW Mental Health Review Tribunal, which conducts about 10,500 hearings annually, and one of the NSW Law Reform Commissioners. The Hon Greg James QC is Adjunct Professor at the School of Law Southern Cross University, and Visiting Professor and Chair of the Curriculum Committee at the Law School University of Western Sydney.

law, in particular in Australia, and in the more far-reaching development of international and global approaches to copyright, including the examination of different philosophical viewpoints which might underlie modern copyright and informed access, as discussed by Professor Lessig and Professor Fitzgerald.

It has become clear to those of us who have spent our lives, as Michael Kirby did, growing up without being almost symbiotically linked to computers, that our concepts both of the technology, and of the application of existing copyright law and philosophy to the dissemination of knowledge, are dramatically out of date. Those who have grown up and lived with the freedom the internet has given bring an entirely different perspective to the concepts of copyright, and to the incentive that the public interest, by recognising property in works and protecting them by copyright laws, affords to creators. The public domain and free access were matters of significance for all concerned with copyright legislation and enforcement, and hence the value of such concepts and how legislation might accommodate them were the focus of much attention.

The conference attempted to accommodate both older conservatism and legalism and more modern liberal attitudes. More modern developments as described in the paper made it plain to those of us not attuned to the freedom of dissemination now available, and not attuned to the degree of control over that freedom of dissemination that States and large corporations might wish to exercise, that we need, in the world's interest, to be well aware of all the issues for debate and their fullest ramifications.

The conference concluded with an examination of current issues raised by Professor Sterling relating to his experiences over 55 years of his work in international copyright law, and to his views for the future. The remarks made in his paper foreshadow the necessity for the principles and values of copyright to be examined continuously globally, rather than nationally, more national recognition, and for the secure protection of those works which, in the global public interest, contribute to international knowledge rights in works.

Professor Sterling set out a list of important current and future issues at Annexure 1 to his paper, and a proposal for global internet licensing in Annexure 2. He had debated during the conference those issues with the conference attendees, and they had been the subject of vigorous examination. They should be re-examined in the context of his proposals for reform to the Australian *Copyright Act* in respect of orphan works and other orphan material, for the formation of an Asian Pacific Copyright Association, and for the development eventually of a global association, which would meet the increasingly realised world needs to secure the original objects of copyright protection.

When one examines the influences that Professor Fitzgerald, who had convened the conference, refers to in his concluding remarks, in the context of the vigorous public debate, private argument and conscientious enquiry that attended the conference, one is left with a high degree of admiration for the contributions made by the authors and the attendees.

I commend to all these papers, and particularly Professor Sterling's proposals, in the hope that, after this conference, the debate will continue, with focus on issues which may enable, at a future conference, a further fruitful discussion of a possible and effective global copyright system.

Greg James

February 2011

INDEX